An Outline of American Literature

Peter B. High
Chubu University, Nagoya, Japan

Longman

London and New York

Longman Group UK Limited,
Longman House, Burnt Mill, Harlow,
Essex CM20 2JE, England
and Associated Companies throughout the world.

© Longman Group Limited 1986
All rights reserved; no part of this publication may be
reproduced, stored in a retrieval system, or transmitted
in any form or by any means, electronic, mechanical,
photocopying, recording, or otherwise, without
the prior written permission of the Publishers.

Published in the United States of America by
Longman Inc., New York

First published 1986
Sixth impression 1991

ISBN 0-582-74502-0

Set in Monophoto Lasercomp Baskerville
Produced by Longman Group (FE) Ltd
Printed in Hong Kong

BRITISH LIBRARY CATALOGUING
IN PUBLICATION DATA
High, Peter B.
An Outline of American Literature
1. American Literature – History
   and criticism
I. Title
810.9 PS88

LIBRARY OF CONGRESS CATALOGING
IN PUBLICATION DATA
High, Peter B.
An Outline of American Literature.
Includes index.
1. American literature – Study and teaching.
2. American literature – history and criticism.
3. English language – Text-books for foreign speakers.
I. Title.
PS92.H54 1986   810'.9   85-19766

Contents

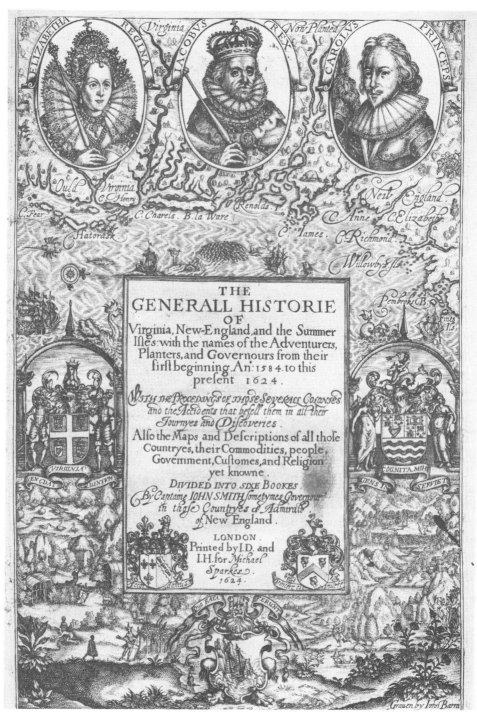

Frontispiece illustration for Captain John Smith's General Historie of
Virginia, New England, and the Summer Isles

Chapter One

Colonial Beginnings

The story of American literature begins in the early 1600s, long before there were any "Americans". The earliest writers were Englishmen describing the English exploration and colonization of the New World (America). THOMAS HARIOT's *Briefe and True Report of the New-Found Land of Virginia* (1588) was only the first of many such works. Back in England, people planning to move to Virginia or New England would read the books as travel guides. But this was dangerous because such books often mixed facts with fantasy[1]. For example, one writer (WILLIAM WOOD) claimed that he had seen lions in Massachusetts. It is probable that these "true reports" had a second kind of reader. People could certainly read them as tales of adventure and excitement. Like modern readers of science fiction[2], they could enjoy imaginary voyages to places they could never visit in reality.

The writings of CAPTAIN JOHN SMITH (1580–1631) probably satisfied readers of both kinds. A real adventurer, he had fought the Turks in Hungary, where he was wounded and taken prisoner. He was sold as a slave and escaped by killing his master. In 1607, he helped found[3] Jamestown, the first English colony in America. Although the details are not always correct, his *True Relation of Virginia* (1608) and *Description of New England* (1616) are fascinating "advertisements" which try to persuade the reader to settle in the New World. The Puritans[4], for instance, studied his *Description of New England* carefully and then decided to settle there in 1620. Smith was often boastful

[1] *fantasy*, imagination.
[2] *fiction*, stories from a writer's imagination.
[3] *found*, start (a colony, college etc.).
[4] *Puritans*, believers in a simple Christian religion without ceremony.

about his own adventures in his books. His *General Historie of Virginia, New England, and the Summer Isles* (1624) contains the story of his rescue by a beautiful Indian princess. The story is probably untrue, but it is the first famous tale from American literature. His Elizabethan[5] style is not always easy to read, and his punctuation was strange even for the seventeenth century. Still, he can tell a good story:

> Two great stones were brought before[A] Powhattan (*the Indian "King"*): then as many as could dragged him (*Smith*) to them, and thereon[B] laid his head, and being ready with their clubs, to beat out his brains, Pocahontas, the King's dearest daughter, got his head in her arms, and laid down her own (*head*) upon his to save him from death: whereat[C] the King was contented[D] he should live.
>
> [A] in front of   [B] on them (the stones)   [C] because of that   [D] agreed

Almost from the beginning, as the English settled along the Atlantic coast of America, there were important differences between the Southern and the New England colonies. In the South, enormous farms or "plantations" used the labor of black slaves to grow tobacco. The rich and powerful plantation owners were slow to develop a literature of their own. They preferred books imported from England. But in New England, the Puritan settlers had come to the New World in order to form a society based on strict Christian beliefs. Like the Puritans in England, who were fighting against the English king (in a war that lasted from 1642 to 1652), they believed that society should be based on the laws of God. Therefore they had a far stronger sense of unity and of a "shared purpose". This was one of the reasons why culture[6] and literature developed much faster than in the South. Harvard, the first college in the colonies, was founded near Boston in 1636 in order to train new Puritan ministers. The first printing press in America was started there in 1638, and America's first newspaper began in Boston in 1704.

The most interesting works of New England Puritan literature were histories. To the Puritans, history developed according to "God's

---

[5] *Elizabethan*, of the time of Elizabeth I (Queen of England 1558–1603).

[6] *culture*, the particular way of living and thinking of a society, including its art.

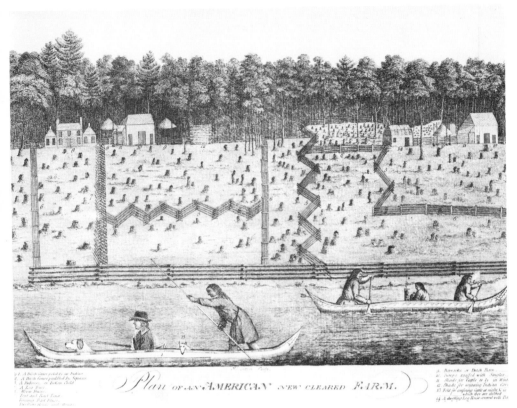

An early farming settlement on former forest land

plan". In all of their early New England histories, they saw New England as the "Promised Land" of the Bible. The central drama of history was the struggle between Christ and Satan.

Of Plymouth Plantation by WILLIAM BRADFORD (1590–1657) is the most interesting of the Puritan histories. It describes the Puritans' difficult relations with the Indians. It also describes their difficulties during the first winter, when half of the small colony died. This is all told in the wonderful "plain style" which the Puritans admired. In order to present the "clear light of truth" to uneducated readers, Puritan writers avoided elegant language. The examples they used were drawn either from the Bible or from the everyday life of farmers and fishermen. At the same time, Bradford's history is deeply influenced by the belief that God directs everything that happens. Each event he writes about begins with, "It pleased God to . . ."

The History of New England by JOHN WINTHROP (1588–1649) is also in the "plain style". But it is far less cheerful. Winthrop was the first governor of Massachusetts Bay Colony and, like most of the Puritan writers, was a minister all his life. His writing style is rather cold. He rarely shows shock or sadness, even when he describes scenes of great unhappiness. Sometimes, the dryness of his "plain style" is very effective. This is his description of the New England coast when he arrived on June 7, 1630:

> We had now fair sunshine weather, and so pleasant a sweet air as did much refresh us, and there came a smell off shore like the smell of a garden.

Like all of the Puritan historians, Winthrop believed that most events could be seen as a sign from God. For example, when a snake was found and killed in a church, people saw this as the victory of New England religion over Satan.

The first Puritans were not very democratic. *The Wonder-Working Providence of Sion's Saviour in New England* (1650), by EDWARD JOHNSON (1598–1672), defends the harsh laws made by the Puritan leaders. Everybody had to obey these church laws. Believers in other forms of Christianity were called "snakes" or even worse names. Puritan society was a "theocracy": the laws of society and the laws of religion were the same. Those who broke the laws were punished severely. *A Survey of the Summe of Church Discipline* (1648) by THOMAS HOOKER (1586–1647) is the most famous statement of these Puritan laws. Less severe was JOHN COTTON's *Way of the Churches of Christ in New England* (1645). In fact, by the beginning of the 1700s, newer Puritan ideas were becoming important to the development of democracy.

Even in the early days, some writers were struggling hard against the Puritan theocracy. ANNE HUTCHINSON (1590–1643) and ROGER WILLIAMS (1603–1683) both desired a freer religious environment. Rogers, who went off to establish his own colony in Rhode Island, was especially important. His *Bloudy Tenent* (1644) became a famous statement of the case for religious freedom. To him, freedom was not only "good in itself", it was a necessary condition for "the growth and development of the soul".

The New Englanders were quite successful at keeping the absolute "purity" of Puritanism during the early, difficult days of settlement. But when the Indians were no longer a danger, the dark forests had become farmland, and more comfortable settlements had grown up, Puritan strictness began to relax. The change was very slow and was not easily recognized by New Englanders at the time. By looking at the early history of the Mather family in New England, we can see how the Puritan tradition[7] grew weaker and weaker.

RICHARD MATHER (1596–1669), the founder of his family in America, was greatly admired as a typical strong Puritan minister. Another preacher, who knew Richard Mather well, described his way of preaching as "very plain, studiously avoiding obscure[8] terms".

INCREASE MATHER (1639–1723), his son, was a leader of the New England theocracy until it began to fall apart at the end of the seventeenth century. He was also a minister at North Church in Boston, the most powerful church in New England. The 1690s was the time of the great witchcraft[9] panic. In the town of Salem, Massachusetts, young girls and lonely old women were arrested and put on trial as witches. A number of these people were put to death for "selling their souls" to the Devil. Increase Mather's best-known book, *Remarkable Providences* (1684), tells us much about the psychological environment of the time. The book is filled with the Puritans' strange beliefs. To Mather and other Puritans, witchcraft and other forms of evil were an absolutely real part of everyday life.

Increase's son, COTTON MATHER (1663–1728), became the most famous of the family. He had "an insane genius for advertising himself". He wrote more than 450 works. Whenever something happened to him in his life, Cotton Mather wrote a religious book. When his first wife died, he published[10] a long sermon[11] called *Death Made Easy and Happy*. When his little daughter died, he wrote *The Best Way of Living, Which is to Die Daily*. Most of these works were quite short and are of little interest to us today. But some, such as his famous *Magnalia Christi Americana* (1702), were very long and were published in many volumes. He was certain that his longest work, *The Angel of*

---

[7] *tradition*, beliefs and customs passed from older to younger people.

[8] *obscure*, not clear.

[9] *witchcraft*, the imagined ability to work magic of certain women (*witches*).

[10] *publish*, print and sell (books etc.); n. *publisher*, *publication*.

[11] *sermon*, religious address.

Cotton Mather

Bethesda (written in 1723), would "prove one of the most useful books that have been published in the World". But the book was so long, no one ever tried to publish it. Cotton's *Diary* gives us a clear picture of the inner life of this strange and often unpleasant man. On almost every page, he speaks of his special relationship with God. When he had a pain in his stomach or teeth, he thought about how he had broken God's law with his stomach or teeth. During his last years, he expressed shock at the "increasing wickedness" of the people around him, including his own children.

The most fascinating part of his *Magnalia Christi Americana* is the description of the Salem witch trials. He makes it clear that he personally believed that this was an "assault[12] from Hell" and that all of New England was filled with evil spirits from hell. At the same time, he admitted that the witch trials had been a mistake and that it was good that they were finally stopped.

[12] *assault*, attack.

The witch trials in Salem, Massachusetts, in the 1690s

The writings of Cotton Mather show how the later Puritan writers moved away from the "plain style" of their grandfathers. The language is complicated and filled with strange words from Latin. Although Mather called his style "a cloth of gold", ordinary people usually found it hard to read.

In the writings of the earliest Puritans, we often find poems on religious themes[13]. ANNE BRADSTREET (1612–1672) was the first real New England poet. Her *Tenth Muse Lately Sprung Up In America* (1650), contained the first New World poems published in England. None of her early poems are very good. Her later poems, written with charming simplicity, show her progress in the art. She refuses "to sing of Wars, of Captains, and of Kings". Instead, she gives us a look into the heart of a seventeenth-century American woman.

The poetry of MICHAEL WIGGLESWORTH (1631–1705), on the other hand, is meant to frighten readers with a picture of the day when the

[13] *theme*, subject (of a piece of writing etc.).

Puritan God will judge mankind. The sound is often ugly, but the images are powerful:

> No heart so bold, but[A] now grows cold
>   and almost dead with fear
> . . .
>
> Some hide themselves in Caves and Delves[B],
>   in places underground

[A] so brave that it does not become   [B] holes dug in hillsides

(*The Day of Doom*, 1662)

The poetry of EDWARD TAYLOR (1645–1729) was unknown to American literary historians until 1937. Written during the last years of the Puritan theocracy, it is some of the finest poetry written in Colonial America. Like Cotton Mather, Taylor hoped for a "rebirth" of the "Puritan Way". Mather wanted stronger leaders for society. Taylor, however, was concerned with the inner spiritual life of Puritan believers. He created rich, unusual images[14] to help his reader "see, hear, taste and feel religious doctrine". In one poem, he describes truly religious people. They are as rare "As Black Swans that in milkwhite Rivers are." Sometimes, he sounds quite modern. In a poem about the making of the universe, he asks, "Who in this Bowling Alley bowled the Sun?"

Throughout American history, even in the twentieth century, there have been many sudden explosions of religious emotion. One of the most famous, called the "Great Awakening", began about 1730. Preachers like George Whitfield toured the country, telling people to "repent[15] and be saved by the New Light". The sermons of JONATHAN EDWARDS (1703–1758) were so powerful – and so frightening – that his church was often filled with screams and crying: "The God that holds you over the fire of hell, much as one holds a spider or some loathsome insect over the fire, abhors[16] you," he said. The sermon from which this line is taken, *Sinners in the Hands of an Angry God* (1733), is still famous for its literary quality. Later in life, Edwards developed into a

[14] *image*, a picture brought into the mind by words; *imagery* = the use of such words.
[15] *repent*, be sorry for one's wrongdoing.
[16] *abhor*, hate; n. *abhorrence*.

great theologian, or religious philosopher. In his *Freedom of Will* (1754), he tried to build a philosophy based on the Puritan faith.

The Puritans admired science as "the study of God's material creation". Edwards developed this idea further. He said that there was a close relation between knowledge of the physical world and knowledge of the spiritual world. This idea created a bridge between the old strict Puritan society and the new, freer culture which came later, with its scientific study of the world.

Although literature developed far more slowly in the South than in New England, a few early writers are worth mentioning. In Virginia, ROBERT BEVERLEY (1673–1722) wrote intelligently about nature and society. His *History and Present State of Virginia* (1705) is written in a plain, clear style, mixing wild humor with scientific observation. Although he was a strong defender of black slavery, his section on the Indians of Virginia is free of race hatred. Even more amusing is the *History of the Dividing Line* by WILLIAM BYRD (1674–1744). Writing for London audiences, Byrd used humor and realism to describe life along the dividing line (or frontier) between Virginia's settled areas and the deep forest. His opinions about the Indians were surprisingly liberal[17] for the time. He felt that the English should marry them rather than fight them. He had a similarly liberal view of blacks: "We all know that very bright Talents may be lodged under a dark Skin." These ideas were certainly not shared by the majority of Southern plantation owners.

[17] *liberal*, ready to understand other people and their opinions.

British soldiers fire on Americans in the Boston Massacre of 1770

Chapter Two

The Birth of a Nation

The most memorable writing in eighteenth-century America was done by the Founding Fathers, the men who led the Revolution of 1775–1783 and who wrote the Constitution[1] of 1789. None of them were writers of fiction. Rather, they were practical philosophers, and their most typical product was the political pamphlet[2]. They both admired and were active in the European "Age of Reason" or "Enlightenment". They shared the Enlightenment belief that human intelligence (or "reason") could understand both nature and man. Unlike the Puritans – who saw man as a sinful failure – the Enlightenment thinkers were sure man could improve himself. They wanted to create a happy society based on justice and freedom.

The writings of BENJAMIN FRANKLIN (1706–1790) show the Enlightenment spirit in America at its best and most optimistic. His style is quite modern and, even today, his works are a joy to read. Although he strongly disagreed with the opinions of the Puritans, his works show a return to their "plain style". At the same time, there is something "anti-literary" about Franklin. He had no liking for poetry and felt that writing should always have a practical purpose.

We can see these ideas even in his earliest work, the *Dogood Papers* (1722), written when he was only sixteen. These are a series of short pieces which are very funny, but full of moral advice (praising honesty and attacking drunkenness, etc.). His *Poor Richard's Almanac* (1732–1757) gives similar advice. Almanacs, containing much useful information for farmers and sailors (about the next year's weather, sea tides, etc.), were a popular form of practical literature. Together with

[1] *Constitution*, statement of how a country is to be governed.
[2] *pamphlet*, short book of a few pages.

the Bible and the newspaper, they were the only reading matter in most Colonial households. Franklin made his *Almanac* interesting by creating the character "Poor Richard". Each new edition continued a simple but realistic story about Richard, his wife and family. He also included many "sayings" about saving money and working hard. Some of these are known to most Americans today:

> Lost time is never found again.
>
> Up sluggard^A, and waste not life; in the grave will be sleeping enough.
>
> God helps them who help themselves.
>
> ^A lazy person

In 1757, Franklin collected together the best of his sayings, making them into an essay[3] called *The Way to Wealth*. This little book became one of the best-sellers[4] of the Western world and was translated into many languages.

During the first half of his adult life, Franklin worked as a printer of books and newspapers. But he was an energetic[5] man with wide interests. As a scientist, he wrote important essays on electricity which were widely read and admired in Europe. His many inventions, his popularity as a writer and his diplomatic activity in support of the American Revolution made him world-famous in his own lifetime.

Although Franklin wrote a great deal, almost all of his important works are quite short. He invented one type of short prose which greatly influenced the development of a story-telling form in America, called the "hoax", or the "tall tale" (later made famous by Mark Twain; see p. 79). A hoax is funny because it is so clearly a lie. In his *Wonders of Nature in America*, Franklin reports "the grand leap of the whale up the falls of Niagara which is esteemed by all who have seen it as one of the finest spectacles in Nature". During the Revolution, he developed this form of humor into a powerful propaganda tool for American independence.

[3] *essay*, short piece of writing on a single subject.
[4] *best-seller*, book that very many people buy.
[5] *energetic*, always active.

Benjamin Franklin, writer and scientist

Franklin's only real book was his *Autobiography*. The first part of the book, begun in 1771, is an entertaining description of his life up to early manhood. The second part was written in 1784 when Franklin was a tired old man and the style is more serious. Franklin now realizes the part he has played in American history and writes about himself "for the improvement of others". As the autobiography of "the father of the Yankees", it is a book of great value.

The period just before the start of the Revolution saw a flood of political journalism[6]. This was mostly in the form of pamphlets rather than newspapers, because the pamphlet was cheap to publish and the author, if he wished, did not have to give his name. JAMES OTIS (1725–1783) was one early propagandist who used violent language more than reason in his attacks on British policies[7]. Other pro-independence writers included JOHN DICKINSON (1732–1808) and JOHN ADAMS

[6] *journalism*, writing for newspapers.
[7] *policy*, a (government's) plan of action.

An American cartoon showing England without her colonies of Virginia, Pennsylvania, New York and New England

(1735–1826). Adams later became the second President of the United States. Other pamphlet-writers, like SAMUEL SEABURY (1729–1796) and DANIEL LEONARD (1740–1829), wrote for the pro-British side. Most of these men had to escape from the United States after the Revolution.

The greatest pamphlet-writer of the American Revolution, THOMAS PAINE (1737–1809), was born in England. When he was thirty-seven, he met Benjamin Franklin in London and was persuaded to go to America. Two years later, he wrote *Common Sense* (1776), the most historically important pamphlet in American history. Its clear thinking and exciting language quickly united American feelings against England. He seemed to express what the readers themselves had been secretly thinking: "There is something absurd[8] in supposing a continent (*America*) to be perpetually[9] governed by an island (*Britain*)." Between 1776 and 1783, he issued a series of thirteen pamphlets, called *The Crisis*. *The Crisis I* appeared the day after the American leader, General George Washington, was defeated in the

[8] *absurd*, very foolish; n. *absurdity*.
[9] *perpetually*, endlessly.

Battle of Long Island. It contains the most famous passage in all of Paine's writings:

> These are the times that try men's souls. The summer soldier and the sunshine patriot[A] will, in this crisis, shrink from the service of his country. . . . Tyranny[B], like Hell, is not easily conquered.
>
> [A] person who loves his country in good times   [B] unjust rule

Paine was also active in the French Revolution and wrote a famous defense of that revolution too: *The Rights of Man* (1791–2).

Only THOMAS JEFFERSON (1743–1826), the chief author of the *Declaration of Independence*, was as important a writer for the American cause as Paine. Thanks to Jefferson's beautiful style, the most important document[10] in the political history of the United States is also a fine work of literature. Although it was written during a difficult time in the war, the *Declaration* is surprisingly free from emotional appeals. It is a clear and logical[11] statement of why America wanted its independence. Jefferson made no attempt to be original. Rather, he built upon the ideas of such philosophers as John Locke. The *Declaration* was revised eighty-six times before it was finally signed on July 4, 1776.

Soon after the war, Jefferson wrote one of the best descriptions of early America: *Notes on the State of Virginia* (1784–1785). Although he himself was a Southerner (and owned slaves at one time), he attacked the slavery system, saying that "nothing is more certainly written in the book of fate than that these people are to be free".

Jefferson was deeply influenced by the ideas of the Enlightenment. He believed that man did not have to depend on God to improve the world, and should use his own wisdom to do the improving by himself. As a typical Enlightenment thinker, Jefferson believed that all humanity is naturally good: "Nature has implanted[12] in our breasts a love of others, a sense of duty to them, a moral instinct." On the other hand, he was afraid that the commercial pressure of city life would

---

[10] *document*, piece of writing that gives support.
[11] *logic*, careful reasoning; adj. *logical*.
[12] *implant in one's breast*, make (something) a part of one's nature.

destroy this goodness. Only "those who labor in the earth", could be the basis of a truly democratic society. Jefferson saw another threat to American democracy in the thinking of the "Federalists", who favored a strong central government for the new American republic (some Federalists even wanted to make George Washington king!). The Federalists wanted a form of government and society which would not be easily upset. Jefferson, however, felt the people should be able to change the form of their society whenever they thought it necessary. He even accepted the idea that a new American revolution might happen someday: "A little rebellion now and then is a good thing, and as necessary in the political world as storms in the physical."

The Federalist Papers (1787–1788) were the major documents of those opposed to Jefferson's thinking. The authors of these eighty-five essays are famous in American history. ALEXANDER HAMILTON (1757–1804), a powerful writer who opposed "extreme democracy", wrote fifty-one of the essays. Written in a calm, clear style, some of them are still studied by American students.

In Revolutionary America, both prose and poetry had a political or "practical" purpose. PHILIP FRENEAU (1752–1832) was perhaps the best poet of his time. He was also a political journalist, and this deeply influenced his early poetry. From the beginning, he wrote in the cause of American independence with strong patriotic feeling. In his poem *Pictures of Columbus* (1771), he mixed gloomy[13] descriptions of nature with sharp attacks on British tyranny. During the war, he wrote about American patriots killed in battle: "None grieved[14] in such a cause to die." He himself fought on an American ship and was captured by the British. He writes about this experience in his *British Prison Ship* (1781):

> Hunger and thirst to work our woe[A] combine,
> And mouldy bread, and flesh of rotten swine[B].

[A] combine to make us suffer [B] bad pig meat

After the war, he wrote poetry supporting Jefferson against the Federalists. In his last and best phase[15], he turned to poetry about

[13] *gloomy*, dark, not hopeful.
[14] *grieve*, feel sorrow.
[15] *phase*, stage of development.

nature. In *The Wild Honey Suckle* (1786), this flower becomes a symbol[16] for unnoticed beauty which quickly passes away. The last lines of the poem compare the shortness of human life to that of the flower:

> For when you die you are the same;
> The space between, is but an hour,
> The frail duration[A] of a flower.
>
> [A] easily destroyed life

But to Freneau, "death is no more than unceasing change". In *The House of Night* (1779), he writes:

> Hills sink to plains, and man returns to dust,
> That dust supports a reptile[A] or a flower;
> Each changeful atom . . .
> Takes some new form, to perish[B] in an hour.
>
> [A] small animal [B] decay and die

Poets of the Revolutionary era often imitated the "neoclassical[17]" style and themes of the great English poets. This style was itself taken from ancient Greek and Roman writers. Usually they wrote in couplets[18], but they also experimented with other forms, like blank verse[19]. The neoclassical poets often used old-fashioned language in their poetry. Words like "blade" and "steed" were preferred to the more common terms, "knife" and "horse". Unfortunately, few American neoclassical poets were very good, and none of them were great.

The "Connecticut Wits" were rather more conservative[20] in both their style and politics. They were America's very first poetic "circle". Although they were strong supporters of the American side in the Revolution, they hated the democratic philosophy of Paine and

[16] *symbol*, something that represents an idea; adj. *symbolic*; *symbolism* = a use in literature of symbols to represent real things, feelings etc.

[17] *neoclassical*, new (*neo-*) or modern style based on ancient Greek or Roman writing.

[18] *couplet*, two lines (of poetry) together, ending in the same sound (*rhyme*).

[19] *blank verse*, poetry (*verse*) without rhymes.

[20] *conservative*, not wanting to change.

Jefferson. Most of them were Federalists in their politics and Calvinists[21] in their religion.

JOHN TRUMBULL (1750–1831) was the best writer of satire[22] among the three major Connecticut Wits. His most famous poem was a criticism[23] of American education, *The Progress of Dulness* (1773). This long poem is about the adventures of Tom Brainless, who enters the university because he is "too dull for vice[24]". Then, becoming a school teacher, he "tries with ease and unconcern / To teach what ne'er himself could learn." Other silly characters in the poem include "Dick Harebrain" and "Miss Harriet Simper". Another story poem, *M'Fingal* (1776), made Trumbull famous during the Revolution. This long, humorous story is set in a small Massachusetts town. M'Fingal, at first a supporter of the British, finally comes to believe that the Americans will win their war for independence. On another level, however, the poem is a satire of the silly language public speakers use.

Another of the Wits was TIMOTHY DWIGHT (1752–1817). He was the grandson of Jonathan Edwards (see p. 12) and a minister himself. He wrote in the neoclassical style of Alexander Pope (the great English poet). Some of his themes are rather Puritan. In *The Triumph of Infidelity* (1788), he describes Satan's efforts throughout history to conquer God's creatures. In *Greenfield Hill* (1794), he tries to persuade the reader that the New World is far better than the Old. To him, America was a land of happiness, while Europe was a land of poverty and war.

JOEL BARLOW (1754–1812), the third famous Wit, was different from the rest. He had hoped to make a living by his poetry, but soon learned that this was still impossible in America. His *Vision of Columbus* (1787) is a long patriotic poem. He compares the civilization of the Incas with that of the English colonies. Inca civilization was the highest achievement[25] of "mere human" progress. The English, however, had the benefit of human intelligence, guided by God. In 1807, he made this long poem even longer and called it *The Columbiad*.

---

[21] *Calvinist*, follower of the religious teaching of Calvin (1509–1564).

[22] *satire*, making the reader laugh at the faults in people or ideas.

[23] *criticism*, judging the good and bad points of writing etc.; a *critic* does this; v. *criticize*.

[24] *vice*, wickedness.

[25] *achieve*, reach successfully; n. *achievement*.

An illustration from The Columbiad, a long patriotic poem by Joel Barlow

Most modern critics agree it is one of the worst long poems in American literature. In 1788, Barlow went to France, where he became a supporter of the French Revolution, writing poems which attacked kings and aristocrats[26]. He later followed Napoleon during his attack on Russia and died of pneumonia during the retreat from Moscow.

His best-loved poem, however, has nothing to do with politics. *The Hasty Pudding* (1793) is a humorous and realistic description of the making of a favorite New England dessert (hasty pudding):

> First in your bowl the milk abundant[A] take,
> Then drop with care along the silver lake
> Your flakes[B] of pudding . . .

[A] in good quantity [B]small, thin pieces

---

[26] *aristocrat*, member of a noble (high-ranking) family; adj. *aristocratic*.

It is what we call a mock-heroic poem, because it uses heroic, neoclassical language and rhythms, usually used for very important subjects, to describe something unimportant and everyday. The effect is often very funny.

In the years immediately after the Revolution, there were also some hopeful beginnings in drama[27]. Although French and Spanish Catholic priests had used drama for religious education among the Indians, drama developed very slowly in the English colonies. The New England Puritans, and some other Protestant groups, believed that the theatre was "an invention of the Devil", bad for the morals of the people. In the South, far away from the Puritan influence, there were a few theatres. America's first theatre was in Williamsburg, Virginia. THOMAS GODFREY's *Prince of Parthia* (written in 1759, produced in 1767) was probably the first American play to be professionally produced. But it wasn't until after Independence that American theatre became interesting.

WILLIAM DUNLAP (1766–1839) was the most active playwright[28], with such successful plays as *The Father* (1789). His *André* (1798), based on the life of a British spy, is considered his best play. *The Contrast* (1787) by ROYALL TYLER (1757–1826), was the first comedy[29] by an American author using characters from his own country. The "contrast" of the play is between the silly British manners of Mr. Dimple and the American manners of Colonel Manly. Their rivalry for the love of a young lady is, of course, won by the American. The plot of *The Contrast* is similar to many British plays of the time. But it introduces an entirely new character "type": the Yankee. Manly's Yankee servant, Jonathan, is extremely self-confident, except with women. He is very patriotic and rather puritanical in his morals. His speech is very colorful. Being a real democrat, he completely ignores class distinctions. We can still see his type in American plays and movies today.

The development of the new American personality can also be seen in the writings of J. HECTOR ST. JOHN DE CRÈVECOEUR (1735–1813). Some might object that he was not really an American and that

---

[27] *drama*, serious (writing of) plays for the theatre.
[28] *playwright*, writer of plays for the theatre.
[29] *comedy*, a play, often amusing, always with a happy ending.

several of his important works were written in French, rather than English. This is true, but it is also true that for most of his adult life he considered himself an American. He was born a French aristocrat and went to America in 1755. In 1764, he settled down as a farmer in New York State. He was against the Revolution when it broke out and returned to France until it was over. His *Letters from an American Farmer* (1782) contain one of the earliest explanations of the American personality, and are still widely read. In one letter, he asks:

> What is this American, this new man? . . . leaving behind him all his ancient prejudices[A], and manners, (*he*) receives new ones from the new mode[B] of life he has embraced[C], the new government he obeys, and the new rank he holds.
>
> [A] fixed opinions [B]way of living [C]accepted

Crèvecoeur did not describe America as a utopia[30], nor did he expect it to become one. Yet he saw far more hope and health in a society where "individuals of all nations are melted into a new race of men" than in the older, closed societies of Europe. At the same time, he was afraid that this happiness would be destroyed by the Revolution. In his *Sketches of Eighteenth Century America* (not published until 1925), he explains these fears. In the most important and interesting part of *Sketches*, Crèvecoeur describes the tragedy[31] of people who have been destroyed by the lawlessness of the Revolution. Neighbors, who were once friends, burned each other's houses and killed each other's families. To Crèvecoeur, the ideal American was quite different: a social man who co-operates with his neighbors, while earning his own living from farming.

---

[30] *utopia*, a perfect country (as described in Sir Thomas More's *Utopia*, 1516); adj. *utopian*.

[31] *tragedy*, (here) a very sad event or situation; adj. *tragic*.

A painting of the poet William Cullen Bryant in the Catskill Mountains

Chapter Three

The Rise of a National Literature

In the early years of the new republic, there was disagreement about how American literature should grow. There were three different points of view. One group was worried that American literature still lacked national feeling. They wanted books which expressed the special character of the nation, not books which were based on European culture. Another group felt that American literature was too young to declare its independence from the British literary tradition. They believed the United States should see itself as a new branch of English culture. The third group also felt that the call for a national literature was a mistake. To them, good literature was universal, always rising above the time and place where it was written. The argument continued for almost a hundred years without any clear decision. As American literature grew and flowered, the greatest writers found a way to combine the best qualities of the literature of the Old and New Worlds. They also gave their works the universality of great literature.

Novels[1] were the first popular literature of the newly independent United States. This was astonishing[2] because almost no American novels were written before the Revolution. Like drama, the novel had been considered a "dangerous" form of literature by the American Puritans. Novels put "immoral" ideas into the heads of young people. In England, however, the Puritan writer John Bunyan had published a great novel-like work, *The Pilgrim's Progress* (part one, 1678). The eighteenth century became a period of greatness for the English novel, with writers like Daniel Defoe (*Robinson Crusoe*), Samuel Richardson

[1] *novel*, book-length story; *novelist* = a writer of novels.
[2] *astonish*, surprise greatly.

(*Clarissa*), and Henry Fielding (*Tom Jones*).

In the early days of independence, American novels served a useful purpose. Unlike poetry, the language of these novels spoke directly to ordinary Americans. They used realistic details to describe the reality of American life. They helped Americans see themselves as a single nation. At the same time, the earliest American novelists had to be very careful. Many Americans still disapproved of the novel. In fact, the first American novel, WILLIAM HILL BROWN's *Power of Sympathy* (1789), was suppressed[3] as "morally dangerous" soon after it was published. As a result, novelists tried hard to make their books acceptable. They filled them with moralistic advice and religious sentiments. SUSANNA ROWSON (1762–1824) called her *Charlotte Temple* (1791) a "tale of truth" and made readers cry over the sad fate of a young girl "lured[4] into sin".

Modern Chivalry (1792–1815) by HUGH HENRY BRACKENRIDGE (1748–1816) was the first important novel. Like Susanna Rowson, Brackenridge wanted to achieve "a reform in morals and manners of the people". The book is a series of adventures in which the author laughs at America's "backwoods[5]" culture. His targets include religious and national groups (the Quakers, the Irish, the Indians), customs (slavery, sword or gun fights), and occupations (law, religion, medicine). The weaknesses of American democracy are also described. As in *Don Quixote*, by the Spanish writer Cervantes, the hero travels around the country with his low-class servant. He experiences problems every step of the way. Although it has been called one of the great forgotten books of American literature, the awkward structure[6] and dialogue[7] of *Modern Chivalry* make it rather hard to read today.

Another novelist who described the nation's western frontier country was GILBERT IMLAY (1754–1828). His *Emigrants* (1793) is an early example of a long line of American novels which showed American culture to be more natural and simple than the old culture of Europe. An English family moves to America to live in a frontier settlement. We see how some members of the family are able to change

---

[3] *suppress*, put down; stop.
[4] *lured*, drawn by a trick.
[5] *backwoods*, land far from towns.
[6] *structure*, the way the parts are put together.
[7] *dialogue*, conversation written down.

Charles
Brockden
Brown

their way of life and find happiness. Others hold on to the "false" old values of English society and are ruined.

Far more interesting and important is the work of CHARLES BROCKDEN BROWN (1771–1810). His interest in the psychology of horror[8] greatly influenced such writers as Hawthorne and Poe many years later. Like these two writers, Brown had the ability to describe complicated (and often cruel) minds. *Wieland* (1798), Brown's best-known work, was a psychological "Gothic novel[9]" in the European style. The hero lives in a world of horror: murders are committed, people speak with the voices of others or suddenly explode into flames. As in all of his works, Brown's story is filled with emotional power. "He seems to believe every word of his own story," admired one nineteenth-century critic, "telling you of it with his face flushed."

Seduction[10] is the central theme of his *Ormond* (1799), in which the evil seducer is finally killed by the heroine. The theme of *Arthur Mervyn* (1799) is the introduction of a young man to the world's evil. The hero meets many people, including a criminal genius, but they all betray[11]

[8] *horror*, fear and dislike.
[9] *Gothic novel*, eighteenth-century story of mystery and horror set in lonely places.
[10] *seduce*, lead a person into evil (usually sexual); n. *seduction*.
[11] *betray*, be unfaithful to.

him. Towards the end, the novel becomes moralistic when the hero decides to spend the rest of his life doing good. *Edgar Huntly* (1799), like many of Brown's other works, has elements of the horror story: the murder of large numbers of people by the Indians; sleepwalking; and the insanity[12] of the hero and narrator[13], Huntly. In the most exciting scene, Huntly wakes up in the total blackness of a cave (he has been sleepwalking) where he must fight a mountain lion. Little by little Brown's heroes discover that they can neither understand nor direct their own lives. Life is "disastrous[14] and humiliating". It is kept that way by the moral blindness of humanity. With this philosophy, it is not surprising that Brown spent his last years writing political pamphlets against the optimistic[15] philosophy of Thomas Jefferson.

ROYALL TYLER, whom we have already mentioned as the author of the play *The Contrast*, also wrote one of the best realistic novels of this period. The hero of his *Algerine Captive* (1797) works on a ship carrying black slaves to America. Then his ship sinks and he himself is made a slave by pirates. The theme of the novel is an attack on the American government for its support of slavery.

In the early part of the nineteenth century, New York City was the center of American writing. Its writers were called "Knickerbockers", and the period from 1810 to 1840 is known as the "Knickerbocker era" of American literature. The name comes from *A History of New York, by Diedrich Knickerbocker* (1809), by WASHINGTON IRVING (1783–1859). Irving's book created a lot of interest in the local history of New York, but it was a humorous rather than a serious history of the city. In the preface, he writes that his purpose is "to clothe home scenes and places and familiar names with imaginative and whimsical[16] associations[17]". Irving actually invented many of the events and legends[18] he writes about in the book. The idea was to give the region of New York City a special "local color". But more importantly, the book is a

---

[12] *insane*, mad; n. *insanity*.
[13] *narrator*, person who tells (*narrates*) the story (*narrative*).
[14] *disaster*, sudden great misfortune; adj. *disastrous*.
[15] *optimistic*, believing that good will win in the end.
[16] *whimsy*, rather strange passing idea; adj. *whimsical*.
[17] *associations*, connections in the mind.
[18] *legend*, old story passed down (possibly based on actual events).

Washington Irving

masterpiece of comedy which laughs at the Puritans and at New York's early Dutch governors. One such governor is described as a man who had almost nothing to say, and who worried more about his own indigestion than the problems of his city:

> It is true he was a man shut up within himself, like an oyster, and rarely spoke . . . but then it was claimed that he seldom said a foolish thing.

Washington Irving's next important work, *The Sketch Book* (1819), contains two of the best-loved stories from American literature: *Rip Van Winkle* and *The Legend of Sleepy Hollow*. The plots[19] of both stories are based on old German folk tales. But Irving fills them with the "local color" of New York's Hudson River Valley. Even today, the real places he mentions are associated with his stories. The Catskill Mountains, on the western side of the Hudson Valley, are still thought of as the place where Rip Van Winkle fell asleep for twenty years. Sleepy Hollow, just north of the city, is still famous as the place where, late one night, Ichabod Crane was chased by the "Headless

---

[19] *plot*, set of events that make up a story.

An illustration from Irving's Rip Van Winkle

Horseman". In this last story, as in many of his others, Irving contrasts the personality of the New England "Yankees" with that of the New Yorkers. Ichabod Crane, a New Englander, is made a comic[20] figure. He is greedy and superstitious. The "Headless Horseman" who frightens him out of the valley is not real. He was invented by local New Yorkers, in order to frighten outsiders.

In all, *The Sketch Book* contains thirty-two stories. The majority are on European subjects, mostly English. Like many important American writers after him, Irving found that the rich, older culture of the Old World gave him a lot of material for his stories. Few of his stories are really original. "We are a young people," he explains in the

[20] *comic*, funny.

preface[21], "and must take our examples and models from the existing nations of Europe." Not surprisingly, many of Irving's later works did just that. *Bracebridge Hall* (1822) is a collection of essays about the old-fashioned English countryside. The stories in *Tales of a Traveller* (1824) are set in Europe. In 1826, Irving went to Spain and lived there for some time. *The Alhambra* (1832), one of his best works, retells the legends of a great Spanish palace, where he lived for many months. Two of his histories, *The Life and Voyages of Christopher Columbus* (1828) and *The Conquest of Granada* (1829) were written during this period.

Irving was the first American to earn his living through literature. He was almost as popular in Europe as he was at home. But there were many who criticized his work. He himself considered "feeling" and language as more important elements in his art than story or character. He regarded the story simply "as a (*picture*) frame on which I sketch my materials". After his death, his reputation began to decline[22]. But even today, we continue to be charmed by Irving's stories and the pleasant personality behind them.

Of the other Knickerbocker writers, only JAMES KIRKE PAULDING (1778–1860) is worth mentioning here. His best novel, *The Dutchman's Fireside* (1831), is an amusing satire set in Colonial America. While he handles his American characters well, he expresses unpleasant social opinions (he is anti-Indian and pro-slavery).

Neither Washington Irving nor any of the other Knickerbockers really tried to speak for the whole country. For them, the American world tended to stop at the borders of New York State. JAMES FENIMORE COOPER (1789–1851), on the other hand, wanted to speak for all America. Although his books are not seen as great literature, they contain much thoughtful criticism of American society. In over thirty novels and several works of non-fiction, he pointed out the best parts of American society and the American personality and severely criticized the worst parts. In Europe, he became known as "the American Walter Scott". (Like Scott, he wrote adventure stories filled with historical details.) But this did not please Cooper because he considered his works to be completely original.

[21] *preface*, the writer's introduction to his or her book.
[22] *decline*, become less; n. *decline*.

Although many of Cooper's best-known works are also set in New York State, their characters are "Americans", not simply "New Yorkers". He describes such American character types as the pioneer[23], the Indian and the Yankee sailor. But the problems they face are not simply American problems. They are problems faced by people everywhere. *The Spy* (1821), his first successful novel, is about a man who moves back and forth[24] between American and British camps during the Revolution, selling things to both sides. He is a tragic character, since almost everyone knows he is really a spy. But which side is he spying for? The Americans are sure he is working for the British and they almost kill him several times. In fact, he is George Washington's most loyal agent. But this secret is kept almost to the end. Up to his death, he is still misunderstood and distrusted by his fellow countrymen.

The Pioneers (1823) was the first novel of Cooper's famous "Leatherstocking" series, set in the exciting period of America's movement westward. Natty Bumppo (who is often called Leatherstocking) appears in all of the novels in the series and is one of the best-known characters in American literature. He is a typical American pioneer figure. He is a master of all the skills needed to live and hunt in the forest. He has an unusually deep love for nature and is afraid of destroying it. His sympathy for all people, including the Indians, is also unusual. Race conflict[25] – especially between whites and Indians – was common in America until the end of the nineteenth century. Cooper makes this conflict a constant theme throughout the series. He fills his novels with battle scenes between whites and Indians. But both the author and his character, Natty, clearly disapprove of those who are simply Indian haters. Such people are always seen as the worst sort of American, because they kill both animals and humans "for the sport of it".

Cooper's Indians, even the "bad" ones, are almost always brave. In general, he divides Indians into two types. His "good" ones – like Uncas and Chingachgook (Natty's best friend) – are loyal and affectionate. Some critics complain that they are too good and that

[23] *pioneer*, one who goes first into new country.
[24] *back and forth*, frequently from one place to another and back again.
[25] *conflict*, disagreement; fighting.

Cooper saw them, wrongly, as "noble savages". The "bad" ones are filled with evil and cannot be trusted. Still, there is always a sadness in Cooper's depiction[26] of the Indians. They are a dying race, sacrificed to the advance of white culture. At the same time, Cooper seems to be warning all of humanity that this could be the fate of other races.

In *The Pioneers*, we see Natty in his old age. He and Chingachgook, now a drunkard, have lost the grace and nobility of their youth. But Chingachgook gets back some of his nobility by returning to the religion of his people before dying. The novel has beautiful scenes describing the seasons and life in a frontier village. The author combines history, adventure and local customs into what he calls "a descriptive tale". *The Last of the Mohicans* (1826), one of America's most famous novels, shows Natty at a much younger age. It is an exciting story, full of action. Characters fight and are taken prisoner, then escape or are rescued. Uncas, the Mohican, is the last of his tribe. He replaces Natty as the hero in the last half of the novel. Uncas is killed by the evil Indian, Magwa. In *The Prairie* (1827), Natty is now in his eighties. He is too old for heroism. But Cooper makes him seem like Moses in the Bible as he guides a group of settlers to their new homeland. His beloved forests have all been cleared and are now farmland. To escape "civilization", he must now live on the treeless plains.

In *The Pathfinder* (1840), we again see Natty as a young man. He almost marries a girl called Mabel Dunham, but decides to return to his life in the wilderness. Cooper also changes his hero's manner of speaking, making him a kind of backwoods philosopher. The idea may have been to make him a more attractive figure for Mabel. But it was not very successful, and the dialogue of this novel is often severely criticized. *The Deerslayer* (1841) shows Natty in his early twenties. Although we see him kill his first Indian, his essential goodness is contrasted with the Indian haters, Hurry Harry and Thomas Hutter. At the end of the novel he visits the scene of its main events, fifteen years after they happened. He finds only a tiny piece of faded ribbon which had belonged to a girl who once loved him. The reader shares Natty's feeling of sadness about the past.

---

[26] *depict*, draw a picture of; describe; n. *depiction*.

*An illustration from The Pathfinder, one of the novels in James Fenimore
Cooper's "Leatherstocking" series*

The victory of time and "civilization" over the wilderness is
beautifully described by Cooper. His weaknesses as a writer, however,
are almost as well known as his strengths. He is most successful in
scenes of violent action or of night-time terror and mystery. But his
character descriptions are often unsatisfactory. His descriptions of

women characters (whom he always calls "females") are especially weak. Only a few of them are interesting as individuals[27]. We rarely get a deep look at their characters. In fact, almost all of them have the same interests and needs: house-cleaning and love. Occasionally, there are also problems with Cooper's descriptions of action scenes. Mark Twain, in his famous essay *Fenimore Cooper's Literary Offenses*, fiercely attacks him for a bad mistake he makes in a scene in *The Deerslayer*. A group of Indians try to jump down onto a riverboat from a tree. According to Cooper's description, however, the boat is no longer under the tree. Still, none of Cooper's "offenses" seriously spoils the reader's enjoyment of his stories.

Cooper was also one of the first writers of sea stories in America. These novels have elements of both romanticism[28] and realism[29]. The author is a romantic when he describes the sudden changes of weather, the beauty of the ocean, and the mysterious ships and seamen. The realism comes from Cooper's personal knowledge of the sea; he had been a sailor in his youth. *The Pilot* (1824) is set in Revolutionary times. It is a kind of Leatherstocking tale set on the sea, with fierce battles, narrow escapes and a wise old sailor similar to Natty Bumppo in his old age. *The Red Rover* (1827) is a tale of pirate adventures, also set in Revolutionary times.

From 1826, Cooper spent seven years in Europe. But he was angered by the way Englishmen spoke unfavorably about his country and, in defense, he wrote *Notions of the Americans* (1828). Back in America, Cooper became a political conservative. His family had been part of the farming aristocracy and he wrote the "Littlepage Trilogy" to support this group. In these three novels, *The Chainbearer* (1845), *Satanstoe* (1845) and *The Redskins* (1846), he depicts the greed of the "common man" in a democracy. He regrets the passing of America's landowning aristocracy and the rise of a new class, the "money-grabbers".

The era of Irving and Cooper had a third important voice, that of the poet WILLIAM CULLEN BRYANT (1794–1878). Although his grand-

---

[27] *individual*, one person, different from all others.

[28] *romanticism*, admiring wild (not man-made) beauty and feelings (emotions) – not thought.

[29] *realism*, showing things as they really are.

parents had been Puritans, Bryant's own philosophy was democratic and liberal. As a poet, he disliked the old neoclassical style. He agreed with the Romantic poets of Europe (such as England's Wordsworth) that the new poetry should not simply copy the forms and ideas of the ancient classics. Rather, it should break away from the old patterns. The new kind of poetry should help the reader to understand the world through his emotions. For Bryant, like other Romantics, "the great spring of poetry is emotion", and its aim is to find a new, "higher" kind of knowledge.

His first great poem, *Thanatopsis* (1817), shows the deep Romantic spirit of Bryant in his youth. In this famous blank verse masterpiece, nature and death are described with a gentle sadness. The title is Greek for "view of death". Bryant's view is that death is the absolute end of the individual:

> And, lost each human trace, surrendering up[A]
> Thine individual being, thou shalt go
> To mix for ever with the elements[B],
> To be a brother to the insensible[C] rock . . .

[A] accepting defeat   [B] simplest things from which the world is made   [C] unfeeling

At first, this might seem a cold and terrifying thought. But, as he explains in later poems, the life of man is part of the wonderful life of nature as a whole. The individual soul is not alone but, as he says in *A Forest Hymn* (1825), part of "the soul of this wide universe". Almost all of his poetry expresses his excitement at the idea of being part of something so vast. *The Prairies* (1832) is an emotional description of the huge flatlands of the American Mid West:

> . . . Lo![A] they stretch,
> In airy undulations[B], far away,
> As if the ocean, in his gentlest swell[C],
> Stood still, with all his rounded billows[D] fixed,
> And motionless forever.

[A] Look!   [B] slight rise and fall of the ground   [C] slight rise and fall of the sea   [D] waves

In such poems as *The Flood of Years* and *The Lapse of Time* Bryant responds to the hugeness of time with similar emotions.

•

Bryant was also a writer with a deep social conscience. As a newspaper editor, he fought hard for the rights of the laborer and of blacks. In such poems as *The Indian Girl's Lament* and *The African Chief*, he praises the qualities that unite all people. But it is his nature poetry which we read with the greatest pleasure today. Furthermore, this poetry prepared the way for the Transcendentalist[30] writers who would soon bring American literature to the attention of the world.

Although literature developed far more slowly in the South than in the North, there were a few important writers. In *Swallow Barn* (1832), JOHN PENDLETON KENNEDY (1795–1870) remembers the old Southern society of his youth. In other novels, Kennedy was greatly influenced by the works of Sir Walter Scott. WILLIAM GILMORE SIMMS (1806–1870), the best of the "romancers of the old South", was also an admirer of Scott. But in his finest novel, *The Yemassee* (1835), he created a highly original work of literature. His subject is a tribe of Indians which is slowly being destroyed by the advance of white society. Unlike Cooper, who was more interested in individuals, Simms describes Indian society as a whole. Their customs and psychology are studied in detail. The book is both literature and history: Simms believed that "it is the artist only who is the true historian".

[30] *Transcendentalist*, one who believes that man can find truth through his own feelings – see Chapter 4.

An illustration from The Raven, *Edgar Allan Poe's most famous poem*

Chapter Four

An American Renaissance

In the 1830s and 1840s, the frontier of American society was quickly moving toward the west. Following in the path of Brackenridge and Cooper, writers were beginning to look at the western frontier for ideas for a literature about American life. But in the cities along the east coast, the older ideal of the nation as an Atlantic community was still very much alive. The feeling there was that the cultures of Massachusetts and Virginia ought to be the models of national culture.

At this time, Boston and its neighboring towns and villages were filled with intellectual[1] excitement and activity. Harvard, in nearby Cambridge, was no longer the only place deeply interested in education. The powerful (and now rather conservative) *North American Review*, founded by Harvard professor Edward Channing in 1818, was also busily spreading ideas. And since 1826, traveling lecturers had been bringing knowledge about culture and science to both the city and the New England countryside. There was a Useful Knowledge Society, a Natural History Society and the Mercantile Library Association. Thanks to them, many New Englanders became regular lecture-goers.

Among the younger people, there was much talk about the "new spiritual era". The young intellectuals of Boston were dissatisfied with the old patriotism. America's power and wealth did not interest them. They wanted to explore the inner life. They studied the Greek, German and Indian philosophers. Many kept diaries about their lives and feelings. Others became vegetarians or nudists.

In the center of this activity were the Transcendentalists. They

---

[1] *intellectual*, concerned with reason and the powers of a developed mind; *an intellectual* is interested more in things of the mind than in feelings.

formed a movement of feelings and beliefs rather than a system of philosophy. They rejected both the conservative Puritanism of their ancestors and the newer, liberal faith of Unitarianism[2]. They saw both religions as "negative, cold, lifeless". Although they respected Christ for the wisdom of his teachings, they thought of the works of Shakespeare and the great philosophers as equally important.

The Transcendentalists tried to find the truth through feeling and intuition[3] rather than through logic. Orestes Brownson, an early Transcendentalist, defined the movement as "the recognition in man of the capacity of knowing truth intuitively . . . an order of knowledge transcending[4] the senses". Henry David Thoreau put it more simply: "Wisdom does not inspect[5], it beholds[6]."

The Transcendentalists found God everywhere, in man and in nature:

> Sea, earth, air, sound, silence,
>   Plant, quadruped[A], bird,
> By one music enchanted[B],
>   One deity[C] stirred.
>
> [A] animal   [B] held by magic   [C] god

(RALPH WALDO EMERSON)

In many ways, nature itself was their "Bible". Birds, clouds, trees and snow had a special meaning for them. Natural images like these created a kind of language. Through this language they discovered ideas already planted in the human soul:

> All things in Nature are beautiful types to the soul that will read them.
>
> . . .
>
> Every object that speaks to the senses was meant for the soul.

(CHRISTOPHER CRANCH)

[2] *Unitarianism*, a branch of the Christian church which does not believe in the Trinity (the union of Father, Son and Holy Spirit in one God).

[3] *intuition*, natural knowledge, not gained through study or reasoning; adj. *intuitive*.

[4] *transcend*, go (or be) above.

[5] *inspect*, examine closely.

[6] *behold*, see.

Ralph Waldo Emerson   *Henry David Thoreau·*

In 1836, RALPH WALDO EMERSON (1803–1882) founded the "Transcendental Club". Its magazine, *The Dial*, was often criticized for its vague[7] or silly ideas. Still, it was the true voice of their thoughts and feelings. For a time, the movement had an experimental community, the Brook Farm Institute. But this came to an end when the Transcendentalists divided into two groups: those interested in social reform[8], and those (like Emerson and Thoreau) who were more interested in the individual.

In 1836, Emerson published *Nature*, the clearest statement of Transcendentalist ideas. In it he stated that man should not see nature merely as something to be used; that man's relationship with nature *transcends* the idea of usefulness. He saw an important difference between *understanding* (judging things only according to the senses) and *"Reason"*:

> When the eye of Reason opens . . . outlines and surfaces become transparent and are no longer seen; causes and spirits are seen through them. The best moments of life are these delicious awakenings.

[7] *vague*, not clear; not well considered.
[8] *reform*, action to improve conditions.

The slow sale of the book showed how small in numbers the Transcendentalists really were. In 1837 Emerson gave a famous speech at Harvard University: *The American Scholar*. He attacked the influence of tradition and the past, and called for a new burst of American creativity. To him, the word scholar did not refer to the man of "book learning", but to the original thinker. Such a man knows himself through intuition and the study of nature, not of books.

A tall, handsome man, Emerson began his career as a Unitarian minister. Even after he left the ministry and turned away from Christianity, he remained a kind of "preacher": he was an enormously popular lecturer. First he would "deposit" ideas in his journal (which he called "my bank account") and then he developed his lectures from the notes in his journal. Next, he rewrote them into essays. *Self-Reliance* (1841) is one of the most famous of these lecture/essays, and is widely read in American high schools today. The essay is filled with memorable lines, familiar to most Americans:

> To believe in your own thought, to believe that what is true for you in your private heart is true for all men, – that is genius[A].

> To be great is to be misunderstood.

> A foolish consistency[B] is the hobgoblin[C] of little minds.

[A] special and unusual power of the mind [B] not changing one's mind [C] spirit that plays tricks and misleads

Equally important is Emerson's essay *The Over-Soul* (1841). The "Over-Soul" is "that unity . . . within which every man's particular being is contained and made one with all things". Flowing out of that unity, "Man is a stream whose source is hidden." From the Over-Soul come all ideas and intelligence: "We do not determine what we think. We only open our senses . . . and suffer[9] the intellect to see."

In his essay *The Poet* (1844), Emerson describes the poet as the "complete man". The poet frees us from old thoughts. A good poem helps us to "mount to paradise / By the stairway of surprise." Emerson

[9] *suffer*, allow.

felt that the form of a poem should grow out of its thought. This is because each poem "has an architecture of its own".

As much as Walt Whitman, Emerson helped open American poetry to new possibilities. His poetry is often criticized as being awkward and unmusical. But for him poetry did not always have to produce pleasant sounds. Harsh sounds could be used to surprise the ear. He also introduced the nation to entirely new poetic material, such as the Hindu idea that we are always reborn into this world each time we die. This is the theme of his *Brahma*:

> If the red slayer think he slays[A],
>   Or if the slain[B] think he is slain,
> They know not well the subtle[C] ways
>   I keep, and pass, and turn again.

[A] kills   [B] killed (person)   [C] clever and hard to understand

But perhaps he is best known as the author of the *Concord Hymn*, which celebrates the Battle of Concord during the American Revolution. The last line of the first stanza[10] is familiar to most Americans:

> By the rude[A] bridge that arched the flood[B],
>   Their flag to April's breeze unfurled[C],
> Here once the embattled[D] farmers stood
>   And fired the shot heard round the world.

[A] rough   [B] river   [C] opened out   [D] under attack

Another literary giant who lived in Emerson's hometown of Concord (thirty miles west of Boston) was HENRY DAVID THOREAU (1817–1862). As a young man at Harvard, Thoreau had been deeply influenced by reading *Nature* and he remained a pure Transcendentalist all his life. He and Emerson held many similar opinions; they even looked alike and for two years, Thoreau lived in Emerson's home. Emerson often remarked that the younger man's ideas seemed like continuations of his own. Over the years, however, the relationship became increasingly difficult. In 1853, Thoreau wrote of a meeting between the two in which Emerson "told me what I already knew". Thoreau felt that he had wasted his time.

[10] *stanza*, one of the groups of lines that make up a poem.

Like Emerson, Thoreau created his lectures and books from notes in his carefully kept journal: "My journal is that for me which would else spill over and run to waste." But what he wrote there – and in his books – was written in a far more lively style than Emerson's. Emerson wrote about nature in the abstract[11]. Thoreau, however, was an experienced woodsman and his works are filled with details about plants, rivers and wildlife.

In 1846, Thoreau was arrested and put in jail for one night because he had refused to pay his taxes. It was a protest against the U.S. government's acceptance of slavery in the South and its war with Mexico. He wrote about his experience in jail in his essay *Civil Disobedience* (1849):

> As I stood considering the walls of solid stone . . . and the iron grating[A] which strained the light, I could not help being struck with the foolishness of the institution which treated me as if I were flesh and bones, to be locked up . . . As they could not reach me, they had resolved[B] to punish my body.
>
> [A] crossed bars [B] determined

The theme of this work – "that we should be men first and subjects afterward" – made it a great influence on Tolstoy, Gandhi and Martin Luther King. It is probably the best-known American essay outside the United States.

From 1845 to 1847, Thoreau lived alone in a hut he built for himself on the north shore of Walden Pond, a few miles from Concord. While there, he wrote *A Week on the Concord and Merrimack Rivers*. The book is loosely organized around the story of a river trip which he had once taken with his brother. Most of the material was actually from his journal. One critic has called it "a heap of good things rather than a book". Its various discussions include a catalog of fish on the Concord River, the poetry of Homer, fights with Indians and the Transcendentalist meaning of sounds.

Later, in 1854, Thoreau wrote his world-famous *Walden*, about his stay in the pondside hut. In its own strange way, it is one of the greatest works of American literature. On the surface, it speaks only of the

---

[11] *abstract*, not concerned with real or solid things; *in the abstract* = as an idea, without considering real examples.

practical side of living alone in the woods, of the plants, animals and insects one finds there, and of the changing seasons. But in fact it is a completely Transcendentalist work. The author tries to "live through the visible to the invisible, through the temporal[12] to the eternal[13]". He rejects the things ordinary people desire in life, such as money and possessions. Instead, he emphasizes[14] the search for true wisdom: "While civilization has been improving our homes, it has not equally improved those who live in them." True enjoyment comes only when one throws off all unnecessary things. Describing his little home, he says, "My best room . . . always ready for company . . . was the pine woods behind my house." *Walden* is a hopeful book, encouraging people to lead sincere, joyous lives. The author sees the world as "more wonderful than it is convenient; more beautiful than it is useful."

Thoreau's poetry is far less important than Emerson's. He seems to apologize for this fact when he writes, "My life has been the poem I would have writ[15] / But I could not both live and utter[16] it." Many of Thoreau's prose[17] sentences, however, sound like poetry. Some are now famous sayings in our literature:

The mass of men lead lives of quiet desperation[A].

As if you could kill time without injuring eternity[B].

[A] lost hope   [B] time without end

Throughout the 1850s, his interest in science increased. But he always felt a basic difference between himself and the scientific naturalist. In 1853, he wrote, "Man cannot afford to be a naturalist, to look at Nature directly . . . It turns the man of science to stone." Also, around this time, Thoreau became deeply interested in the Abolition-ist[18] movement. His home became a meeting place for anti-slavery groups. He was an active member of a group which helped slaves escape to freedom.

[12] *temporal*, (the world) ruled by time.
[13] *eternal*, timeless; lasting for ever.
[14] *emphasize*, give special force to.
[15] *writ*, written [old use].
[16] *utter*, put into words.
[17] *prose*, written language which is not poetry.
[18] *abolition*, putting an end to (something); the *Abolitionists* wanted to end slavery.

There were other, less important Transcendentalist poets and writers. One of these was AMOS BRONSON ALCOTT (1799–1888), an important pioneer in American education and the author of *Conversations with Children on the Gospels* (1836). His method was to "trust the intelligence of children" in educating them. His greatest success was with his own daughter, LOUISA MAY ALCOTT (1832–1888). Later, Louisa wrote *Little Women* (1868–1869), an extremely famous and charming novel about a family just like her own. MARGARET FULLER (1810–1850), editor of the Transcendentalist magazine *The Dial* from 1840–1842, was also an important female voice in nineteenth-century American literature. Her *Woman in the Nineteenth Century* (1845) was a powerful call for equal rights for women. WILLIAM ELLERY CHANNING (1818–1901) is best remembered as the close friend of Thoreau. His *Thoreau, The Poet-Naturalist* (1873) is a masterpiece of American biography. GEORGE RIPLEY (1802–1880) and THEODORE PARKER (1810–1860) were Transcendentalist writers who tried to lead the movement toward social reform.

The Transcendentalists had their enemies, too. Oliver W. Holmes (whom we will look at in the next chapter) made a cruel attack on them in his *After-Dinner Poem* (1843):

> Portentous[A] bore[B]! their "many-sided" man –
> . . .
> Deluded[C] infants! Will they never know
> Some doubts must darken o'er the world below?

[A] wanting to sound important [B] dull person [C] deceived

NATHANIEL HAWTHORNE (1804–1864) also attacked the Transcendentalists for ignoring those doubts which "darken o'er the world". His *Celestial Railroad* (1843) is an ironic[19] short story about Christian, the hero of John Bunyan's *Pilgrim's Progress*. In Bunyan's story, Christian must travel the difficult road of life on foot. Along the way, he meets such problems of life as pain, sin and doubt. In Hawthorne's tale, however, Christian's journey to the Celestial City (heaven) is far simpler: the railroad takes him straight there. The railroad symbolizes

---

[19] *irony*, a use of words which are clearly opposite to one's meaning, often laughingly (as when one says "What beautiful weather!" on a day of very bad weather); adj. *ironic, ironical*.

A portrait of Nathaniel Hawthorne, painted in 1852

the Transcendentalists' failure to deal with such difficulties as doubt and sin in human life. Christian's trip ends with him being thrown into a lake of cold water ("Reality"). As we can see in *The Celestial Railroad*, Hawthorne's stories usually have a strong allegorical[20] quality. (One modern critic complained that, "Half of him entered the world of allegory and could never get out.")

Hawthorne always writes about man in society, rather than simply about man in nature. His characters usually have some secret guilt or problem which keeps them at a distance from other people. They are troubled by pride, envy[21], or the desire for revenge. This interest in the dark part of the human mind causes Hawthorne to create tales similar to those of the Gothic novelists.

Hawthorne carefully describes the psychology of his characters. Loneliness and waste are the themes of his first novel, *Fanshawe* (1828). It is about a young genius who dies before he can create a work of greatness. The novel tries to copy the Gothic fiction still popular at the time, and Hawthorne himself considered it a failure. With the publication of *Twice-Told Tales* (1837), he showed his mastery of the short story. *The Minister's Black Veil*, one of the stories, contains the

[20] *allegory*, a story (etc.) in which the characters and events represent good and bad qualities; adj. *allegorical*.

[21] *envy*, dislike for a person who has more (money, success etc.) than oneself.

themes of aloneness and evil which run through his whole work. A New England minister puts on a black veil as a symbol of the evil hiding in every human heart. He wears it for the rest of his life, but it separates him from the rest of society and from woman's love. The author repeats this theme of aloneness, or isolation[22], in the stories *Wakefield* (1835) and *Lady Eleanore's Mantle* (1838).

Mosses from an Old Manse (1846), in which *The Celestial Railroad* appears, contains some of Hawthorne's best and best-known tales. *The Birthmark* (1843) and *Rappaccini's Daughter* (1844) are early examples of the "mad scientist" story in American fiction. Both tell of intellectual men who are ruined when they interfere with the sacred mysteries of life. In *Young Goodman Brown* (1835), the hero believes that all the people in his village are Devil-worshippers. Actually he is only hiding from his own sinfulness, by dreaming of sin in others. In *The Snow Image* (1851), another collection of short stories, the hero of *Ethan Brand* (1851) kills himself by throwing himself into a fire. He had been searching for the "unpardonable sin" and had found it in his own soul. His "vast[23] intellectual development" had destroyed the balance between his mind and heart. Although he did not personally share the Puritan view of life, the problem of sin is common in this author's work.

Hawthorne's best work usually has a strong feeling for the Puritan past of seventeenth-century New England. This is the setting of *The Scarlet Letter* (1850), considered his masterpiece. It is the study of the effects of the adultery[24] of Hester Prynne and Arthur Dimmesdale, a Puritan minister. Hester is forced to wear a red letter "A" on her dress, showing the world that she is an adulteress. Hester's husband tries to get revenge by destroying Dimmesdale's mind and soul. Dimmesdale, the father of Hester's child, tries to hide his guilt. In the end, he confesses and dies immediately afterward, praising God. The theme of the novel is that it is useless to hide guilt in order to avoid punishment. The novel asks the question of whether the act of Hester and her lover was really sinful. The author gives no clear answer. But by the end of the novel, Hester's "A" seems to symbolize the sinfulness of all people.

---

[22] *isolation*, being (kept) alone or separate.

[23] *vast*, very great.

[24] *adultery*, the sin when a husband or wife is unfaithful.

Hawthorne's *House of the Seven Gables* (1851) is read in all American high schools. In the seventeenth century, the founder of the Pyncheon family had committed a terrible crime. The "curse" of this ancient guilt finally destroys the family in the nineteenth century. The novel is really an allegory. Each character represents a different quality and each episode[25] is used to show these qualities. The effect of the novel is more pictorial than dramatic. Scenes remain in the reader's mind like age-darkened photographs.

The Blithedale Romance (1852) is a criticism of the Transcendental-ists' Brook Farm community. While *The House of the Seven Gables* attacks the failure to correct past evils, this book attacks the mistakes of modern reformers. Many critics praise the book's technical experi-ments, such as the way the narrator learns as the story progresses. Hawthorne's *Marble Faun* (1860) is set in Italy. It was written when the author returned from a seven-year stay in Europe. The plot includes Hawthorne's favorite theme: the effects of sin (murder, in this case). When Donatello throws an evil-seeming stranger off a cliff, each of the characters is somehow involved[26]. Some critics suggest that it is a kind of Garden of Eden story and that Donatello is a kind of Adam. It is also an interesting example of the "international" novel which Henry James later made famous, setting many of his works in Europe. Hawthorne contrasts Puritan New England (represented by the American art student Hilda) with Catholic Italy (Miriam, the mysterious woman with a guilty past).

In his famous review of Hawthorne's *Mosses from an Old Manse*, HERMAN MELVILLE (1819–1891) noted that despite the "sunlight on the hither side of Hawthorne's soul, the other side . . . is shrouded[27] in blackness, ten times black". This statement is even more true of Melville himself. In his fiction, man lives in a world divided into two warring parts: good against evil, God against Satan, the "head" against the "heart". There is no way to overcome these opposites. Melville has a tragic view of life: he seems to feel that the universe itself is working against human happiness and peace of mind.

Melville's most important experiences in life started when he

[25] *episode*, one event or happening in a book.

[26] *involved*, (be) mixed up in; (be) connected or concerned with.

[27] *shrouded*, covered (as a dead body is covered with a sheet or *shroud*).

became a sailor at age twenty. On board ship, he was deeply shocked by the life of the low-class sailors. Their personal morality was completely different from anything his family had taught him. But when he began to write, life at sea became the most important material for his books and short stories. Later, he called this experience, "my Harvard and my Yale".

Melville's stories are always more than simple sea adventures. In a sense, the voyages of his heroes are always searches for the truth. His first novel, *Typee* (1846), was quite popular because of its realistic detail. The hero escapes from his ship and lives among a tribe of cannibals (the Typee). He finds them happy, morally pure and "better than Europeans". But they do kill and eat other human beings. The book raises the question of whether happiness is always united with morality. Typically, Melville leaves the question unanswered. *Omoo* (1847) continues the adventures of Tom, the hero of *Typee*. Both novels contrast civilization with primitive[28] life. On a deeper level they show the clash between the values of Christianity and those of the tribal religions.

Mardi (1849) was too abstract and difficult to be popular. In this novel, the sea voyage is no longer real, but allegorical. The hero first visits imaginary South Sea islands, which represent various countries of the world. The section on the island of "Vivenza" is actually an important criticism of the United States. Vivenza rejects[29] the past too easily, and thinks that its own civilization will last forever. But Vivenza will also decline, like all other nations of the past. The voyage next moves to more abstract levels, where places represent philosophies.

Next, Melville wrote *Redburn* (1849), about a young man's first experiences as a sailor. Its theme – how people are drawn into evil – is a major theme in American literature. It is a deeply humanitarian[30] novel, emphasizing that people do not belong to just one nation, but to all of humanity. In *White-Jacket* (1850), Melville makes important progress as a writer. He moves from allegory to symbolism (an important development in American literature). The central symbol

[28] *primitive*, in an early stage of development.
[29] *reject*, throw away; refuse to accept.
[30] *humanitarian*, concerned with improving life for human beings.

The great whale in Melville's Moby-Dick

is the hero's white jacket. It shows that he is different from his fellow sailors. Although he tries to get rid of it, he can't, because it has become the symbol of his own identity[31].

Writing these novels helped prepare Melville for *Moby-Dick* (1851), perhaps the greatest novel of American literature. Equally important was the encouragement Hawthorne gave Melville while he was writing it. From the beginning, it is clear that the voyage of the whaling ship *Pequod* will be a symbolic voyage. It is also clear that Moby-Dick, the great white whale, represents God or fate, although Melville gives the reader a great deal of factual information about whale-hunting in order to make the world of *Moby-Dick* seem real. Captain Ahab, the central character, is "a grand, ungodly, God-like man". He is torn between his humanity and his desire to destroy the

---

[31] *identity*, existence as a particular person.

white whale. These two sides – the light and the dark – fight each other in Ahab. The dark side wins. To Ahab, Moby-Dick is part of a "universal mystery" which he hates, because he cannot understand it. When Ahab finds the whale and attacks him, his ship is destroyed. Ahab himself is pulled down into the sea to his death. Melville seems to say that personal identity is only an illusion[32]:

> There is no life in thee now. Except that rocking life imparted[A] by a gentle rolling ship; by her, borrowed from the sea; by the sea from the inscrutable[B] tides[C] of God.
>
> [A] given   [B] mysterious   [C] movements of the sea

Unfortunately, the public didn't like *Moby-Dick*. It was many years before the genius of its author was recognized. Melville's next book, *Pierre* (1852), was also not popular. The subtitle of the book is *The Ambiguities* and it is the tale of a man caught in the "ambiguities of life". Whenever he thinks he is doing good he finds his true motives[33] are really evil. *The Confidence-Man* (1857) has a similar theme: the tension between the apparent confidence and charity[34] of society, and its "darker half" (suspicion and lies).

After the failure of *Pierre*, Melville's themes became less ambitious. His style became more humorous and conversational. But, as we see in his short story, *Bartleby the Scrivener* (1853), his philosophy never changed. The young hero, like Ahab, feels that evil fills the world and spoils everything. But instead of actively hating it, he becomes completely passive. It is the sad story of a young man who is unable to act. In the end, he even refuses to eat and so dies. The hero of *Benito Cereno* (1855) is equally unhappy with reality. The theme is that every comfortable view of life refuses to see the darker half, which will destroy it in the end. *Billy Budd*, Melville's last important work, was published in 1924, over thirty years after his death. It is the story of the young sailor Billy (who represents the goodness of human nature) and his evil enemy, Claggart. In the end, they destroy each other. Melville seems to be saying that the world has no place for pure goodness or pure evil.

[32] *illusion*, seeing something that is not there, or that does not really exist.

[33] *motive*, cause (reason, desire etc.) of a person's actions.

[34] *charity*, kindness.

Edgar Allan Poe

Another novelist who wrote about the sea was RICHARD HENRY DANA (1815–1882). His *Two Years Before the Mast* (1840) was written to show the public the hardships[35] of the common sailor. It was an instant popular success and quickly became an American classic, read by young Americans for over a century. Filled with humor, factual details and strong, fresh descriptions, it was a big influence on Melville when he wrote his *Redburn*. Dana later became a lawyer and his *Seaman's Friend* (1841) became the standard work on the law of the sea. He was also an active Abolitionist.

EDGAR ALLAN POE (1809–1849) was yet another writer interested in psychology and the darker side of human nature. His fiction belongs to the Southern, rather than the New England, writing tradition. It is far more romantic in language and imagery. Both Poe's parents had been actors and had died by the time he was three. His bad relationship with his foster father was one of many unhappinesses in his brief life. His *MS Found in a Bottle* (1833), which he wrote at the age of twenty-four, shows how quickly Poe had mastered the art of the short story. The theme of this strange sea story was used in many later Poe stories: a lonely adventurer meets with physical and psychological horrors.

Poe made important contributions to American literature in three areas: the short story, literary criticism, and poetry. Many of Poe's tales of horror are known throughout the world. His method was to put his characters into unusual situations. Next, he would carefully

---

[35] *hardship*, suffering and difficult conditions.

describe their feelings of terror or guilt. The greatest examples of this kind of story are *The Pit and the Pendulum* (1841), *The Tell-Tale Heart* (1843) and *The Black Cat* (1843). The author here rarely shows the actual object of horror. Rather, the reader must use his imagination.

The Fall of the House of Usher (1839) is the best known of Poe's tales. It is a successful example of his theory that in short stories, "unity of effect is everything". The story's setting and its symbols reveal[36] the character of the hero. A crack in the house symbolizes the relationship between the adult twins, Roderick and Madeline Usher. When Roderick buries his twin sister before she is really dead, she returns to the house from the grave. When Roderick dies, the house sinks into the black lake surrounding it. Poe's heroines often "return from the grave" by various means. In *Ligeia* (1838) the ghost of the hero's first wife returns to life by stealing the body of his second wife.

Poe was also one of the creators of the modern detective story. Instead of examining characters and feelings these stories examine mysteries or problems. Examples include *The Murders in the Rue Morgue* (1841), *The Mystery of Marie Rogêt* (1842), *The Purloined Letter* (1845) and *The Gold Bug* (1843). Except for the last of these, each of the stories has the same hero, the brilliant French detective Monsieur Dupin. This character is one of Poe's finest creations. The author shows us how Dupin's brilliant mind works. The not very intelligent narrator seems to be as confused by the complicated plot as the reader. This makes Dupin's genius seem even greater. In many ways, such a narrator reminds one of Doctor Watson, Sherlock Holmes's friend, who narrates the tales about that great detective. Poe's detective stories are written in a simple, realistic style. Perhaps this is why they were more popular during his lifetime than his tales of horror.

The interest of Poe's poetry is in its sound, rather than its content. He constantly experimented with ways to make it musical, and defined poetry as "the rhythmic creation of beauty". Even the names he uses have a musical sound: Eulalie, Lenore, Ulalume. In *The Bells* (1840), he chooses his words for the quality of their sound. Try reading the poem aloud to yourself. Try to hear the sleigh[37] bells and the rhythm of the horse's footsteps in the snow:

---

[36] *reveal*, show (what was or would be hidden).

[37] *sleigh*, a horse-drawn carriage without wheels for traveling over snow.

How they tinkle, tinkle, tinkle,
    in the icy air of night!
While the stars, that oversprinkle[A]
All the heavens, seem to twinkle[B]
    with a crystalline[C] delight.

[A] scatter themselves over   [B] make quick flashes   [C] as of clear colorless jewels

Similarly, in his most famous poem, *The Raven* (1845), the rhythm allows us to hear the bird's beak hitting the door:

While I nodded, nearly napping[A], suddenly there came a
    tapping,
As of someone gently rapping – rapping at my chamber[B] door.

[A] asleep   [B] room

The unhappy young man asks if he will again meet his dead loved one, Lenore. "Nevermore!" is the repeated, machine-like answer of the big black bird.

Poe felt that the real goal of poetry is "pleasure, not truth". But for him, "pleasure" did not mean happiness. Rather, a good poem creates in the reader a feeling of gentle sadness. In *Ulalume* (1847), another of his many poems about beautiful women who are now dead, Poe mixes sadness with horror. Again, the sound is more important than the theme (conflict between physical and spiritual love).

Poe's literary criticism is also important. His reviews[38] for the *Southern Literary Messenger* were read everywhere in America. He wanted to help develop a national literature for the young country and felt that intelligent criticism was the key. He hated bad books and bad writing. His criticisms were usually accurate[39]. But, as James Russell Lowell complained, they also had "the coldness of mathematical demonstrations". This made him many enemies. Even after his death, other writers continued to attack him and tell lies about his personal life. Poe's unhappy life ended in 1849, when he was found in a Baltimore street, drunk and dying.

---

[38] *review*, critical essay on new books etc.; *to review* = to consider or reconsider the value of.

[39] *accurate*, correct.

Henry Wadsworth Longfellow, by the British photographer Julia Margaret Cameron

Chapter Five

The Boston Brahmins

Nineteenth-century America mostly ignored – or tried to ignore – the importance of Edgar Allan Poe. Americans at the time were very patriotic and they often felt his art was too "foreign". They simply could not understand the excitement he caused in France. Poe was an important influence on such great French poets as Charles Baudelaire and Arthur Rimbaud.

While Poe was exploring the unhappy depths of the inner self, the poetry of HENRY WADSWORTH LONGFELLOW (1807–1882) was speaking directly to the hearts of ordinary Americans. Part of his popularity came from saying – and saying beautifully – exactly the things most Americans wanted to hear. As if to answer Poe, he recommended an active, healthy life:

> Life is real! Life is earnest[A]!
> And the grave is not its goal . . .
> [A] serious

In poems like *A Psalm of Life* (1838), he expresses the hardworking, optimistic philosophy of his countrymen:

> Not enjoyment, and not sorrow,
> Is our destined[A] end or way;
> But to act, that each tomorrow
> Find us farther than today.
> [A] decided by fate

"Let us, then, be up and doing," is his famous conclusion. Typically, he doesn't tell us exactly what we should be doing. In *Excelsior* (1842), he encourages idealism[1]. The metaphor[2] is that of a young man climbing a mountain in the Alps. A terrible storm is coming but this does not stop him. When a beautiful maiden invites him to rest with her, he does not stop, but climbs higher:

> A tear stood in his bright blue eye,
> But still he answered, with a sigh,
> Excelsior[A]!

[A] climb higher

Few people today can enjoy this sort of sentimentalism[3]. It is more funny, now, than inspiring[4]. But when he turns to American history, he makes it sound so exciting that it is hard to resist him: "Listen, my children, and you shall hear / Of the midnight ride of Paul Revere." (*Paul Revere's Ride*, 1861) His great ballads[5] were *Evangeline* (1847), *The Song of Hiawatha* (1855) and *The Courtship of Miles Standish* (1858). In these, he borrowed (or invented) legends of Colonial times and made them into popular stories known to all Americans. His language is always simple and easy to understand. He could change his rhythms with ease to fit his subject exactly. When picturing a riding horseman like Paul Revere, the meters[6] gallop like a running horse. In the beginning of *Evangeline*, he describes the setting in a slow-paced, six-beat measure. This prepares us for the tragic love story he is about to tell:

> This is the forest primeval[A]. The murmuring[B]
>   pines and the hemlocks,
> Bearded with moss, and in garments green,
>   indistinct[C] in the twilight[D]

[A] which has been here since the earliest times [B] trees (pines and hemlocks) making a low sound [C] not clearly seen [D] half-light at sunrise or sunset

[1] *idealism*, living according to one's *ideals*: what one considers perfect; adj. *idealistic*.

[2] *metaphor*, a way of expressing one idea by naming another thing to which it can be compared (not using "as" or "like") – example: "the *roses* in her cheeks".

[3] *sentimental*, expressing (too much of) tender feelings; *sentimentalism* = too great an interest in such feelings.

[4] *inspire*, cause a flow of fine feelings or great thoughts.

[5] *ballad*, short story told in the form of a poem.

[6] *meter*, arrangement of words in regular groups of strong and weak beats in poetry.

In his *Hiawatha*, the unrhymed, trochaic[7] meter sounds like the beat of an Indian tom-tom drum. By not rhyming his lines, he gives his poem a rather primitive, uncivilized feeling. This is precisely the effect Longfellow wants. He is telling the story of an Indian hero, before the coming of the white man. Hiawatha is the poet's ideal of manhood.

> Évery húman heárt is húman,
> Thát in éven sávage[A] bósoms
> Thére are lóngings, yéarnings[B], strívings[C],
> Fór the góod they cómprehénd not[D]

[A] uncivilized hearts [B] strong desires [C] reaching out towards something [D] do not understand

Longfellow turned to more religious themes later in life. In his poem *The Tide Rises, The Tide Falls* (1879), he describes the end of a man's life. It is like a traveler who walks along a seashore and disappears into the distance. The water covers his footsteps and wipes them away.

Like Washington Irving, Longfellow took most of his ideas from other writers. Still, the modern complaint that there was nothing original about his work is not completely fair. Longfellow had mastered several European languages and creatively used material he found in German, Dutch, Finnish and other national literatures. A more serious problem is pointed out in Emerson's gentle criticism of this poet: "I have always one foremost satisfaction in reading your books – that I am safe." Longfellow never surprises or shocks us with new truths. With his calm and clear voice, he prefers to express "the simple dreams of average humanity". They were the comfortable dreams and ideals of nineteenth-century America.

Longfellow was the most famous member of a group of aristocratic Boston writers called the "Brahmins". Most Brahmins came from rich, old Boston families. Although they looked to England for "excellence" and often copied English literary styles, they considered Boston "the thinking center of the (*American*) continent, and therefore the planet". Their "Saturday Club" met one Saturday a month for dinner. Gathered together were "most of the Americans whom educated foreigners wished to see". Their membership included

---

[7] *trochaic*, using *trochees*, feet of two sounds, stressed followed by unstressed (´ ˘).

Tremont Street, Boston, in the 1830s

Longfellow, Hawthorne, O. W. Holmes, J. G. Whittier, James Russell Lowell and the famous historians Prescott and Motley. In 1857, the club started its own magazine, the *Atlantic Monthly*. Through this magazine, Boston's literary establishment[8] tried to influence the intellectual life and tastes of the new American republic. For the next twenty or thirty years, it was the leading intellectual magazine of the United States.

OLIVER WENDELL HOLMES (1809–1894), who had invented the name "Brahmin" for this group, was among the first to write for the magazine. His *Autocrat of the Breakfast Table* essay series, which he

---

[8] *establishment*, group of people who control, as a *literary establishment* may try to control taste in books etc.

began publishing in the first issue of the *Atlantic Monthly* in 1857, quickly made him one of America's most famous writers. It takes the form of imaginary conversations at a Boston boarding house. The "Autocrat[9]" is clearly Holmes himself. Through this character, Holmes expresses opinions on many different subjects. The superiority of Boston culture is one of his favorite subjects. The essays are almost always humorous; often they contain surprising opinions. We can see both elements in the Autocrat's statement that, "Stupidity often saves a man from going mad." The series was a popular success, partly because readers enjoyed laughing with Holmes at people they saw as less intelligent or cultured than themselves.

Holmes was especially good at humorous poetry and is known as one of America's best writers of light verse[10]. Deep, original thought was not his strong point. Like his essays, his light verse uses humor to express his strong likes and dislikes.

The Deacon's Masterpiece (1858) uses typical Holmes humor, but the subject is a serious one. The poem is a clever attack on Puritan Calvinism. His image is a horse carriage which has been perfectly put together, just like the Calvinist religion:

> Have you heard of the wonderful one-hoss shay[A],
> That was built in such a logical[B] way
> It ran a hundred years to a day . . .

[A] two-wheeled carriage with one horse [B] carefully reasoned

But Calvinism is based on untrue principles, and is certain to fall apart some day. After a hundred years, the carriage collapses[11]:

> . . . went to pieces, all at once, –
> All at once, and nothing first, –
> Just as bubbles do when they burst.

Holmes was also the author of several novels, each centered around an unusual medical problem. Because of such themes, he called them

[9] *autocrat*, a single person with the power to rule.

[10] *light verse*, poetry without a (very) serious purpose.

[11] *collapse*, fall to pieces.

James Russell Lowell

"medicated novels". *Elsie Venner* (1861), his best novel, was really an attack on the Calvinist idea of moral responsibility. Elsie, a beautiful young woman, has an unnaturally cold personality. But this isn't really her fault. Her mother had been bitten by a poisonous snake just before Elsie was born. This had a lasting influence on the girl's personality after she was born. Both this novel and Holmes's next one, *The Guardian Angel* (1867), express strong anti-Calvinist opinions. *A Mortal Antipathy* (1885) has a rather modern psychological theme. A terrible experience in early childhood causes a young man to fear women.

JAMES RUSSELL LOWELL (1819–1891) was the third famous Brahmin poet. In his era[12], he was admired nationally as the perfect aristocratic man of literature. In his early career, Lowell's poetry often had a political message. In *The Biglow Papers*, written during the Mexican War (1846–1848), he attacked American policy. To him, the war was "a national crime". The book's main character, Hosea Biglow, speaks in a New England dialect[13] and often expresses humorous opinions. At other times, however, he is completely serious: "Ez fer (*as for*) war, I call it murder." Another humorous character, Birdofredom Sawin, is silly enough to join the army full of hopes. He returns home as a

[12] *era*, period in history.
[13] *dialect*, local way of speaking the national language.

"*Birdofredom Sawin, with*
only one leg to stand upon" –
frontispiece illustration
for an 1859 edition of
Lowell's Biglow Papers

Birdofredom Sawin, with
only one leg to stand upon.

physically and morally destroyed man. The second series of *The Biglow Papers* was written to support the North during the Civil War (1861–1865), but it is far less interesting to read.

In *A Fable for Critics* (1848), Lowell makes fun of many of his fellow writers. He describes Poe as "three-fifths of him genius and two-fifths sheer fudge[14]". W.C. Bryant is "as quiet, as cool, and as dignified, / As a smooth silent iceberg." Emerson, who was influenced by the philosophy of Plato, has "a Greek head on right Yankee shoulders". Thoreau "watched Nature like a detective". Later in life, Lowell became an important literary critic. He had wider interests than the other Brahmins and several of his essays are still read and studied today.

Among the Brahmins, there were several important historians. One was GEORGE BANCROFT (1800–1891), whose *History of the United States* (published in ten volumes, 1834–1874) was the first successful effort to "place American history in the mainstream of historical events". WILLIAM HICKLING PRESCOTT (1796–1859) wrote the classic *History of Ferdinand and Isabella* (1837). He followed this with exciting narratives

---

[14] *fudge*, putting old ideas together roughly.

An illustration from J. G. Whittier's poem Snow-Bound, showing the children at the fireside

of Latin America. The Brahmin historians thought of history as literature, as "art". Their purpose was to present a drama of great men and great events. Perhaps the greatest of them was FRANCIS PARKMAN (1823–1893), who wrote *The Oregon Trail* (1849). He actually traveled the trail himself and describes his experiences among the Plains Indians. Although he did not particularly like the Indians, he disliked the new white settlers more. To his civilized Bostonian mind, they were "the rudest and most uncivilized part of the frontier population".

JOHN GREENLEAF WHITTIER (1807–1892) was a New England poet who came from a family of ordinary farmers, rather than from the Boston aristocracy. His best poetry always spoke of the beautiful, simple things of life. He was a strong supporter of Abolitionism and he wrote many poems against slavery. But when the Civil War ended, he returned to a softer tone. *Snow-Bound* (1866), Whittier's greatest poem, describes a time when Whittier, his parents and family were "shut in from all the world" by a snowstorm. The first part of the poem describes the coming of the storm:

> The sun that brief December day
> Rose cheerless over hills of gray . . .

The next morning, they wake to find a changed world:

> And when the second morning shone,
> We looked upon a world unknown.
> . . .
> A universe of sky and snow!
> The old familiar sights of ours
> Took marvellous[A] shapes . . .
> [A] wonderful

In the middle of this cold, wintry world, the poet invites us to:

> Sit with me by the homestead[A] hearth,
> And stretch the hands of memory forth
> To warm them at the wood-fire's blaze!
> [A] farmhouse fireplace

But the fire isn't the only kind of warmth in the house. More important is the warmth of family affection, which the poet values so highly.

A soldier and his family during the Civil War, 1861–1865

Chapter Six

The Civil War and the "Gilded Age"

In July of 1855, Emerson received in the mail a small book of poems in a completely new form. "I rubbed my eyes a little to see if this sunbeam were no illusion," the delighted Emerson wrote to the book's author; "I greet you at the beginning of a great career." The book was *Leaves of Grass* by WALT WHITMAN (1819–1892). "Bearded, sun-burnt, gray-necked, forbidding[1], I have arrived," the author announces in one of his poems. He wanted "to define America, her athletic democracy". The Boston Brahmins disliked his boldness and vulgarity[2]. In fact most critics attacked his work, while the reading public simply did not read it. But today, Whitman's work is considered an extremely important achievement of American literature.

Like Benjamin Franklin and Mark Twain, most of Whitman's education came from early jobs in printing shops and newspapers, rather than from schools. At a time when most young Americans were working hard to rise in the world, Whitman seemed a rather lazy youth. He took long walks in the country and by the seashore. He describes this way of life:

> I loafe[A] and invite my soul,
> I lean and loafe at my ease observing a spear of summer grass,
> . . .
> I am enamoured of[B] growing out-doors,
> Of men that live among cattle or taste of the ocean or woods . . .

[A] waste time   [B] in love with   (*Song of Myself*, 1855)

---

[1] *forbidding*, having an unfriendly look.
[2] *vulgar*, of the common people; not polite; n. *vulgarity*.

Throughout his work, he maintains a joyous curiosity about almost every detail of life. Often his poems contain lists of sights and objects any nineteenth-century American could recognize. His two favorite words are "sing" and "absorb[3]". First he "absorbs" the sights, sounds, smells and tastes of the world around him, and then he "sings" them out in poetry. A wonderful little poem in the early part of *Leaves of Grass* describes his non-systematic way of studying the world:

> Beginning my studies the first step pleased me so much
> The mere fact of consciousness, these forms, the power of motion,
> The least insect or animal, the senses, eyesight, love,
> The first step I say awed[A] and pleased me so much
> I have hardly gone and hardly wished to go any further,
> But stop and loiter[B] all the time to sing it in ecstatic[C] songs.

[A] made humble   [B] move only a few steps   [C] delighted

Leaves of Grass was Whitman's life work. The book grew and changed as he and his country, America, grew and changed. He called it "a passageway to something rather than a thing in itself concluded". He saw reality as a continuous flow, without a beginning or end. He disliked the stiffness and "completeness" of nineteenth-century poetic forms. Therefore, from 1855 until his last revisions in 1892, *Leaves of Grass* remained an incomplete "work-in-progress[4]". One of the earliest inclusions was his important *Song of Myself*. This extremely long poem announces all of the major themes of Whitman's work. In the first lines, he begins with himself: "I celebrate myself and sing myself." But this "self" soon grows to include friends, the entire nation and, finally, humanity. He then introduces himself as "Walt Whitman, a Cosmos". To him, the real "self" includes everything in the universe. "Nothing, not God, is greater than the self is." This is a Transcendentalist idea of "self". In fact, the whole poem is an expansion[5] of Emerson's idea of the "Over-Soul".

The word "expansion" here is important. Whitman moves beyond

---

[3] *absorb*, take in.

[4] *progress*, moving on.

[5] *expand*, make (or become) wider, larger; n. *expansion*.

Walt Whitman

Emerson's world in many areas. "I launch[6] all men and women forward with me into the Unknown," he says. One great "Unknown" is death. To him, it is delightful and desirable:

> Has anyone supposed it lucky to be born?
> I hasten to inform him or her it is just as lucky to die,
>   and I know it.

Out of the Cradle Endlessly Rocking (1859) expands and deepens this idea by connecting it with the ocean ("the fierce old mother"):

> The word final, superior to all . . .
> Are you whispering it, and have been all the time,
>   you sea waves?
> . . .
> (*The sea*) Whispered me through the night, and very
>   plainly before daybreak,
> Lisped[A] to me the low and delicious word death,
> And again death, death, death, death . . .
>
> [A] spoke softly

Whitman announces, "I am the poet of the Body and I am the poet of the Soul." As "poet of the Body", he boldly brings sex within the area of poetry:

> Urge and urge and urge,
> Always the procreant[A] urge of the world,
> Out of the dimness[B] opposite equals advance, always substance
>   and increase, always sex.
>
> [A] life-producing [B] dull light

This development shocked most nineteenth-century Americans, including Emerson. Many were embarrassed and angered by the two groups of poems about sex – *Children of Adam* and *Calamus* – which he included in the third edition[7] (1860) of *Leaves of Grass*.

---

[6] *launch*, send out (over the sea).
[7] *edition*, printing (of book) with changes.

An even more important development was in the area of poetic form. Through Whitman, American poets finally freed themselves from the old English traditions. In his famous autobiographical essay, *A Backward Glance o'er Travel'd Roads* (1889), he says, "the time had come to reflect all themes and things, old and new, in the lights thrown on them by the advent[8] of America and democracy". To do this, he invented a completely new and completely American form of poetic expression. To him, message was always more important than form, and he was the first to explore fully the possibilities of free verse[9]. In his poetry the lines are not usually organized into stanzas; they look more like ordinary sentences. Although he rarely uses rhyme or meter, we can still hear (or feel) a clear rhythm[10]. If you look back over the poems included here, you will find that words or sounds are often repeated. This, along with the content, gives unity to his poetry.

Whitman developed his style to suit his message and the audience he hoped to reach. He wrote without the usual poetic ornaments, in a plain style, so that ordinary people could read him. He strongly believed that Americans had a special role to play in the future of mankind. Although he often disapproved of American society, he was certain that the success of American democracy was the key to the future happiness of mankind.

Even the Civil War (1861–1865) did not disturb this faith. Whitman was a strong supporter of the North. Too old to fight, he went down to the battlefield in Virginia to work as a nurse. He felt great pity for the victims[11] of war: "I saw battle corpses . . . And the white skeletons of young men, I saw them." He greatly admired President Lincoln and saw him as a symbol of the goodness of mankind. Two of Whitman's greatest poems – *O Captain! My Captain!* and *When Lilacs Last in the Dooryard Bloom'd* – were written about the murder of Lincoln in 1865.

In 1863, when Lincoln met HARRIET BEECHER STOWE (1811–1896) in Washington, he greeted her with, "So you're the little woman who made the book that made the great war." There was some truth in

---

[8] *advent*, arrival; coming.

[9] *free verse*, poetry in a form that does not follow any regular pattern.

[10] *rhythm*, expected beat or movement.

[11] *victim*, one who suffers as a result (of war etc.).

this. Just as Paine's *Common Sense* had unified American feeling for the Revolution, Stowe's *Uncle Tom's Cabin* (1852) united Northern feelings against slavery. As soon as it was published, it became a great popular success. Hundreds of thousands of copies were sold in America before the Civil War; since then it has been translated into over twenty languages and millions of copies have been sold worldwide. It is the story of an old black slave, Uncle Tom, who has the hope of freedom held before him but who never escapes from his slavery. In the end, he welcomes the death caused by his cruel master, Simon Legree. As a masterpiece of Abolitionist propaganda, the book had its effect. It helped expand the campaign in the North against Southern slavery which led to the Civil War. During the war, Lincoln himself made a contribution to American literature, his *Gettysburg Address* of 1863. He gave this address on the field where one of the great battles of the Civil War had been fought. He stated that the purpose of the war was:

> That government of the people, by the people, for the people, shall not perish from the earth.

EMILY DICKINSON (1830–1886) was another New England woman who wrote during the Civil War era. But we find no mention of the war

Emily Dickinson

or any other great national event in her poetry. She lived a quiet, very private life in a big old house in her little hometown of Amherst, Massachusetts. Of all the great writers of the nineteenth century, she had the least influence on her times. Yet, because she was cut off from the outside world, she was able to create a very personal and pure kind of poetry. Since her death, her reputation has grown enormously and her poetry is now seen as very modern for its time.

At first this might seem surprising. Like Anne Bradstreet and the other old Puritan poets, Dickinson "seldom lost sight of the grave":

> I heard a fly buzz when I died.
> . . .
> With blue, uncertain, stumbling^A buzz,
>   between the light and me;
> And then the windows failed, and then
>   I could not see.
>
> ^A uneven

Dickinson's own Calvinist childhood gave her this way of looking at life in terms of death. In nineteenth-century America, with its steam engines and big factory chimneys, such a view probably seemed old-fashioned. It did, however, allow her to see things freshly. As one recent critic notices, she seems to be looking at the world "for the first and *last* time".

Although she rejected her family's old-fashioned religion early in life, she made the "search for faith" one of the great themes of her work. Apart from the Bible, her most important guide in this search was the philosophy of Ralph Waldo Emerson. Many, in fact, try to classify her as one of the Transcendentalists. Like the Transcendentalists, she saw "the possible" as more important than "the actual". She felt that people had to "move outward towards limits shrouded in mystery". To grow as human beings we must be brave, because we can "cling[12] to nothing". This idea comes from Emerson's *Self-Reliance*. Dickinson never came to any firm conclusions about the nature of faith. In one famous poem, she seems to think of it as a temporary "prop" for the soul. After it grows stronger, the soul (seen

[12] *cling*, hold firmly.

here as a house) no longer needs this prop of faith at all. As always, she writes in the meter of the hymns of her childhood church days:

> The props assist the house
> Until the house is built
> And then the props withdraw
> And . . .
> The house supports itself.

In 1879, she returned to the subject of faith. Sometimes her definition is far less confident (or "self-reliant"). Still, it is quite characteristic of her own personality:

> Not seeing, still we know –
> Not knowing, guess –
> Not guessing, smile and hide
> And half caress[A]

[A] touch lovingly

Dickinson's poetry is filled with images and themes taken from Emerson's essays. But almost always, she gives them a new and exciting interpretation. In the early 1860s, however, a rather different theme began to show in her work: pain and limitation. With Emerson, these things were hardly ever discussed. (Melville once described Emerson as "a man who had never had a toothache".) This new theme in Dickinson was her way – probably her only way – of expressing the terrible suffering of the Civil War. But with her, it was always the pain of the lonely person at night, never that of the whole battlefield. It was the pain of the modern Existentialist (see p. 181). The world is "a place where God and nature are silent", and the universe is a "design of darkness".

New England had another important woman writer, SARAH ORNE JEWETT (1849–1909). All of her realistic short stories are set in New England. In fact, she was one of the leaders of the "local color" school of realism. In the period soon after the Civil War, "local color" became an important part of American literature. It tried to show what was special about a particular region[13] of the nation. Jewett's

[13] *region*, part of the country.

characters are usually ordinary people, living in ordinary little New England towns. The way they speak and the details of their lives give us a strong feeling for New England as a place.

Jewett describes her characters realistically, and deepens them with symbolism. In *A White Heron* (1886), for example, the heron[14] becomes a symbol of freedom and beauty. The young heroine imagines that a certain tree, which rises above the rest in the forest, is "a great mainmast to the voyaging earth". She climbs to the top of the tree and sees the white heron flying among distant trees. This becomes one of the most precious experiences of her life. *The Country of the Pointed Firs* (1896), set in a town on the coast of Maine, is Jewett's masterpiece. Again, she describes her characters realistically, and deepens them with symbolism. Mrs. Todd's role as "an interpreter of nature's secrets" is symbolized by the fact that she gathers herbs for medicine. Most of the characters have never been out of their "salt-aired, white-clapboarded[15] little town". But a few, like Captain Littlepage and Mrs. Fosdick, have traveled the world. They are all old people now, and they seem content in their tiny world of townsmen and neighbors.

The South, which was economically and spiritually destroyed by the Civil War, produced very little important literature in the post-war years. The best (or, as one critic puts it, "the least bad") poet was SIDNEY LANIER (1842–1881). He is remembered for his *Marshes of Glynn* (1878). It describes how a poet comes closer to nature as he approaches old age. He learns from nature that death is the doorway to eternity: "Belief overmasters doubt, and I know that I know." At last, the poet looks forward to death, not with fear, but with curiosity. Lanier also wrote an important book on how to write poetry, *The Science of English Verse* (1880).

GEORGE WASHINGTON CABLE (1844–1925) was another Southern writer. He was a close friend of Mark Twain and often toured the country with him, giving lectures. An important "local color" writer, he specialized in the life of the Creoles (French whites living in the New Orleans region). In such stories as *Parson Jove*, he showed the amusing differences between Creole culture and the neighboring Protestant culture of the South.

---

[14] *heron*, long-legged bird living beside water and catching fish etc.
[15] *clapboard*, wood covering the outside walls of a house.

JOEL CHANDLER HARRIS (1848–1908) was the most interesting Southern writer in the post-Civil War period. Although he was white, he popularized Negro folklore[16]. His *Uncle Remus* tales, written between 1880 and 1892, are known and loved by most Americans, even today. In them, an old slave tells stories to a white child. Like *Aesop's Fables*, they are all animal stories, but all the animals act just like humans. The hero is usually a little rabbit, "Brer Rabbit", who uses many tricks to escape from his old enemy, "Brer Fox". ("Brer" means "Brother".) Although he is weaker, the rabbit is much smarter than the fox. In one story, Brer Fox has caught him and is going to eat him. Then the little rabbit shouts, "Eat me if you wish, Brer Fox, but *please* don't throw me into that thorn bush!" Of course the fox does just that, and the rabbit escapes. In all Chandler's stories, the weak use their brains to resist the strong and powerful. This was exactly how the black slaves resisted their masters in the Old South.

After the Civil War, the center of the American nation moved westwards and American tastes followed. The new literary era was one of humor and realism. The new subject matter was the American West.

The trend started with BRET HARTE (1836–1902), another leader of "local color" realism. He was a New Yorker who had moved to California during the "Gold Rush" days of the 1850s. He achieved his first success with his short story, *The Luck of Roaring Camp* (1868). It is set in a dirty mining camp, filled with gamblers, prostitutes and drunks during the Gold Rush. The camp and its people are completely changed (or "reborn") when a baby is born there. The story combines frontier vulgarity with religious imagery and yet still manages to be quite funny. Harte's *Outcasts of Poker Flat* (1869) describes the fate of two prostitutes, a professional gambler and a teenage girl in a snowstorm.

The reading public loved Harte's stories about the Far West and many other writers followed his lead. The real importance of his stories is that they provided the model for all the "Westerns" which have since appeared as novels and movies. In Harte's work, we see all the main characters of the movie Western: the pretty New England school teacher, the sheriff, the bad man, the gambler and the bar girl.

---

[16] *folklore*, stories (*folk tales*), customs and beliefs of a racial or national group.

Mississippi riverboats at the time of Mark Twain

The bank robberies and bar room fights he describes have all become part of a well-known genre[17].

William Dean Howells (see p. 85) once remarked that the American West could be described "without the sense of any older civilization outside of it. The East, however, was always looking fearfully over its shoulder at Europe." Because of this freedom, the writers of the West were able to create the first "all-American" literature, representing the entire nation. The work of MARK TWAIN (1835–1910; real name Samuel Clemens) is the best example of this new outlook.

Charles Dickens, the English novelist, had described the Mississippi River as a "horrible ditch". With Twain, however, it became "all existence" and an important symbol of "the human journey". He had grown up on the river in Hannibal, Missouri. Although the little town

---

[17] *genre*, particular kind of writing.

was far from the centers of East Coast culture, it was the perfect place for the young Twain to grow up. There, he could hear many Indian legends and listen to the stories of the black slaves. But the life of the river itself influenced him the most. The arrival of the big steamboats excited his boyhood dreams of adventure.

For four years, from 1857, Twain worked as a river pilot on one of these boats. Much later, he wrote his famous *Life on the Mississippi* (1883), based on his romantic memories. When the Civil War destroyed the riverboat business, he went to Nevada with his brother. From there, he went on to California, where he worked on a newspaper. In 1865, he became nationally famous with his short story, *The Celebrated Jumping Frog*. Based upon stories he heard in the California mining camps, the story is about an apparently innocent stranger who cheats a famous frog racer and beats him. The stranger fills the stomach of the other man's frog with tiny metal balls. It is a typical Western humor story called a "hoax". Like all the Western humorists, Twain's work is filled with stories about how ordinary people trick experts, or how the weak succeed in "hoaxing" the strong. Twain's most famous character, Huck Finn, is a master at this.

In 1867, Twain's newspaper sent him to Europe and the Holy Land. When his letters were published, he became an American literary hero. The letters then became his first major book, *The Innocents Abroad* (1869). The book clearly shows his "democratic" hatred of the European aristocracy. When he is taken to see the great old paintings, he refuses to praise them. In fact, he plays a "hoax" on his guide by asking very stupid questions. Although he is critical of Europeans, he is much more critical of American tourists in Europe. He laughs at tourists who pretend to be excited by the art treasures they see there. They are only excited because their guide books tell them they should be. He also attacks tourists in Jerusalem who show false religious feelings. In 1880, Twain tried to write another humorous book about travel in Europe, *A Tramp Abroad*, but it was not as fresh or as funny as the first one.

The Innocents Abroad created the pattern for Twain's next important book, *Roughing It* (1872), about his travels in the Far West. This book also began as a series of newspaper articles. He gives us clear pictures of the people he met: the cowboys, the stagecoach drivers, the criminals and the "lawmen". Although it isn't one of Twain's great works, it is very funny. It features many hoaxes and also another form of Western humor, the "tall tale". In one episode an angry buffalo climbs a tree to chase a hunter, and in another a camel chokes to death on one of Twain's notebooks.

The period of the Civil War was a time when a small number of millionaire businessmen held great power in American society. The city homes of the very rich looked like palaces and many people thought of this period as a new "Golden Age". But the gold was only on the surface. Underneath, American society was filled with crime and social injustice. It was, in fact, only a "Gilded Age": the gold was just a thin layer. Mark Twain created this phrase for his next novel, *The Gilded Age* (1873), co-written with Charles Warner. It was one of the first novels which tried to describe the new morality (or *im*morality) of post-Civil War America. One of the new elements of this novel is that it creates a picture of the entire nation, rather than of just one region. Although it has a number of Twain's typically humorous characters, the real theme is America's loss of its old idealism. The book describes how a group of young people are morally destroyed by the dream of becoming rich.

Twain's *Adventures of Tom Sawyer* (1876) was a story about "bad boys", a popular theme in American literature. The two young heroes, Tom and Huck Finn, are "bad" only because they fight against the stupidity of the adult world. In the end they win. Twain creates a highly realistic background for his story. We get to know the village very well, with its many colorful characters, its graveyards and the house in which there was supposed to be a ghost. Although there are many similarities[18] between Tom and Huck, there are also important differences. Twain studies the psychology of his characters carefully. Tom is very romantic. His view of life comes from books about knights in the Middle Ages. A whistle from Huck outside Tom's window calls him out for a night of adventures. Afterwards, Tom can always return to his Aunt Polly's house. Huck has no real home. By the end of the novel, we can see Tom growing up. Soon, he will also be a part of the adult world. Huck, however, is a real outsider. He has had a harder life and never sees the world in the romantic way that Tom does.

[18] *similar*, like; *similarity* = being like.

Mark Twain with a farm worker at the home of his wife's family in Elmira, New York

Some critics complain that Twain wrote well only when he was writing about young people. They say that his psychology was really only child psychology. This may be true. But in his greatest novel, *The Adventures of Huckleberry Finn* (1884), Twain gives his young hero very adult problems. Huck and an escaped slave, Jim, are floating down the Mississippi River on a raft. During their trip, in the various towns and villages along the way, Huck learns about the evil of the world. Huck, meanwhile, is facing a big moral problem. The laws of society say he must return Jim to his "owner". But, in the most important part of the book, he decides that the slave is a man, not a "thing". He thinks deeply about morality and then decides to break the law. After that, he is not a child any more. Many see *The Adventures of Huckleberry Finn* as the great novel of American democracy. It shows the basic goodness and wisdom of ordinary people. The novel has also been called "the school of many late Western writers". One of these, Sherwood Anderson (see p. 119) used it as a model for his own *Winesburg, Ohio* (1919). Ernest Hemingway, whose own style is based on Twain's, once said, "All modern American literature comes from *Huckleberry Finn.*"

In his later novels, Twain seems less hopeful about democracy. In *A Connecticut Yankee in King Arthur's Court* (1889), the hero is the boss of a factory. He is hit on the head and wakes up in sixth-century England. Because he is a nineteenth-century inventor, he begins to modernize this world, and because he knows so much, he becomes a kind of dictator, called "the Boss". In many ways, Twain seems to be praising both the technology and the leadership of the bosses of American business during the "Gilded Age". Like Twain's hero, these bosses thought they knew more than the ordinary people of society.

Twain's pessimism[19] grew deeper and deeper. In *The Man That Corrupted Hadleyburg* (1900), he describes a town that had been famous for its honesty. In the end, everybody in town has lied in order to get a big bag of gold. *The $30,000 Request* (1904) is another story with the same theme. In *The Mysterious Stranger* (published in 1916, after Twain's death), an angel visits three boys in an English village in the Middle Ages. He becomes their friend and shows them the evil of mankind. After destroying their innocent happiness, he finally announces that he is Satan. Twain saw human nature as a kind of machine: "I see no great difference between a man and a watch, except that a man is conscious and a watch is not." Human evil comes from something being wrong with that machine.

Throughout all of Twain's writing, we see the conflict between the ideals of Americans and their desire for money. Twain never tried to solve the conflict. He was not an intellectual. He was like a newspaperman who reports what he sees. His humor was often rather childish. After you read some of Twain's work, see if you agree with the opinion of one critic (P. Abel): "Twain was a boy and an old man, but never was he a man."

---

[19] *pessimism*, the belief that in this world evil is more powerful than good.

Henry James, by the artist John Singer Sargent

Chapter Seven

The Era of Realism and Naturalism

By 1875, American writers were moving toward realism in literature. We can see this in the true-to-life descriptions of Bret Harte and Mark Twain. But Twain's stories still had many unrealistic qualities: "tall tales" and unlikely coincidences[1]. He was never a pure realist. Meanwhile, in France, realism had become a very serious literary movement. Such French novelists as Zola were changing the relationship between literature and society. For them, realism was an ideology[2] and the novel had the power to become a political weapon.

WILLIAM DEAN HOWELLS (1837–1920) created the first theory for American realism. He had many important followers. Under him, realism became the "mainstream" of American literature. In 1891, he became the editor of *Harper's Monthly* in New York City. He made *Harper's* into a weapon against literary "romanticism". He felt that such works created false views about life. And as editor, he was able to help younger novelists like Hamlin Garland and Stephen Crane. He was also a friend and supporter of Mark Twain and Henry James.

Howells put his realist theories into practice in his novels. The theme of *A Modern Instance* (1882), one of his earlier novels, shocked the public. It was about divorce, a subject which was not talked and written about openly. His characters are very complex and very unromantic. The author blames society for their troubles. This is a position he took in many of his later novels as well.

Howells's next novel, *The Rise of Silas Lapham* (1885), is about an ordinary, uneducated man who becomes rich in the paint business. It describes his unsuccessful attempt to join Boston's "high society". In

---

[1] *coincidence*, two events that happen, by chance, at the same time.
[2] *ideology*, set of ideas that may point the way for society.

the end, his paint business is ruined because he refuses to cheat other people. The novel contains a famous scene at a dinner party, in which the characters discuss literature. A silly young lady is talking about a popular romantic novel: "There's such a dear old-fashioned hero and heroine in it, who keep dying for each other all the way through and making the most unnecessary sacrifices for each other." Many of the romantic novels of the time were written for young female readers. "Old-fashioned heroes" and "unnecessary sacrifices" were common elements in the pretty pictures of life they created for such readers. Another character, Mr. Sewell, expresses Howells's own opinions. He attacks such romantic nonsense. He complains about the power of these novels to form "the whole intellectual experience" of large numbers of people. Then he goes on to say: "The novelists might be the greatest possible help to us if they painted life as it is, and human feelings in their true proportion and relation."

Howells hated the romantic literature of such popular writers as Frank Stockton (1834–1902) and such historical romances as *Ben-Hur* (1880, by Lew Wallace). Such novels "make one forget life and all its cares and duties", he wrote. Novels "should make you think . . . and shame you into wishing to be a more helpful creature than you are". Like most Americans in the 1880s, he realized that business and businessmen were at the center of society, and he felt that novels should depict them. The good realist should be interested in "the common feelings of commonplace[3] people". On the other hand, he felt that authors should not make society look more ugly than it is. He disapproved of the way that French realists filled their novels with murder, crime and "guilty sex". American novels should depict the "more smiling aspects of life".

However, in *A Hazard of New Fortunes* (1890), Howells seems to turn away from the "smiling aspects" of society. It is the story of a man who, little by little, learns about the terrible suffering of poor people in society. From about this time, Howells himself was becoming a kind of socialist. This new outlook made him add a new law to his ideology of realism: art and the artist must serve the poor people of society. From then on, he began attacking the evils of American capitalism. Like Tolstoy, he argued for kindness and the unity of all people in society,

[3] *commonplace*, ordinary.

An 1875 picture showing different trades at a time of rapid industrialization

rather than selfish competition. A little later, Howells began to write "utopian" novels about an ideal society with perfect justice and happiness. These included *A Traveler from Altruria* (1894) and *Through the Eye of the Needle* (1907).

EDWARD BELLAMY (1850–1898) wrote the most famous American "utopian" novel. In his *Looking Backward, 2000–1887* (1888), a man goes to sleep and wakes up in the year 2000. He finds an entirely new society which is much better than his own. The author's purpose is really to criticize capitalist America of the 1880s. He is showing his fellow Americans a picture of how society could be. Today, the book seems a little too optimistic. Bellamy was sure society's problems could be solved by a higher level of industrialization. Today, many people are not so sure.

In the 1890s, many realists became "naturalists". "Naturalism[4]" was a term created by the French novelist, Emile Zola. In studying

[4] *naturalism*, the idea that art and literature should present the world and people just as science shows they really are.

Stephen Crane, author of The Red Badge of Courage

human life, the naturalist used the discoveries and knowledge of modern science. He believed people were not really "free". Rather, their lives, opinions and morality were all controlled by social, economic and psychological causes.

STEPHEN CRANE (1871–1900), the first American naturalist, was not much influenced by the scientific approach. He was a genius with amazing[5] sympathy and imagination. At the age of twenty-two, he became famous as the author of the novel *Maggie: A Girl of the Streets* (1893). It is the sad story of a girl brought up in a poor area of New York City. She is betrayed by her family and friends and finally has to become a prostitute. Almost every day she experiences the violence and cruelty of society. Finally, she goes to the river and looks down at the water, "lapping oilily against the timbers". Then she jumps in.

Like Maggie, all of Crane's characters are controlled by their environment. This is what makes Crane a "naturalist". Although Maggie wants to be good, the accidents of life make her seem bad. In *The Red Badge of Courage* (1895), Crane's greatest novel, the accidents of war make a young man seem to be a hero. The story is set in the Civil War. In the view of the author, war changes men into animals. Seeing that he is about to be killed, young Fleming (the hero) runs like an animal to save his life. After running, he hates himself for being a coward. Then, he is accidentally hit on the head. The other soldiers think it is a battle wound. They call it his "red badge of courage". Later, in another battle, Fleming again behaves like an animal. But

---

[5] *amazing*, very surprising.

this time he is a fighting, "heroic" animal. The world, like the battlefield, is filled with meaningless confusion. Good and bad, hero and coward, are merely matters of chance, of fate.

Similarly, in his short story, *The Open Boat* (1898), Crane shows how even life and death are determined by fate. After a shipwreck, four men struggle to stay alive. In the end, three live and one dies; but again, there is no pattern. There is not even a God, only fate . . . and the sea.

Crane's descriptions of places and events are both realistic and poetic. His style is far more exciting than that of the other naturalists. He uses colors and word-sounds to create brilliant "impressions[6]". Not surprisingly, he was also a good poet. In 1899, at the very end of his tragically short life, Crane wrote a collection of poems called *War Is Kind*. This one expresses the theme which lies at the heart of his novels:

> A man said to the universe,
> "Sir, I exist!"
> "However," replied the universe,
> "The fact has not created in me
> A sense of obligation[A]."

[A] owing something

As we can see, Crane's naturalism caused him to move far away from Howells's "more smiling aspects of life". In fact, this was the trend[7] for all of the realists. One very important group went in the direction of social criticism. In *The Damnation of Theron Ware* (1896), for example, HAROLD FREDERIC (1856–1898) attacks contemporary[8] religion. An idealistic young minister goes to a small town. The members of his little church there are not real Christians. They hate Jews, blacks, Catholics and "book-learning". Their only religion is "the religion of cash", of money. This is the ugly side of America's common people. Like other novels written in the 1890s, this one expresses deep doubts about the progress of American society.

[6] *impression*, effect produced on the mind; *impressionistic* = trying to give an impression without describing in detail.

[7] *trend*, direction of development.

[8] *contemporary*, of (or at) the same time – today or when an author was writing.

The naturalism of HAMLIN GARLAND (1860–1940) was filled with a deep sympathy for the common people. His literature was a form of social protest[9]. In such books as *Main-Travelled Roads* (1891), Garland protests against the conditions which made the lives of Mid-Western farmers so painful and unhappy. Although he saw life as "determined" by outside conditions, he hoped his novels would help change those conditions. He developed a writing method which he called "veritism" (from the word verity, meaning "truth"). He described people, places and events in a careful and factual manner. This is how he would describe a poor, sad, farming town: "unpaved streets, drab-colored, miserable rotting wooden buildings". The style of his descriptions is often impressionistic, like Crane's: he mixes emotions, colors and sights. But there is always a message behind these descriptions: that there is something very wrong with American society. The farmers lead desperate lives. In *Up the Coulé*, one of the short stories in *Main-Travelled Roads*, a character expresses the message directly:

> A man like me is helpless. . . . Just like a fly in a pan of molasses. There ain't any escape for him. The more he tears[A] around, the more liable[B] he is to rip[C] his legs off.
>
> [A] runs in fear   [B] likely   [C] tear

At the end of the nineteenth century, Hamlin Garland was describing the failure of the "American Dream". Like many twentieth-century naturalists, he felt that the forces of American capitalism had destroyed the individual's freedom: "In the world of business, the life of one man seems to be drawn from the life of another man, each success springs from others' failures."

AMBROSE BIERCE (1842–1914) was one of the few important writers in late nineteenth-century America who was not a realist or a naturalist. The struggles of ordinary people in the everyday world did not interest him. Like Edgar Allan Poe, he loved to describe terrifying events and strange forms of death. His famous short stories about the Civil War – in *Tales of Soldiers and Civilians* (1891) and *Can Such Things Be?* (1893) – are actually horror stories. Irony is an important element

---

[9] *protest*, speak, write or act against something that one believes is wrong; n. *protest*.

in each of them. Things rarely happen the way a character hopes or expects they will. Fate often makes people do things they don't want to do. In *A Horseman in the Sky* (1891), a young soldier in the Northern army (who was born in the South) meets his father near his old home. But there is no joy at the meeting. Because the father is an officer in the Southern army, the son must kill him.

Bierce is also similar to Poe in his control of details. Each detail in a story is part of the single, clear impression created by the whole story. Each additional detail gives us a clearer impression of the ironic fate waiting for a character. In *The Devil's Dictionary* (1911), Bierce uses humor to express his ironic view of the world. Here are his unusual and unexpected definitions for a few common words:

> Patience: a form of despair, disguised as a virtue
> Realism: the art of depicting nature as it is seen by a toad
> Reality: the dream of a mad philosopher
> Twice: once too often
> Year: a period of three hundred and sixty-five
>   disappointments

HENRY JAMES (1843–1916) was a realist, but not a naturalist. Unlike Howells and the naturalists, he was not interested in business, politics or the conditions of society. He was an observer of the mind rather than a recorder of the times. His realism was a special kind of psychological realism. Few of his stories include big events or exciting action. In fact, the characters in his last (and finest) novels rarely do anything at all. Things happen to them, but not as a result of their own actions. They watch life more than they live it. We are interested in how their minds respond to the events of the story. What do they see? How do they try to understand it? The changing consciousness of the character is the real story. Henry's older brother, the philosopher William James, gave this kind of literature a name. He called it "stream-of-consciousness" literature. In the late nineteenth century, most readers were not ready for such a new approach and so Henry James's greatest novels were not very popular. But in twentieth-century literature, the "stream-of-consciousness" method has become quite common. Thanks to modern psychology and writers like Henry James, we are now more interested in the workings of the mind. We know that events inside one's head can be as dramatic as events in the outside world.

We usually divide James's career as a writer into three stages: early, middle and mature. James developed toward his mature – or fully developed – style rather slowly. The novels of his early period deal with his thoughts and feelings as an American living in Europe. James himself spent most of his life in England and, in 1915, he finally became a British citizen. *Roderick Hudson* (1876) tells of the failure of a young American artist in Italy. Although he has genius, the young man fails because he lacks moral strength. *The American* (1877) contrasts[10] American "innocence" with European "experience". James uses this contrast throughout his work. Like many of James's later American heroes, Christopher Newman (in *The American*) is a rich young man who goes to Europe in search of culture and a better life. There he meets a young woman, and wants to marry her. The woman wants to marry him too. But even though he is a fine, intelligent man, her family will not allow it. They are the worst kind of European aristocrats. They value their family name more than the happiness of their daughter. They have a "destructive, life-hating honor". Unlike most of James's later novels, this one is rather easy to read. The story moves quickly and clearly.

Daisy Miller (1879) is another novel about American innocence defeated by the stiff, traditional values of Europe. Daisy brings her "free" American spirit to Europe. She looks at people as individuals, rather than as members of a social class. Despite her goodness, she is completely misunderstood by the European characters. She meets a young American, who has lived in Europe a long time and has taken on the same kind of coldness. The coldness of these people finally leads Daisy to her death.

The Portrait of a Lady (1881) is the best novel of James's "middle period". Again, a young, bright American girl goes to Europe to "explore life". After many good offers of marriage, she chooses the wrong man. The most important part of the book is where she realizes her mistake. She sits all alone, late at night, in her "house of darkness". James shows her inner consciousness in this quiet moment. There is great drama in his description of her "motionlessly *seeing*" the mistake

---

[10] *contrast*, (show) the difference between (one thing and another).

A cartoon showing Henry James returning to Europe

she has made. The drama is not created by her actions but by the thoughts in her mind. This description marks the beginning of James's "mature" period.

After this, little by little, dramatic action almost disappears from James's novels. Characters usually spend their time talking about the different aspects and possibilities of the situations they are in. Sometimes the drama comes when a character changes from one way of looking at the world to another way. In *The Princess Casamassima*

(1886), the hero is a revolutionary who wants to destroy the European aristocracy. But gradually, he falls in love with the aristocrat's "world of wonderful precious things". This change of heart leads to his suicide[11]. In *The Ambassadors* (1903), a middle-aged American goes to Paris to rescue the son of a friend from the "evils" of European society. When he arrives, he is still a moralistic New Englander. He disapproves of everything he sees. But slowly, he begins to see Europe in an entirely different way. In the end, the boy is happy to be "rescued" and to go back to America. The man, however, wants to stay in Europe.

Henry James never tries to give a large, detailed picture of society. Rather, in his stories, he selects a single situation or problem: often, the problem is about the nature of art. Then, using his imagination, he studies that one problem from various points of view. In his excellent short stories, we can clearly see how this method works. In *The Real Thing* (1893), the problem is how art changes reality. An artist wants to create a picture of typical aristocrats. When he tries to use real aristocrats as his models, he fails. He discovers that lower-class models are better for his purposes than "the real thing". The real aristocrats are so real that he can't use his imagination. In *The Death of the Lion* (1894), a famous writer faces the problem of being too popular. He becomes too busy with his admirers to write.

Another kind of problem that Henry James deals with in both his short stories and novels is the "unlived life". The hero may be so afraid of life that he cannot really live. In *The Beast in the Jungle* (1903), the hero is sure something terrible is going to happen to him. Much later, he discovers that the terrible fate waiting for him "is that nothing is to happen to him". A further problem James often studied was the introduction of children to the evil and immorality of the world around them. This is the theme of *What Maisie Knew* (1897) and *The Turn of the Screw* (1898). The latter is a famous ghost story about two children and their nurse. The nurse is sure the children are being haunted[12] by ghosts, but it is not clear to the reader whether these ghosts are real or only in the nurse's mind.

For James, in his private life and in his literature, being an

[11] *suicide*, killing oneself.
[12] *haunt*, visit regularly, as *ghosts* (the spirits of dead people) are thought to do.

American was a great problem. "It is a complex fate, being an American," he wrote. Although he lived most of his life abroad, this was always a central theme. In his writings, Americans are always being "tested" by European civilization. And, similarly, the achievements of European civilization are always being tested by the new possibilities of American civilization.

*Life for rich Americans (left)
and poor Americans (below)
in the early 1900s*

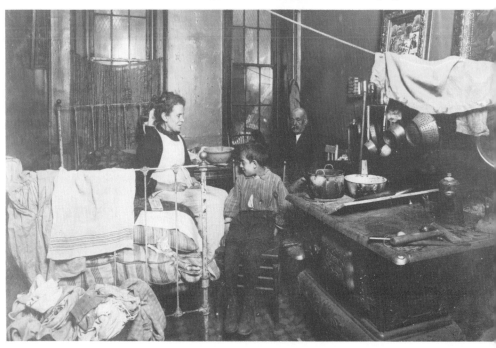

Chapter Eight

At the Turn of the Century

By the mid-1880s, the happy, well-educated world of the Boston Brahmins was dead and gone. Rich businessmen had replaced the old "aristocrats of literature" as the leaders of Boston life. This change deeply saddened HENRY ADAMS (1838–1918), one of the youngest members of the Brahmin group. Both his grandfather and his great-grandfather had been Presidents of the United States. He had hoped that, like them, he also would live in the White House some day. Adams moved to Washington D.C. in order to make a career in politics. But all his political plans failed. Instead, he wrote two novels. The first was *Democracy* (1880), a satire on the political and social life of the nation's capital. His *Esther* (1884) was about the cultural education of a young woman. Although he was skillful as a novelist, Adams's real love and talent was for history. He found it "wildly interesting". He spent twelve years researching[1] and writing his *History of the United States of America during the Administrations of Jefferson and Madison* (1889–1891). It is both a work of history and a work of art. Like Prescott and Parkman, the Brahmin historians, he used a poetic style to help his readers to feel the "mood" of great events. But like the naturalist novelists, he tried to give a scientific interpretation of the forces in human history.

Adams is best remembered for his *Mont-Saint-Michel and Chartres* (1904). On the surface, it is a guide book to two famous French religious sites. Actually, however, it is a deep study of medieval[2] culture. As one critic (Van Wyck Brooks) has noticed, Adams's "contempt for the present grew with his love of the past". In the

[1] *research*, close study to find the facts about something.
[2] *medieval*, of the Middle Ages in European history (about 1100–1500).

architecture, poetry and philosophy of the twelfth and thirteenth centuries, he found peace. The old culture of Europe had a calm unity; the new culture of America, however, had neither calmness nor unity. When the book was published, Adams was surprised to find that he had become the leader of a popular movement. Many young people shared his dissatisfaction with the present world.

The Education of Henry Adams (1907) is an equally beautiful book. The author describes his education as a journey. First he is in search of a career, then he is in search of meaning in the modern world. Both searches end in failure. The present world has too many "meanings". Nineteenth-century education cannot explain this new world. To Adams, the naturalist, inhuman and uncontrollable forces rule our lives: "Chaos[3] is the law of nature; order, the dream of man." In medieval times, man's dream of order was achieved by the Christian Church. But in the new age of rapid change and progress, that order has been lost. Adams often uses the image of the Virgin Mary to represent the old ideal: she represents unity and the force of the inner spirit. Electricity and steam engines represent the new "silent and infinite forces" which now rule the modern world. But these machines – and the forces used to run them – can never achieve man's old dream of order in life. They have no inner spiritual meaning: "All the steam in the world could not, like the Virgin, build Chartres."

At the Turn of the Century[4], words and phrases like "uncontrollable forces", "energy", and "evolution" were appearing in other novels. Writers were greatly influenced by Zola's "scientific" study of man, by Darwin's theory of evolution and by the ideas of the German philosopher Friedrich Nietzsche, which attacked Christianity. Writers at the Turn of the Century were beginning to think about traditional social morality in a new way. Traditional values had been based on the idea of individual responsibility: the individual can and must choose between good and evil. But now writers were asking whether the individual could really make such a choice. When they looked at the many outside forces influencing a person, the area of individual choice and responsibility seemed quite small. Nietzsche suggested that there were also other forces which worked *inside* the

---

[3] *chaos*, lack of all order; total disorganization.

[4] *turn of the century*, the end of one century and the beginning of another (example: 1898–1901).

Frank Norris

individual. Each person, he said, has a "will to power". This "will" – or desire to control oneself, other people and the world around one – is "beyond good and evil" (Nietzsche's phrase). It is a force of nature, like hunger, or sex.

The novels of FRANK NORRIS (1870–1902) are clearly influenced by this new way of thinking. His characters are often unable to control their own lives. They are moved around by "passions" or by "fate". The whole world, natural and human, is a battlefield between uncontrollable forces. In *McTeague* (1899), he describes a California landscape[5] in which "A tremendous, immeasurable Life pushed steadily heavenward without a sound, without a motion." In the next paragraph, he describes the mechanical power which opposes it. It is a mining machine, which is like a monster: "gnashing[6] the rocks to powder with its long iron teeth, vomiting them out again in a thin

[5] *landscape*, stretch of country that can be seen at one time.
[6] *gnash*, put the teeth together fiercely.

stream of wet gray mud". McTeague, the "hero" of the novel, is also animal-like: "Below the fine fabric[7] of all that was good in him ran the foul stream of hereditary[8] evil, like a sewer[9] . . . The evil of an entire race flowed in his veins." His wife, whom he kills, had won a lot of money in a lottery. This act of "fate" makes her crazy. She enjoys sleeping naked on top of her gold coins.

The Octopus (1901) is a novel about the battle between California wheat farmers and the Southern Pacific Railroad. As in *McTeague*, we see the conflict between the power of nature (the farmers) and a mechanical monster (the railroad). The farmers are defeated by "inevitable[10]" economic forces. In *The Octopus* and then in *The Pit* (1903), Norris uses wheat as the symbol of life. He makes it an almost religious symbol. In this sense, he is different from the "scientific" naturalists. His writing style is also different from that of the other naturalists. Many of his techniques for description (his repetitious and powerful language) seem closer to such romantic writers as Hawthorne.

JACK LONDON (1876–1916), like Norris, was deeply influenced by Darwin's ideas of constant struggle in nature and "the survival of the fittest". Not surprisingly, the heroes of some of London's best stories are animals. In his famous *Call of the Wild* (1903) the dog, Buck, is taken from his easy life in California and brought to the frozen environment of Alaska. He survives because he is a "superior individual". In the end, he returns to the world of his ancestors. He becomes the leader of a pack of wolves. Wolf Larsen, the hero of *The Sea-Wolf* (1904), is not simply a man, he is a "superman". The beautiful poetess Maude Brewster becomes fascinated with him after he rescues her and takes her on board his ship. His knowledge of the sea makes him seem like a master of nature. But in the end, even this superman dies. London himself once explained that his point was that a man like Wolf Larsen could not survive in modern society.

The laws of nature govern everything and everybody inside or outside society in London's novels. Sometimes people are defeated by

[7] *fabric*, material.
[8] *hereditary*, passed from parents to children.
[9] *sewer*, underground pipe carrying away waste from toilets etc.
[10] *inevitable*, unavoidable.

Jack London

An illustration from London's novel The Call of the Wild

these laws. In his great short story, *To Build a Fire* (1910), a man stupidly goes out into the terrible cold of an Alaskan storm. Since he has matches, he thinks he can build a fire any time. But in the end Alaskan nature defeats him and he freezes to death.

It seems that Jack London saw himself as a kind of superman hero, too. Despite the fact that he died when he was forty, he had had an amazing career. He was largely self-educated. He had been a seal hunter, an oyster pirate, an explorer, a war correspondent, a gold miner and a rich farmer. During a cold winter in the Alaskan Klondike, he had read the books that became the basis of his thought and writing. Sometimes he was a Darwinian naturalist. Sometimes, as in his novels *The People of the Abyss* (1903) and *The Iron Heel* (1907), he was a Marxian socialist. Later he rejected socialism and seemed to support a kind of white racism. Although he often changed his philosophy, the quality of his writing was always high. As H. L. Mencken (see p. 123) wrote, London's work had "all the elements of sound fiction: clear thinking, a sense of character, the dramatic instincts and . . . words charming and slyly[11] significant[12]".

The Turn of the Century was an exciting moment in American intellectual history. American novelists and poets were no longer simply copying British and European writers. They were now sharing ideas with the whole world. America was about to become an important contributor to world literature. A similar thing was happening in philosophy and sociology. JOHN DEWEY (1859–1952) and WILLIAM JAMES (1842–1910) developed their philosophy of "Pragmatism". They believed that there are no fixed truths; that whatever works (in theory or reality) is right; and that ideas are instruments which are useful only when they help change society. William James, Henry James's elder brother, greatly influenced European philosophers with his *Varieties of Religious Experience* (1902) and, especially, his *Pragmatism* (1907). In sociology, THORSTEIN VEBLEN (1857–1929) made an important contribution to the growing attack on the capitalist economic and social system with his *Theory of the Leisure Class* (1899). According to this theory, America's very rich do not produce the wealth of the nation; they simply use it. The

[11] *sly*, clever but deceptive; adv. *slyly*.
[12] *significant*, full of meaning.

American economic system, Veblen says, encourages competition in making money rather than in making products. After they have made their money, the rich use it wastefully. They buy expensive things in order to show other people how rich they are.

Big Business and the Big Capitalists like Rockefeller and Carnegie were becoming the "bad guys" of American society. The American public began to feel that "dirty politics" and "dirty business" had gone too far in American society. At the Turn of the Century, even the President expressed this idea. In a speech in 1902, President Theodore Roosevelt announced that the government must lead a war against the nation's political, social and economic evils. In politics, this was the "Progressive era". In newspapers and literature, from 1900 to 1914, this was the "Muckraker[13] era".

Inexpensive, popular magazines like *McClure's*, *Everybody's* and *Cosmopolitan* sent their reporters out to find the wrong-doers of politics and business. The job of these "Muckrakers" was to print the truth, however unpleasant, in their magazines. They quickly moved from magazine articles to books. In her *History of the Standard Oil Company* (1904), IDA TARBELL (1857–1944) attacks the methods John D. Rockefeller used to crush his competitors. DAVID G. PHILLIPS (1867–1911) covered all kinds of social evils, from politics (*The Plum Tree*, 1905) to finance (*The Cost*, 1904, and *The Deluge*, 1905). Some writers, like LINCOLN STEFFENS (1866–1936), had a social philosophy very close to that of the naturalist novelists. "The struggle for existence is very animal-like," Steffens wrote. After two years of careful research, he published his *Shame of the Cities* (1904), which described America's "invisible government" (the secret co-operation between big business and national political leaders). Some writers, like the novelist ROBERT HERRICK (1868–1938), seemed to have a tragic view of life. In *The Common Lot* (1904) and other novels, he describes the evil growth of the "commercial spirit" in America, from the 1890s. In great sadness, he says that the soul of the middle class is being destroyed. These people now lead empty, meaningless lives. Like many writers after him, Herrick seemed to be filled with hopelessness and despair.

UPTON SINCLAIR (1878–1968), the most famous of the Muckrakers, was the opposite of Herrick. He believed in human goodness and was

---

[13] *Muckraker*, one who collects the shameful facts (*muck* = dirt) about people.

Upton Sinclair, author of The Jungle

sure society could be changed: "The deepest instinct[14] of the human heart is the longing[15] for justice between man and man." For him, Muckraking was "almost a religious mission". His greatest novel, *The Jungle* (1906), was a successful weapon in his fight for justice. It tells the story of an immigrant family, the Redkuses, who come to America with dreams of a better way of life. But they only experience a series of horrors and tragedies. Sinclair shows the terrible conditions the family experience in Chicago's meat-packing industry. Jack London described the novel as "the *Uncle Tom's Cabin* of wage-slavery". Indeed, it did have a similar practical effect. Millions of Americans were shocked by his descriptions. Even President Theodore Roosevelt was

---

[14] *instinct*, natural feeling that does not depend on teaching.
[15] *longing*, deep (and often sad) desire.

shocked. All this attention forced the reform of America's food industry. As literature, however, *The Jungle* is not very satisfactory. In almost all of his many novels, Sinclair's characters seem rather flat and lifeless. But perhaps Sinclair's main interest was not as much in his characters as in his message. His novels were always a form of propaganda. They tried to force society to change. Because Sinclair's books did succeed in correcting many of the evils they described, however, they no longer create the excitement they once did.

The same cheap magazines that started the Muckrakers gave the world another writer of interest, O. HENRY (1862–1910). During 1904 and 1905, O. Henry wrote one short story a week. His first collection of stories, *Cabbages and Kings* (1904), made him a popular hero. He usually used his own experiences as ideas for stories. He had lived in Texas and Central America. He had even spent some time in prison. He loved New York City and knew how to describe it for Americans who lived in other parts of the country. It was a magic place, "inhabited by four million mysterious strangers". Like Mark Twain, he wrote in an easy-to-understand, journalistic style. His stories begin with action and move quickly toward their conclusion. They are filled with deep, loving portraits of the lives of ordinary people. Like Twain, he takes the side of the "little people" and the weak "under-dogs" against the strong or important. The plots often seem to be written according to a formula. One such formula is the "reversal": an action by a character produces the opposite effect from the one he had been hoping for. When, for example, a little boy is kidnapped by some bad men, we know what will happen. The boy will "reverse" the situation before the end of the story and make the men his prisoners.

Another O. Henry formula is to keep an important piece of information from the reader until the very end (as in *The Gift of the Magi*, 1906). In 1914, the *New York Times* praised his story *Municipal Report*. The newspaper said, "It is the greatest American short story ever written." But other critics hated O. Henry's stories. In 1920, H. L. Mencken complained that "there is not a single recognizable human character" among any of his works. Even O. Henry once wrote, "I am a failure. My stories? No, they don't satisfy me." Still, they satisfied (and still satisfy) millions of readers. Even today, O. Henry is recognized as one of America's finest early short story writers.

American newspapers and magazines had become very powerful

by this period. They were patriotic; they wanted the United States to grow in strength, and attacked peace-lovers as "unhealthy and un-American". Some historians say that the Spanish–American War (1898) was started by American journalists. The newspapers wanted something exciting to write about. Stephen Crane and Frank Norris were newspaper correspondents in that war. Correspondents like RICHARD HARDING DAVIS (1864–1916) pleased readers with stories of courage and red blood. Davis's descriptions of battle were particularly good, like the battle of Santiago, "when (*the Spanish*) empire was wiped off the map in twenty minutes". He later collected his reports into his very popular *Notes of a War Correspondent* (1910). Each report told the tale of a courageous hero; sometimes a soldier, sometimes a journalist. Like Hemingway, who also started as a war correspondent, Davis was admired by women readers. He was a hero; brave, manly.

LAFCADIO HEARN (1850–1904) also began as a newspaper writer. He was born in Greece and his father was British. At nineteen, he arrived in America without any money, and had to find a way to make a living. Soon he was a reporter for the Cincinnati *Enquirer* and then, later, on a New Orleans paper. His best writing described mood[16] rather than action. He loved the contrast between brilliant light and darkness. He described New Orleans at night: "the shadow of a pedestrian makes a moving speck in the moonlight on the pavement".

Later, he went to the Caribbean islands. In his *Martinique Sketches* (1890), he "painted" this world of sunshine and bright colors with words. He described "the blinding whiteness of linen laid out to bleach[17] for miles on huge boulders[18]". His best descriptions are like romantic photographs: "Sundown approaches; the light has turned a rich yellow; long black shapes lie across the curving road, shadows of palm, shadows of tamarind . . . shadows of giant-fern."

But the world knows and loves best the Lafcadio Hearn who went to Japan, changing his name to "Koizumi Yakumo", and becoming a Japanese citizen. He also changed his style and subject matter. He had always been interested in legends and folk tales. Now he began collecting Japanese ghost stories. To tell these tales – in such books as

[16] *mood*, a state of the feelings.
[17] *bleach*, make (or become) white.
[18] *boulder*, rock made round by the action of water.

In Ghostly Japan (1899) and *Kwaidan* (1904) – he departed from his old poetic style and began using words simply. He began writing for the ear, rather than for the mind's eye. "Listen" to this passage from his *Mimi-nashi-Hoichi*:

> At that instant, Hoichi felt his ears gripped by fingers of iron, and torn off! Great as the pain was, he gave no cry. The heavy footfalls receded^A, along the verandah, – descended into the garden, – passed out to the roadway, – ceased.
>
> ^A went away

Lafcadio Hearn didn't simply translate the stories, he made them into a new kind of literature. The Japanese love him for this. They have translated such books as his *Kwaidan* back into their own language. Every Japanese school child knows his name and at least some of his work. Although Hearn admired Japan, he wrote about both the good and the bad in that country. In *Japan: An Attempt at Interpretation* (1904), he praises its old society and criticizes its new industrial society. He also predicted[19] the conflict between Japan and the West. But in the history of American literature, he is the man who made the legends and tales of an unknown culture a part of our own literature. As one critic says, "He is the only writer in our language who can be compared with Hans Christian Andersen."

[19] *predict*, say what will happen.

Theodore Dreiser in later years

Chapter Nine

The Turning Point of American Literature

As the new century entered its second decade[1], the forward movement of American literature seemed to have stopped. The realist novels of W. D. Howells and Hamlin Garland were beginning to seem old-fashioned. Among the exciting young writers of the Turn of the Century, Jack London seemed to have lost his genius and Frank Norris and Stephen Crane were already dead. People were again asking what was wrong with American literature.

Part of the problem was that most American readers and writers had not yet "outgrown" the nineteenth century. The novels of WINSTON CHURCHILL (1871–1947); (*not* the famous British Prime Minister) were typical of the tastes of America's reading public. His most popular works – *The Crisis* (1901) and *The Crossing* (1904) – had old-fashioned, romantic plots. They expressed sadness at the passing of the aristocratic culture of the South after the Civil War. Also popular was JAMES BRANCH CABELL (1879–1958). His novels were romantic, written in an elegant, nineteenth-century prose style. By creating his own mythical[2] kingdom of "Poictesme" (where knighthood and poetry ruled), he helped his readers escape from the reality of the present into an unreal past. In such novels and collections of stories as *Gallantry* (1907), *Chivalry* (1909) and *The Soul of Melicent* (1913), he succeeded in his desire to "write beautifully of beautiful happenings". Although his books are often delightful in themselves, they did not provide the new direction needed by the new generation of American writers.

In the 1840s, Emerson had shown American literature the way

---

[1] *decade*, period of ten years.

[2] *myth*, ancient story with magic elements; *mythical* = of or like myths; *mythology* = collection of myths.

forward. In the 1880s, W. D. Howells gave similar leadership to the realist movement. Starting in 1915 (with his *America's Coming-of-Age*), the critic VAN WYCK BROOKS (1886–1963) opened a period of "self-criticism", in which writers looked at what was wrong with the nation and its literature:

> There is a kind of anarchy[A] that fosters[B] growth and there is another kind of anarchy that prevents growth – all our contemporary literature in America cries out of this latter kind of anarchy.
>
> [A] having no rule   [B] helps

Brooks knew that such literary criticism would "sooner or later become social criticism . . . because the future of our art and literature depends upon the complete reconstruction of social life". American society was "united in a sort of conspiracy[3] against the growth and freedom of the spirit". For too long, he wrote, American life had been divided between the businessman (who only thinks of making money) and the intellectual (who only has unpractical theories and ideals). "The professor and the businessman between them hold in their hands a great part of human destiny[4]," Brooks wrote. But, because they don't understand each other, there is no "middle ground" where they can meet. The new generation of American writers must construct (or reconstruct) this "middle ground".

Young writers took notice of Brooks's criticism. The result was the "new realism" which lasted up to the 1950s. It made American literature one of the most exciting and most influential literatures of the world. Van Wyck Brooks, meanwhile, went on to the job of providing American writers with a "usable past". That is, he reviewed and reorganized the history of American literature. He wrote famous biographies of Mark Twain (1920) and of Henry James (1925). His theory was that they were failures because their environment had prevented their development as true artists. With *The Flowering of New England: 1815–1865* (1936), which won the Pulitzer Prize, Brooks became recognized as America's first serious literary historian.

[3] *conspiracy*, secret plan to break the law or do harm.
[4] *destiny*, fate.

In a sense, the nineteenth century didn't end in America until about 1913. Around this time, the new critics – Brooks, H. L. Mencken and Hanna Larson – began celebrating the death of "puritanism" (strict morality like that of the old New England Puritans). "Until recently," Hanna Larson wrote in 1913, "American fiction was so moral as to be immoral, because it had no place for truth." Truth, in this case, included truth about sex. Hiding the truth about human sexuality – and punishing those who tried to talk about it – was part of America's "puritanical" morality. In the nineteenth century, there was a "double standard" in both public and private morality: people had to "talk one way while acting in a completely different way".

But this was beginning to change. American readers were beginning to lose their fear of those who looked below the surface of human relationships. Intelligent readers, at least, were now able to accept even ugly truths about human nature. In 1919, Sigmund Freud, the great Austrian psychologist, had given a famous lecture series in America. This series was both a liberation and an inspiration for American artists. But even before Freud's arrival, two American novelists were starting to destroy the "double standard" of America's puritanical morality: Edith Wharton and Theodore Dreiser.

EDITH WHARTON (1862–1937) was born into an old New York family. She married a man of her own class, but later she left him and moved to Europe to begin a career as a writer. All of her stories are set in the puritanical world of the upper classes. Many people notice a strong similarity between her stories and those of her friend and teacher, Henry James. They both wrote psychological novels, usually about the problems of women in upper-class society.

However, Wharton's style is more direct than James's. She can describe a whole way of life by describing a few surface details. In *The House of Mirth* (1905), Lily Bart looks down from a stairway into the main hall of a large house: "the great central lantern overhead shed a brightness on the women's hair and struck sparks from their jewels as they moved". Similarly, in a very few words she can "catch" (often humorously) the personality[5] of one of her upper-class characters: "she had a way of looking at you that made you feel as if there was something wrong with your hat". In her wonderfully funny short

[5] *personality*, character.

story about a ladies' culture circle – *Xingu* (1916) – she describes one of the members:

> Her mind was a hotel – where ideas came and went like transient[A] guests, without leaving their address behind.
>
> [A] coming and going

Like the major works of James, many of Wharton's novels are about the life and customs of upper-class society. But angry social criticism is not far beneath the surface. The life of Lily Bart, heroine of *The House of Mirth*, is actually a battle. She has been brought up to see herself as a decorative object for wealthy men. But she hates having to spend time with boring men, "all on the chance that (*such men*) might decide to do her the honor of boring her for life". When she tries to act with a little bit of freedom, society rejects her as immoral. In the end, she fails to get a husband, and kills herself. Undine Spragg, the heroine of *The Custom of the Country* (1913), is quite open about her own sexual desires. Unlike Lily Bart, she knows exactly how to use her attractions to get a wealthy husband. Wharton is attacking here the Victorian world of her own youth. Even the littlest suggestion of sexuality had to be hidden. For example, it was considered bad manners for a man to offer a lady his chair: the chair might still have some warmth from the man's body. The upper classes claimed to be highly moral, but often their actions – towards women as well as in business – were not moral at all.

Wharton continues her theme of dishonesty about one's emotions and sexual feelings in her most famous novel, *Ethan Frome* (1911). As in all of her work, this theme is never expressed directly. Instead it lies just below the surface in scenes of great tension[6]. Ethan, a New England farmer, has a cold, unsatisfactory relationship with his wife. A young cousin, Mattie, comes to live with them. Ethan and the girl Mattie are drawn to each other. But in scene after scene, we see them denying[7] their desires. Finally, they try to kill themselves, but they fail. In the end Mattie (now a cripple), Ethan (now elderly) and the cold wife all share a strange and terrible life together in the tiny farmhouse. At the time it was published, most readers thought

[6] *tension*, anxiety in a situation or between people.
[7] *deny*, refuse to allow.

Edith Wharton

Wharton was punishing her characters for their desires. Today, we might interpret it differently: their unhappy lives are the result of ignoring[8] those desires. *The Reef* (1912) and *Summer* (1917) are two more Wharton novels about sexual passion. In all of her works, the natural instincts of people are crushed by an untruthful society. But her characters still have some room for moral choice. This makes her different from the pure naturalist writers like Crane and Dreiser. Their characters have no real choice.

THEODORE DREISER (1871–1945) was one of America's greatest writers, and its greatest naturalist writer. He and his characters did not attack the nation's puritanical moral code: they simply ignored it. This attitude shocked the reading public when his first novel, *Sister Carrie*, came out in 1900. Although we now see it as a masterpiece, it was suppressed until 1912. The heroine, Carrie Meeber, leaves the poverty of her country home and moves to Chicago. She is completely honest about her desire for a better life: clothes, money and social position. Dreiser himself had been born in poverty, and therefore doesn't criticize her for this. Nor does he criticize her relationships with men. Carrie is quite modern in the way she moves from one

[8] *ignore*, take no notice of.

relationship to another. She tries to be faithful to them, but circumstances make this impossible. Almost by accident, she becomes a success as an actress. In the end, however, she learns that even money and success are not the keys to true happiness.

As in all of his novels, Dreiser's real theme in *Sister Carrie* is the purposelessness of life. While looking at individuals with warm, human sympathy, he also sees the disorder and cruelty of life in general. While one character, Carrie, gains fame and comfort, another character in the novel, Hurstwood, loses his wealth, social position and pride. This character's tragedy is just as accidental as Carrie's success. Dreiser does not try to explain why these things happen. In his form of naturalism, the workings of fate can never be explained. In *Jennie Gerhardt* (1911), his next novel, the theme is the same. One character puts it this way: "The individual doesn't count much in the situation . . . We are moved about like chessmen . . . we have no control." It is a "most terrible truth" that "the purposes of nature have no relation to the purposes of men".

In romantic novels, characters often earn rewards – sometimes money, sometimes glory – by having a good moral character. In the pure naturalist novel, goodness is punished more often than it is rewarded. It is almost a kind of weakness in the character. Dreiser's Jennie Gerhardt has good intentions and a good character. But these are not enough to reward, or even save her. The accidents of life have made her immoral in the eyes of society. Actually, the reader does not see her that way at all. Christian morality demanded that she act in one way. Life itself made it necessary for her to live in another way. Christian morality has created a false sense of guilt. The morality is wrong, not Jennie. The morality itself causes Jennie's tragedy. Therefore Dreiser sees such morality as evil.

Dreiser's "Trilogy[9] of Desire" – *The Financier* (1912), *The Titan* (1914) and *The Stoic* (published in 1947, after his death) – shows a new development in his thinking. He had already found life to be meaningless, and morals to be absurd. Now, under the influence of Nietzsche, he stressed "the will to power". The trilogy tells the story of F. A. Cowperwood, a "superman" of the modern business world. Although he is writing about the achievements of a single, powerful

[9] *trilogy*, a group of 3 books related in subject but each complete in itself.

individual, Dreiser does not forget the basic principles of his naturalism. On the one hand, the author says that "the world only moves forward because of the services of the exceptional individual". But on the other hand, Cowperwood is also a "chessman" of fate. Like Carrie, his success is mostly the result of chance.

Dreiser's greatest novel, *An American Tragedy* (1925), reveals a third stage in his thinking: social consciousness. Much more than in *Sister Carrie*, he sees his characters as victims of society. Clyde Griffiths, the hero (or "anti-hero"), has the same dream as Carrie: he thinks money and success will bring him happiness. When a pregnant[10] girlfriend threatens to destroy this dream, he plans to kill her. At the last moment, he changes his mind, but the girl dies accidentally anyway. Since Clyde had decided not to kill her, is he really responsible for her death? This becomes the main question during his trial. The trial itself is not really fair. The newspapers stir up public anger against him. In the end, Clyde is executed[11]. Clearly, Dreiser believes that Clyde is not really guilty. Society and its false moral code are far more guilty. Dreiser calls his novel a tragedy, and in certain ways it is similar to classical Greek tragedy. It concentrates on a single individual, which gives it unity; and this individual is eventually[12] destroyed by forces which he cannot control.

Dreiser's novels were very long. They were filled with details about factories, banks, cities and business life. Some people complained about his style. There were too many details, they said, and his language was not clear. But nobody could deny his importance. He and his books were like a huge mountain. In a sense this was a problem for younger writers. Each of them had to find his (or her) way around the mountain of Dreiser's naturalism. Some of them rejected the whole tradition of naturalism in literature.

This is what WILLA CATHER (1873–1947) did. She was almost the same age as Dreiser, but more conservative. She disagreed with his criticisms of society and hated his "detail-piling". She believed the novel should be without "social furniture" (details about business, politics, etc.). The author and reader should concentrate on the emotional life of the central character.

[10] *pregnant*, going to have a baby.
[11] *execute*, put to death.
[12] *eventually*, in the end.

Willa Cather

Cather's speciality was portraits of the pioneer men and women of Nebraska. She had grown up there, and the values of the old pioneer people were her values. Her famous short story *Neighbor Rossicky* is about the last days of a simple, hard-working immigrant farmer. After much struggle, he has a successful farm and a loving family. Then he dies and is buried in the Nebraska land he had loved so much. A visitor looks at his grave and the beautiful land around it:

> Nothing but the sky overhead, and the many-colored fields running on until they met the sky. The horses worked here in the summer: the neighbors passed on their way to town.

Cather's most famous novels – *O Pioneers!* (1913), *The Song of the Lark* (1915) and *My Ántonia* (1918) – all have the same Nebraska setting. Each is a success story. The heroine of *My Ántonia* is a poor immigrant girl who had come to Nebraska as a child. The hardships of farm life kill her father and almost destroy her. But she has a "great gift for life". She lives on, marries and raises a large, happy family. As with Rossicky, her life "seemed complete and beautiful". But there was a darker side to life on the American prairie. *A Wagner Matinée* (1920) shows its harsh loneliness and lack of opportunity to enjoy art and culture. After a thrilling hour at a music concert, a farmer's wife turns to her husband and weeps: "I don't want to go, Clark. I don't want to go!" Outside the little concert hall are "the black pond . . . the tall, unpainted houses . . . the dishcloths hung to dry . . . the thin turkeys picking up refuse about the kitchen door."

Between 1923 and 1925 – in *A Lost Lady* and *The Professor's House* – Cather describes the decline and fall of the great pioneer tradition. It is being defeated by the new spirit of commerce and the new kind of man: the businessman. The greed of such people is destroying "the great, brooding spirit of freedom, the generous easy life . . . The space, the color, the princely carelessness of the pioneer they would destroy and cut up into profitable bits." After 1927, with her famous *Death Comes for the Archbishop*, Cather turned to historical fiction. Some say that in writing of the past she was trying to escape from the ugliness of the present.

ELLEN GLASGOW (1874–1945) is often compared with Willa Cather. Both novelists examined the problem of change. Glasgow, who grew up in Virginia, spent her life writing novels about her state's past. *The Battle-Ground* (1902), *The Deliverance* (1904), *Virginia* (1913) and *Life and Gabriella* (1916) form a social history of Virginia from the Civil War to World War I. We see the ruling aristocracy of Virginia being replaced by the new middle class. In a sense, Glasgow is a rebel against the old traditions of the South. Her male characters, mostly typical Southern gentlemen, are all childish and/or evil. Their society humiliates[13] women and keeps them in ignorance. But Glasgow does not direct all her criticism at the men. Like their husbands, the wives are "capable of dying for an idea, but not of thinking of one".

The Romantic Comedians (1926) centers on the marriage of an old man to a young girl. It is an amusing attack on Southern customs. Virginius Littlepage in *They Stooped to Folly* (1929) is a "model Virginia gentleman". He is crushed by his wife: "she preserves his place in the community and keeps him from enjoying it". *The Sheltered Life* (1932) is a novel about the breakdown of the false world of the South. The marriages, all based on "the ideal of Southern woman-hood", are unhealthy and unhappy. Then, in the thirties, big factories move into the region. When factory smoke enters their homes, the wives talk of moving. "After living here all our lives," one husband shouts, "shall we be driven out by a smell?" Once, these people had been the aristocratic rulers of the region. In one scene Glasgow gives us comedy, irony and sadness.

[13] *humiliate*, lower the social position of.

In the teens and early twenties, a number of other important American writers were treating life in small-town America. Some praised it, but most condemned its stupidity and prejudice. As early as 1899, BOOTH TARKINGTON (1869–1946) had been describing the small-town world as "one big jolly family". His books are about "the good old days". *The Magnificent Ambersons* (1918) is a loving portrait of a great, rich family which "rules" its town. Industrialism brings changes and the family begins its decline. In 1942, Orson Welles made it into a famous movie.

In 1915, the poet EDGAR LEE MASTERS (1869–1950) began the "Revolt from the Village" movement. His *Spoon River Anthology* is a collection of poetry which shows the many ways in which people are damaged by the narrowness of life in small-town America. In each of the 243 poems, a dead person from the town of Spoon River speaks from the grave. Depending upon the speaker, the language can sound very educated or low-class and vulgar. We find here a wide variety of social types: upper-class women, prostitutes, Christians, teachers, scientists, lovers, haters, and shy people. The picture they give of small-town life is usually not very attractive:

> When I died, the circulating[A] library
> Which I built up for Spoon River,
> And managed for the good of inquiring minds
> Was sold at auction in the public square,
> As if to destroy the last vestige[B]
> Of my memory and influence.
> [A] book-lending   [B] sign

He goes on to attack the "narrow and cruel" puritanism of small-town America. He expresses a feeling shared by many other American writers at this time:

> And often you asked me,
> "What is the use of knowing the evil of the world?"
> . . . I could never make you see
> That no one knows what is good
> Who knows not what is evil;
> And no one knows what is true
> Who knows not what is false.

When it was published, Masters's book was welcomed as "the most read and talked about volume of poetry that has ever been written in America". Today, however, we remember it chiefly as the inspiration for Sherwood Anderson's *Winesburg, Ohio*.

SHERWOOD ANDERSON (1876–1941) was another writer looking for a way around the "mountain" of Dreiser's naturalism. He brought the techniques of "modernism" to American fiction. These techniques included a simpler writing style, very much like ordinary spoken English; more emphasis on the *form* of the story than on its content; and a special use of time (in which past, present and future are mixed together, as in a dream). Many younger writers were greatly influenced by Anderson's "modernist" ideas. We can clearly see his influence on the style of Ernest Hemingway. William Faulkner called Anderson "the father of my generation of writers". Thomas Wolfe said he was "the only man in America who ever taught me anything".

In certain ways, Anderson was better at teaching other writers than writing his own novels. Only one of his books is really important in American literature: *Winesburg, Ohio* (1919). The book is actually a collection of connected short stories. All of the characters live in the same small town. Almost all of them are lonely people. They are cut off from other people and cannot communicate what is in their hearts. This loneliness makes them act in strange ways. Alice Hindman is a shy woman who has waited many years for the return of her lover. Then, one rainy night, "a wild, desperate mood took possession of her". She took off all her clothes, and:

> Without stopping to think what she intended to do, she ran downstairs through the dark house and out into the rain . . . and felt the cold rain on her body. . . . Not for years had she felt so full of youth and courage. She wanted to . . . find some other lonely human and embrace him. On the brick sidewalk before the house a man stumbled homeward. . . . "Wait!" she cried. "Don't go away. Whoever you are, you must wait." . . . He was an old man and somewhat deaf[A]. Putting his hand to his mouth he shouted. "What? What say?" Alice dropped to the ground and lay trembling.
>
> [A] he could not hear well

Later that night, Alice wept sadly. "What is the matter with me?" she cried. Then, "turning her face to the wall", she told herself bravely: "Many people must live and die alone, even in Winesburg."

Each of Anderson's tales contains a moment of self-understanding like the one above. In his autobiography, *A Story-Teller's Story* (1924), Anderson explains this technique: "I have come to think that the true history of life is a history of moments. It is only at rare moments that we live." This is a new and interesting idea of time in a story. These moments are like windows into the true nature of a character. Such moments are timeless. "What happens next" is not important. Anderson rejects traditional ideas about how a story should develop.

Anderson gave *Winesburg, Ohio* a second title: *The Book of the Grotesque*. There is something grotesque[14] about each character. This may be the result of their loneliness, their sexual disappointment or their strong but mistaken beliefs. Each of these "grotesques" has his or her timeless moment of deep experience. The whole purpose of the plot is to prepare us for this moment. Anderson's aim is to "leave a definite impression". He wants to give the feel of "a story grasped as a whole, like one would pick up an apple in an orchard". Perhaps because of this technique, Anderson's novels – *Marching Men* (1917), *Poor White* (1920), *Dark Laughter* (1925), etc. – "tend to break apart into episodes". The novels seem to be made up of a series of little stories, rather than being united by one large story. His style was much better suited to the short story.

Half a million young Americans died in World War I. President Woodrow Wilson had called it "a war to make the world safe for democracy". But afterwards, many younger Americans were not so sure that American democracy was worth saving. A new mood of anger entered the work of young writers. The "Revolt from the Village" became a revolt against the new commercial culture of post-war America. But the main target[15] was still the small town. In 1920, three important novels were published on this theme. *Miss Lulu Bett*, by ZONA GALE (1874–1938), and *Moon-Calf*, by FLOYD DELL (1887–1969), both describe the unhappy fight of intelligent young people

---

[14] *grotesque*, so strange as to appear foolish or frightening.
[15] *target*, the thing one aims at (in satire etc.).

against the stupidity of their hometowns. But it was *Main Street* by
SINCLAIR LEWIS (1885–1951) which created the most excitement of the
three.

Lewis's *Main Street* (1920) "is the continuation of Main Streets
everywhere. The story would be the same in Ohio . . . or in the hills of
Carolina." This is because Lewis's real subject is American culture:
"our comfortable tradition and sure faith". Carol Milford, a young
city woman, marries a Mid Western doctor called Kennicott and
moves to Gopher Prairie, Minnesota. The "spirit" of this tiny town
makes her very unhappy. Lewis's purpose is satire (and sometimes
pure comedy). His method is a kind of "photographic realism". His
scenes are usually "catalogs" (lists) of details. Often, these details
create a kind of drama in themselves. Here is Carol, sitting alone at
night, soon after coming to Gopher Prairie:

> There was only the hum of motor tires crunching the road, the
> creak of a rocker[A] on the Howlands' porch, the slap of a hand
> attacking a mosquito . . . the precise[B] rhythm of crickets, the
> thud of moths against the screendoor[C] – sounds that were a
> distilled[D] silence. It was a street beyond the end of the world,
> beyond the boundaries of hope. Though she should sit here
> forever . . . no one who was interesting would ever come by.
>
> [A] rocking-chair   [B] exact   [C] a door to let air in but to keep insects out
> [D] making (the silence) more noticeable

Carol tries to "reform" the town by re-educating the people. But she
fails. In the end, she gives up all her hopes. She joins the community
and tries to become just like everybody else. She "conforms".

Babbitt (1922), Lewis's next famous novel, is the story of the perfect
conformist; a man who tries to act the same way everybody else does.
The story opens with the hero rising out of bed and going into the
bathroom. He washes his face, and:

> Then George F. Babbitt did a dismaying[A] thing. He wiped his
> face on the guest-towel! It was a pansy-embroidered trifle[B]
> which always hung there to indicate[C] that the Babbitts were in
> the best . . . society. No one had ever used it. No guest had ever
> dared to.
>
> [A] fearful   [B] an almost useless thing with needlework flowers   [C] show

A scene from the movie of Lewis's novel Babbitt

Babbitt is a typical small businessman. Machines are "symbols of truth and beauty for him". His "philosophy of life" sounds like the names of products on a supermarket shelf: he believes in "Pep, Punch, Vigor, Enterprise, Red Blood, He-Men, Fair Women . . . American-ism and Pointing with Pride." Like *Main Street*, the novel is extremely funny satire. But it is also an important sociological study of American business culture. Today, "Babbitt" is part of our language. It means a "joiner", a "conformist". The novel has no real plot. But near the end, a kind of story does develop. Babbitt begins to doubt his way of life. "He beheld it as incredibly[16] mechanical. Mechanical business – a brisk selling of badly built houses. Mechanical religion – a dry, hard church, shut off from the life of the streets . . . mechanical friendships."

[16] *incredible*, unbelievable.

Like Carol Kennicott, Babbitt tries to revolt against the values of his town. He, too, fails. He finds that when he is free, he is "nothing at all". The novel ends with his return to being a conformist.

Although *Babbitt* was extremely popular among readers in America and Europe, some people criticized it. The American philosopher George Santayana (1863–1952) complained that "there is no suggestion of the direction in which salvation[17] may come". Lewis severely condemns the values of middle-class America, but he does not suggest any other values which can take their place. There is no "salvation", no way out. In *Elmer Gantry* (1927), Lewis's novel about an evangelist (a man who devotes his life to teaching people about religion), there is no character who is free from evil. No one shows us a different set of values. Around the time *Elmer Gantry* was being published, Ernest Hemingway was trying to create his own answer to this problem. In time, Hemingway succeeded in developing his own set of American values. This was something Sinclair Lewis could never do.

H. L. MENCKEN (1880–1956), America's most powerful social and literary critic in the twenties, also hated the middle class. In articles for the magazines *The Smart Set* and *The American Mercury*, he called them the "booboisie", a mixture of the words "bourgeoisie" (meaning the middle class) and "boob" (meaning a very stupid person). In many of his best articles, Mencken seemed almost anti-democratic. For him, stupidity was just as evil as dishonesty. America needed "a civilized aristocracy . . . superior to the sentimentality of the mob", he wrote. To him, "the mob" included those lower-class Americans who "hate all learning, all human dignity, all beauty, all fine and noble things". On the other hand, Mencken loved the rich, expressive language of common Americans. He wrote *The American Language* (1919, later revised several times), a serious study of "the development of English in the United States".

The 1920s was the decade of a "Lost Generation" of American writers (see Chapter 11). Many of the nation's best minds were moving away to foreign countries. Those who stayed at home were also deeply disappointed with American society. They knew American society did not value its artists and intellectuals. This made them lonely and angry.

[17] *salvation*, saving; way of escaping.

Gertrude Stein (right) with Lord Berners, composer, writer and artist

Chapter Ten

Poetry from 1900 through the 1930s

In the early twentieth century, American poetry began experimenting with new forms and content. EDWIN ARLINGTON ROBINSON (1869–1935) uses nineteenth-century poetic forms to express twentieth-century fears and problems. He loves the older forms – the traditional sonnet[1] and quatrain[2] – and he often uses the old-fashioned language of romantic poetry. But even his earliest poetry is filled with a very modern "sense of loss": the old values are gone, and there is nothing to replace them. The house in the poem *The House on the Hill* (1894) represents the New England Transcendentalism of Emerson and his followers. Once, it was the home of idealism and certainty. But now the Transcendentalists are all dead and "gone away":

> There is ruin and decay
> In the House on the Hill:
> They are all gone away,
> There is nothing more to say.

Robinson's poetry often expresses the uncertainty and lost beliefs of his own era. Sometimes he contrasts these feelings with the optimism of Emerson. In a famous poem of 1844, Emerson had looked joyfully into the future, seeing hope in the form of a star: "I see the coming of the light! I see (*its*) scattered gleams!" Fifty years later, in *Credo* (1896),

---

[1] *sonnet*, 14-line poem with definite rhyme patterns.
[2] *quatrain*, group of 4 lines of poetry in fixed form.

Robinson has far less hope for the new century:

> I cannot find my way: there is no star
> In all the shrouded[A] heavens anywhere;
> And there is not a whisper in the air
> Of any living voice . . .
>
> [A] cloud-covered

Robinson believes that man's fate is wrapped in "the black and awful chaos of the night". Some of his best poems are like little short stories in verse. Sometimes he shows a character, like Richard Cory, getting lost in life's "awful chaos". Cory seemed to have all of the best things in life. In fact he "glittered when he walked":

> And he was rich – yes, richer than a king,
>   And admirably schooled in every grace:
> In fine, we thought that he was everything
>   To make us wish that we were in his place.
>
> So on we worked, and waited for the light,
>   And went without the meat, and cursed the bread;
> And Richard Cory, one calm summer night,
>   Went home and put a bullet through his head.
>
> (*Richard Cory*, 1897)

The poet does not tell us why. Richard Cory, it seems, had simply decided that life was meaningless. Another of Robinson's famous characters, Miniver Cheevy, "wept that he was ever born, / And he had reasons." He cursed ordinary, modern life and "sighed for what was not". The age of romantic idealism is dead. Due to the rise of modern science, even religious faith has become weak. Now each individual must stand alone and face "the dark tideless floods of nothingness" (death). Is life still worth living? According to Robinson, we must each answer this for ourselves.

"Aloneness" is a common theme in the poetry of ROBERT FROST (1874–1963), another New Englander. In style, he also loved "the old way of being new": he always worked in the traditional forms of poetry. But there the similarity stops. Robinson is often difficult to understand. Frost speaks directly. He uses "a language absolutely unliterary". And, although he is a realist, his moods are rarely as black as Robinson's. Frost liked to say he was only having a "lover's quarrel with the world". These various qualities made him one of the best-loved poets of twentieth-century America.

Most of Frost's well-known poetry is nature poetry. It has a surface smoothness and simplicity. Then, suddenly, the surface breaks under our feet, like ice on a pond. We look down into unexpected depths of meaning. This is certainly true of *Stopping by Woods on a Snowy Evening* (1923):

> Whose woods these are I think I know.
> His house is in the village though;
> He will not see me stopping here
> To watch his woods fill up with snow.
>
> My little horse must think it queer[A]
> To stop without a farmhouse near
> Between the woods and frozen lake
> The darkest evening of the year.
>
> He gives his harness bells a shake
> To ask if there is some mistake.
> The only other sound's the sweep
> Of easy wind and downy flake[B].
>
> The woods are lovely, dark and deep
> But I have promises to keep,
> And miles to go before I sleep,
> And miles to go before I sleep.
>
> [A] unusual   [B] feathery snow

Each of the quatrains is carefully rhymed. But we get the feeling we are reading a story rather than a poem. When Frost repeats the last line, we are reminded that everything in the poem has a deeper meaning. "Miles to go before I sleep" probably means that he – and we – have important duties to finish before we die. Looking back, we can see that the poem is filled with images of stillness: "The woods are lovely, dark and deep", etc. This may represent a desire for the stillness of deep sleep, or even for death.

According to Frost, a good poem "begins in delight and ends in

Robert Frost towards the end of his life

wisdom". It cannot give us a complete philosophy of life. But it can sometimes help us to live with the confusions of human life. In fact, we can see a kind of philosophy in Frost's poetry. It has much in common[3] with Emerson's idea of "self-reliance". *The Road Not Taken* (1916) shows how individuals are forced to make choices in their lives:

> Two roads diverged[A] in a yellow wood,
> And sorry I could not travel both
> And be one traveler, long I stood
> And looked down one as far as I could
> To where it bent in the undergrowth;
> Then took the other . . .
>
> [A] separated

This little decision "has made all the difference". "Knowing how way leads to way", he realizes he can never go back again. In his blank verse play *A Masque of Mercy* (1947), Frost says, "The saddest thing in life / Is that the best thing in it should be courage." Still, the individual is not completely alone in this world. "Countless ties of love and thought" connect him "to everything on earth".

Later in life, with his pure white hair and old-fashioned manner, Frost became a kind of "folk hero". He made Americans think of the "good old days" and they expected him to be a little bit conservative. Frost's conservatism made him reject the new "free verse" styles of poetry. Free verse is "like playing tennis with the net down", he once remarked.

[3] *in common with*, that is the same as.

CARL SANDBURG (1878–1967) always excels in free verse. He uses the form successfully to treat many "unpoetical" subjects. He loves the everyday life of common people. Like Walt Whitman, Sandburg exclaims: "I am the People, the Mob!" He often uses the rhythmic repetitions of free verse to "sing" about factories and the building of skyscrapers. His *Chicago* (1914) is very like Whitman's poetry. Here, he actually sees hope and joy in the brutality of the city. Notice how he describes the city as a strong, muscular man, filled with the joy of living:

> Hog[A] Butcher for the World,
> Tool Maker, Stacker of Wheat,
> Player with Railroads and the Nation's Freight[B] Handler;
> Stormy, husky, brawling[C],
> City of the Big Shoulders:
> They tell me you are wicked, and I believe them . . .

[A] seller of pig meat   [B] goods sent by rail or road   [C] street fighting

Several of Sandburg's poems are known and read by American school children (his anti-war poem, *Grass* (1916) is one of these). But perhaps in the future he will be remembered best for his fine biography *Abraham Lincoln* (1926; 1939). Sandburg's deep love for Lincoln is another similarity with Whitman.

ROBINSON JEFFERS (1887–1962), unlike Sandburg, uses free verse to attack the human race. Only the powerful forces of physical nature have his respect. This was the main theme of his poetic career. "Man will be blotted out . . . Yet stones have stood for a thousand years," he wrote in his *To the Stone-Cutters* (1924). Twenty-three years later – in *Their Beauty Has More Meaning* (1947) – he is still saying exactly the same thing:

> . . . And when the whole human race
> Has been like me rubbed out[A], they will still be here: storms,
>   moon and ocean,
> Dawn and the birds. And I say this: their beauty has more
>   meaning
> Than the whole human race and the race of birds.

[A] removed like pencil marks

Jeffers's father taught him how to read Greek when he was five years old. At fifteen, he could speak a number of modern languages. In his twenty-seventh year, he moved to a lonely place on the California coast. For half a century he lived there. It was at the "Continent's End", facing "the final Pacific". He had turned away from Western civilization. Below his stone cottage were the waves: "wide-throated, the heavy-shouldered children of the wind / Leap at the sea-cliff." He often wrote about ancient myths, and always filled his poems with beautiful descriptions like the one above. He used the natural scenery around his home to give his poems a "feeling of real place". But always, "home" meant a place away from all other people.

Jeffers's famous long poem, *Roan Stallion* (1925), is about the strange, passionate love of a woman for a huge horse. In the poem, Jeffers expresses his philosophy of "inhumanism":

> Humanity is the mould[A] to break away from, the crust to break
>   through, the coal to break into fire,
> The atom to be split.

[A] fixed shape

GERTRUDE STEIN (1874–1946) had her own war with civilization. Her enemy was the tired old civilization of the nineteenth century. In 1902, she moved to Paris. There, she became close friends with Picasso, Braque and Matisse. Soon her apartment became one of the centers for the "modernist revolt" in art. The idea was to find a new way of looking at the world. When other American writers (like Hemingway) began moving to Paris in the twenties, they were all influenced by her ideas and opinions about writing. For example, William Faulkner's special treatment of time probably comes from Gertrude Stein. Most twentieth-century writers are very interested in the nature of consciousness. How can the writer *show* the conscious mind in writing? Stein tried to answer this with her strange experiments. In a way, she made her own English language into an entirely new language. She threw away the rules of traditional grammar, and made her words act in completely new ways.

In *Useful Knowledge* (1928), Stein makes this strange (but impor-tant) statement: "one and one and one and one and one and one . . ." She goes on counting this way. She does not stop until she announces that we have reached "One Hundred". She is telling us that this is the *reality* of the term, "One Hundred". Each "one" is a completely independent existence. In Stein's writing, each *word* has the same completely independent existence. Therefore we must read her writings *word by word*. Each word (and each meaning) must appear before the reader's eye as if it is new. The word is happening to us *now*. Coming one after another, the words and meanings in her sentences create something she calls "the continuous present". Here is Stein's most famous sentence. Try to follow the above instructions as you read it:

rose is a rose is a rose is a rose.

To understand this line, think of a strip of movie film. A film strip has a series of frames. Each frame shows the object in a separate moment. Stein shows her rose in a similar way. We are looking at it *moment-by-moment*.

We have to read her descriptions of scenes in the same way. Each moment or object is complete in itself. In any scene, a writer shows us a variety of objects and actions together. The writer might say: "At a dinner party, I greatly enjoyed a pudding with a spicy sauce." The writer has *organized* the experience for the reader. But Stein does not organize. Each object or event has the same importance or "weight" for her. Here is how she would describe the same scene:

All the pudding has the same flow and the sauce is painful, the tunes are played, the crinkling[A] paper is burning, the pot has a cover and the standard is excellence.

[A] the kind of paper used for table fireworks

(*An Acquaintance with Description*, 1928)

Stein never uses generalizations. She always writes about the reality which she finds directly in front of her eyes. The result, of course, is confusion. But the experience of *now* is never immediately understandable: it is confusing. Stein says, "What is strange is this." (By "this", she means the new or unfamiliar experience of *now*.)

One critic has said that Stein's language "seems to have no past. Things seem to speak directly and immediately." This is the "modernist" element in her writing. Writers in the nineteenth century were still interested in causes, purposes and explanations. They believed in progress: that history was moving toward a goal. Most modernists reject these ideas about time. Like Gertrude Stein's work, their work lives in the "continuous present". It has no "future" and no "past".

T. S. ELIOT (1888–1965) and EZRA POUND (1885–1972) were "traditionalists". In a way, their ideas reject Stein's "past-less" writing. Perhaps because they valued a "sense of history", they both lived most of their lives in Europe. In his famous essay, *Tradition and the Individual Talent* (1920), Eliot says:

> The historical sense involves a perception[A], not only of the pastness of the past, but of its presence. The historical sense compels[B] a man to write not merely with his own generation in his bones, but with a feeling that the whole of the literature of Europe, from Homer, . . . composes a simultaneous[C] order. . . . No poet . . . has his complete meaning alone . . . You cannot value him alone; you must set him, for contrast and comparison, among the dead.
>
> [A] power of seeing   [B] forces   [C] all at one time

To both Eliot and Pound, knowledge of tradition is necessary for the poet to create "new" poetry. If he does not understand the past, he will not know what is new. This is Pound's meaning in his *Credo* (1911):

> If a certain thing has been said once for all[A] in 450 B.C. or in 1290 A.D., it is not for us moderns to go saying it over, or to go obscuring the memory of the dead by saying the same thing with less skill.
>
> [A] perfectly

Another principle of the Pound–Eliot philosophy was "impersonalism". "The progress of an artist is a continual self-sacrifice, a continual extinction (*destruction*) of personality," Eliot wrote. He believes it is important to look carefully at the poetry, not at the poet. "We can only say that the poem, in some sense, has its own life . . . The feeling, or emotion, resulting from the poem is something different from the feeling or emotion in the mind of the poet."

The poetry of T. S. Eliot (which is covered in *An Outline of English*

Ezra Pound in the garden of his Paris studio in 1923

Literature) is certainly much greater than the poetry of Ezra Pound. Still, as Eliot realized, Pound had taught him a lot. Pound's rather long poem *Hugh Selwyn Mauberley* (1920) may have been the inspiration for Eliot's poem *The Waste Land* (1922). Both describe the spiritual emptiness of the world after World War I. Pound's poem describes the anger of the young soldiers who:

> walked eye-deep in hell
> believing in old men's lies, then unbelieving
> came home, home to a lie,
> home to many deceits . . .

The money-hungry post-war society causes the symbolic death of Mauberley. Similarly, the characters in *The Waste Land* are spiritually dead:

> . . . I was neither
> Living nor dead, and I knew nothing,
> Looking into the heart of light, the silence.

In 1946 Eliot wrote:

> It was in 1922 that I placed before him (*Pound*) in Paris the
> manuscript of a sprawling[A], chaotic[B] poem called "The Waste
> Land" ... (*it left Pound's*) hands reduced to about half its size, in
> the form in which it appeared in print ... This is irrefutable[C]
> evidence of Pound's critical genius.
>
> [A] carelessly spread out   [B] disorganized   [C] proof beyond doubt

Pound's critical theories have influenced many important American and British poets. From 1909 through the twenties, he was
involved in most of the major artistic movements. The main idea of his
theory is that: "Literature is language charged[4] with meaning."
(*ABC of Reading*, 1934) He had been a leader of the "Imagist" school of
poetry. He believed that good poetry was based in images (pictures of
solid, real things) rather than ideas. He was also influenced by Asian
literature. In fact, his most famous Imagist poem, *In a Station of the
Metro*, is rather like a Japanese *haiku*:

> The apparition of those faces in the crowd;
> Petals on a wet, black bough
>
> (1915)

On the surface, this poem has two separate images: the crowd and the
branch. Actually, Pound is placing one image on top of the other, so
that we see them as a single image. Therefore, the faces in the crowd
become beautiful, like flower petals on a rainy day. The petals,
meanwhile, become faces in a crowd. This new, combined image is the
real "apparition" – it floats before our eyes like a ghost which lives in
no particular time or place.

As he grew older, Pound's quarrel with Western society grew much
worse. During World War II, he lived in Italy and made anti-
American radio broadcasts for Mussolini. After the war, the Americans arrested him. He worked on his *Cantos*[5] (1925–1972) until he
died. This extremely long poem was left unfinished. *Canto VII* shows
his feelings about the twentieth century. The image for "today" is a

---

[4] *charged*, loaded.
[5] *canto*, one of the main divisions of a long poem.

Amy Lowell, leader of the Imagists

beer-bottle; the image for "the past" is a statue. This time, however, they do not unite into a single happy image. Pound places the two images "against" one another. This lack of harmony represents the "contemporary" world:

> "Beer-bottle on the statue's pediment[A]!
> "That Fritz, is the era, today against the past,
> "Contemporary."
> [A] base

HILDA DOOLITTLE (1886–1961; known as "H.D.") and AMY LOWELL (1874–1925) were two other important Imagists in the World War I period. Amy Lowell was a woman of great energy. She created an unusual image for herself by always appearing in public with a cigar in her mouth. She quickly took the leadership of the Imagist movement away from Pound. After that, Pound called the Imagists "the Amygists". Lowell's most famous poem is her *Patterns* (1915). It ends with her remembering her lover, who had died in the war:

> Fighting with the Duke in Flanders,
> In a pattern called a war.
> Christ! What are patterns for?

The poetic experiments of MARIANNE MOORE (1887–1972) were also deeply influenced by Ezra Pound and Imagism. Pound defined the "image" in Imagism as: "an intellectual and emotional complex in an instant of time". Such images are always drawn from the real world of science and fact. Similarly, Moore always uses images which are "hard, clear, cold, exact and real". In *Silence*, she describes a person she knows as:

> Self-reliant like the cat –
> that takes its prey[A] to privacy,
> the mouse's limp tail hanging like a shoelace from its mouth –
> they sometimes enjoy solitude[B] . . .
>
> [A] caught (mouse)   [B] being alone

Moore loved to choose unusual subjects (monkeys, steamrollers, elephants, snails) and study them from strange angles. Her poems have a rather "anti-poetic" spirit. At first, they seem to have no form at all. Extremely short sentences are mixed with extremely long ones (as we see above). In fact, however, she is always experimenting with new forms of rhythm, rhyme and content. She loves to include in her poems pieces of the real world: quotes from business documents, school books or newspaper articles. Genuine poetry, she once said, shows us "imaginary gardens with real toads in them".

The Pound–Eliot influence is also very strong in the work of the doctor–poet WILLIAM CARLOS WILLIAMS (1883–1963). His images are not symbols of some larger idea. His words, in *To A Poor Old Woman* for example, mean exactly what they say:

> munching[A] a plum on
> the street a paper bag
> of them in her hand
>
> They taste good to her
> They taste good
> to her. They taste
> good to her
>
> [A] using her teeth on

The influence of Eliot's "impersonal" style is also apparent here. Williams tries to become as "invisible" as possible. He does not want to weaken the effect. There are:

> . . . no ideas but in things –
> nothing but the blank faces of the houses
> and cylindrical trees

> (*Paterson, Book One*, 1946)

For Williams – and for most poets in the early twenties – the appearance of T. S. Eliot's poem *The Waste Land* was an extremely important event. Eliot "returned us to the classroom", Williams wrote. However, he did not stay in that "classroom" very long. The poetry of Eliot and Pound used the language and myths of Classical literature. But Williams was more interested in the language and scenes of everyday life. Williams's poems have a warmer feeling for real people and real life than Pound's. Even though he never describes the old woman in the poem *To A Poor Old Woman*, we can still "see" her face. Compare that with the faces in Pound's poem *In a Station of the Metro* (see p. 134), which have no individuality. Williams's deep concern for people makes his poetry more interesting to the average reader. He is more optimistic than Pound or Eliot. For him, poetic imagination gives the individual the power to face death bravely:

> Through this hole
> at the bottom of the cavern
> of death, the imagination
> escapes intact[A].
> It is the imagination
> which cannot be fathomed[B].
> It is through this hole we escape . . .
> [A] unharmed   [B] fully understood

> (*Paterson, Book Four*, 1951)

In his last volume of poetry, *Pictures From Brueghel* (for which he received the 1963 Pulitzer Prize), Williams sums up his philosophy of life:

> Only the imagination is real!
> I have declared it
> time without end.
> If a man die
> it is because death
> has first
> possessed his imagination . . .

"Imagination" is also the central idea in the poetry of WALLACE STEVENS (1879–1955). Just as Williams was a full-time doctor, Stevens remained a full-time businessman in an insurance company most of his life. In his spare time, he created thoughtful and "sensuous" poetry. Words are often used for their sound, rather than for their meaning. This sometimes makes the poems difficult to understand. But beyond the difficulty, there is very deep meaning. A single philosophy runs through Stevens's work, from his first volume of poetry, *Harmonium* (1923), onwards. Unlike Eliot – but like most modern writers – Stevens was sure that God does not exist and that all religions are false. When a man dies:

> Darkness, nothingness of human after-death,
> Receive and keep him in the deepnesses of space –
>
> *(Flyer's Fall)*

But Stevens is not sad about the basic meaninglessness of life. He is excited and joyful. It gives freedom to the poetic man. We can create our own patterns, our own order, our own gods. These are the "Supreme[6] Fictions" which we create to give meaning to our lives. Stevens often shows us this pattern-making in his own poetry. In *Anecdote of the Jar* (1923), the jar is one of the "Supreme Fictions" of the poet. It is like a new god. Placed in the "wilderness of the world", it organizes that wilderness, giving it order and meaning. The language

---

[6] *supreme*, highest (in power or degree).

of the poem sounds like the language of a myth:

> I placed a jar in Tennessee,
> And round it was, upon a hill.
> It made the slovenly[A] wilderness[B]
> Surround that hill.
>
> The wilderness rose up to it
> And sprawled around, no longer wild.
> The jar was round upon the ground
> And tall and of a port[C] in air.
>
> It took dominion[D] everywhere.
> The jar was gray and bare.
> It did not give of bird or bush,
> Like nothing else in Tennessee.

[A] untidy   [B] land with little life   [C] importance   [D] control

ARCHIBALD MACLEISH (b. 1892) is another poet who began under the influence of the Pound–Eliot "classroom". His famous *Ars Poetica* (1926) is really a statement of Eliot's "objective" and "impersonal" theory of poetry:

> A poem should be wordless
> As the flight of birds.
>
> A poem should be motionless in time
> As the moon climbs,
>
> Leaving, as the moon releases
> Twig[A] by twig the night-entangled[B] trees,
>
> Leaving, as the moon behind the winter leaves,
> Memory by memory the mind –
>
> A poem should be motionless in time
> As the moon climbs.

[A] thin branch   [B] tied in an inseparable mass by the night

The poet should *show* us things, not talk about them. This is exactly what MacLeish is doing in the above poem. He gives us images and then stands away to let the images speak for themselves: the wordless flight of birds, the climbing moon "motionless in time". Just as the moon "releases" the twigs of the "night-entangled trees," the poet sheds light on objects and lets us see them with our own eyes. This is the role of the poet, because:

> A poem should not mean
> But be.

Like Pound and Eliot, MacLeish often uses ancient myth for completely new purposes (as in his *Pot of Earth*, 1925). Similarly, he uses the literature of the past as a part of his own work, such as in his poem *The Hamlet of A. MacLeish* (1928) and his verse play *J. B.* (1958), based upon the Book of Job in the Bible. After writing a lot of social and political poetry in the 1930s and 1940s, MacLeish began writing excellent poems about old age. He speaks of the deep tiredness of old people and the weakening power of memory. In *Ship's Log* (1968), he writes:

> Mostly I have relinquished^A and forgotten
> Or grown accustomed, which is a way of forgetting.
> ^A allowed to escape

The poetry of EDNA ST. VINCENT MILLAY (1892–1950) began as a lonely voice of social rebellion in the Jazz Age of the twenties. Her book *A Few Figs from Thistles* (1920) made her an instant success, with a great number of readers. Unlike the experimental modernists, she is lyrical[7], romantic and easy to understand. She was one of the "new, liberated women". She wanted freedom: freedom in thought and freedom in love. She "sings" about this new freedom in bittersweet songs that always, somehow, seem old-fashioned:

> What lips my lips have kissed, and where, and why, ·
> I have forgotten, and what arms have lain
> Under my head till morning; but the rain
> Is full of ghosts tonight, that stop and sigh^A
> Upon the glass and listen for reply . . .
> ^A breathe sadly

[7] *lyrical*, expressing strong feelings, usually in song-like form; also *lyric* as adjective.

ELINOR WYLIE (1885–1928) was another woman poet of the same period. She was proud of her "small clean technique". Completely lacking the large emotions of Millay, she preferred to make poems with "crisp and sharp edged forms". Her poems have less warmth and human feeling than Millay's. In *Eagle and the Mole* (1921), for example, she tells the reader to "avoid the reeking herd (*the sweaty crowd*)" and to live alone on a mountain top, like an eagle on the rock.

The poetry of VACHEL LINDSAY (1879–1931) had a very different feeling. Like Whitman, he loved the "reeking herd" of humanity. Perhaps he loved crowds too much. In his last years, he became famous as an entertainer. He had a wonderful voice and loved to recite his poetry before crowds anywhere. His early poems, however, were important experiments. They use the rhythms of jazz music. *The Congo* (1914) is the most famous of these. The sound, rather than any meaning, is important here:

> "BLOOD" screamed the skull-faced, lean witch
>   doctors,
> "Whirl ye the deadly voo-doo rattle,
> Harry the uplands,
> Steal all the cattle
> Rattle-rattle, rattle-rattle,
> Bing.
> Boomlay, boomlay, boomlay, BOOM."
> A roaring, epic, rag-time tune
> From the mouth of the Congo
> To the Mountains of the Moon.

In Lindsay's later writings, meaning becomes more important. Like many American artists, he hoped to give the American people a message. He wanted them to see that the "American Dream" was dying. He wanted people to join him in an effort to restore America to its original purity. But people preferred him to remain an entertainer. No one listened to his message. In 1931, Vachel Lindsay killed himself.

Ernest Hemingway

Chapter Eleven

The Writers of the "Lost Generation"

The twenties were strange and wonderful years in America. "The uncertainties of 1919 were over – there seemed little doubt about what was going to happen – America was going on the greatest, gaudiest spree[1] in history." These are the words of F. SCOTT FITZGERALD (1896–1940). Fitzgerald's best books form a kind of spiritual history of the "Lost Generation" (a phrase first used by Gertrude Stein). Many young people in the post-World War I period had "lost" their American ideals. At the same time America "lost" many fine young writers – like e. e. cummings and Hemingway – because they had moved to Paris. Fitzgerald's first novel, *This Side of Paradise* (1920), describes this new generation. They had "grown up to find all gods dead, all wars fought, all faiths in man shaken". Two concerns now filled their lives: "the fear of poverty and the worship of success". From the beginning, Fitzgerald had a feeling that the twenties would end badly, both for himself and for America. Therefore, "All the stories that came into my head had a touch of disaster in them."

Fitzgerald's life was like the plot of one of his novels. He was born of rich parents in the Mid West and educated at Princeton University. This made him a part of the best society. In 1917, he became a fashionable army lieutenant, but he was never sent to fight in Europe. Instead, he wrote *This Side of Paradise*. By the age of twenty-four he was a famous novelist. Throughout the twenties, he wrote an enormous amount of fiction. This provided the money for many of Fitzgerald's own "sprees": all-night parties and wild trips to Europe. His fiction was extremely popular in the twenties because it was modern and easy to read. Then, in 1929, America's economy collapsed (starting the

[1] *spree*, a time of wild fun.

Great Depression). This happened at a time when Fitzgerald himself began to have serious mental and physical health problems. In *The Crack-Up* (published in 1945, after his death), he describes this period of troubles.

Flappers and Philosophers (1920) and *Tales of the Jazz Age* (1922) are collections of the best of Fitzgerald's short stories about the early twenties. (The term "flapper" refers to the modern young ladies of that period who smoked, drank whisky and lived dangerously free lives.) *The Diamond as Big as the Ritz* is the best known of these stories. Great wealth causes an evil family to become crazy. At the end of the story, there is a big earthquake[2] and the family diamond mine begins to collapse. Old Braddock Washington tries to save his diamond mine. He stands on a mountain top and shouts up at the sky: "OK, you up there!" Behind him, two slaves are holding a huge diamond. He is offering a bribe[3] to God. Washington is convinced that even "God has His price[4], of course".

Jay Gatsby, the hero of *The Great Gatsby* (1925), has a similar belief in the absolute power and "natural goodness" of money. The novel is considered by many critics to be one of the great twentieth-century novels. Through the eyes of Nick Carraway, the narrator, we see both the glamor[5] and the moral ugliness of the twenties. Nick's neighbor is Gatsby, a rich and successful man (and possibly a criminal). But Gatsby is also a true romantic. He has spent his whole life dreaming of his childhood sweetheart. He gives large, expensive parties at his home. He hopes that she will come and fall in love with him again.

The novel combines symbolism with psychological realism. The descriptions of the house, the parties, the music and the guests give them a "symbolic glow". They seem to be part of an unreal world: "Men and girls came and went like moths[6] among the whisperings and the champagne and the stars." The novel is famous for its unusual and interesting use of colors: "The lights grow brighter and now the orchestra is playing yellow cocktail music." Gatsby symbolizes the American belief that money can buy love and happiness. His failure

[2] *earthquake*, shaking of the earth.
[3] *bribe*, money offered to persuade someone to do wrong.
[4] *have one's price*, can be bribed if enough is offered.
[5] *glamor*, attractive charm.
[6] *moth*, winged insect which flies towards lights at night.

F. Scott Fitzgerald
in happier times,
celebrating Christmas
with his wife Zelda
and daughter Scottie

makes him a rather tragic figure. The following scene symbolically describes the emptiness of his hopes and dreams. His guests have just gone home:

> A wafer[A] of a moon was shining over Gatsby's house . . . surviving[B] the laughter and the sound of his still glowing garden. A sudden emptiness seemed to flow now from the windows and the great doors, endowing with complete isolation[C] the figure of the host, who stood on the porch, his hand up in a formal gesture of farewell.
>
> [A] thin curve   [B] living on after   [C] giving the appearance of being quite alone to

According to one critic, *The Great Gatsby* is "a symbolist tragedy". The hero tries – and fails – to change the world of hard material objects (and of hard, materialistic[7] people) into the ideal world of his fantasy. His world, like the world of many of his fellow Americans, is "material without being real, where poor ghosts, breathing dreams like air drifted about . . ." Still, there is something heroic about Gatsby. To the

[7] *materialistic*, enjoying the pleasures that money can buy, not matters of the mind or spirit.

end of his life he continued to believe and to hope. He believed in:

> the orgiastic[A] future that year by year recedes[B] before us. It
> eluded[C] us then, but that's no matter – tomorrow we will run
> faster, stretch our arms out farther . . . and one fine morning –
>
> [A] wildly exciting [B] moves away [C] escaped from

The rich symbolic nature of Fitzgerald's best novels and short stories often makes us stop to re-read passages. Only this way can we see the real meaning of colors and other details. *Babylon Revisited* (1931), one of his best late short stories, describes the Lost Generation after its moral and economic collapse. The hero and his wife had lived wildly in Paris in the twenties. Now, "the party is over". It is a sad, memorable story. Fitzgerald's novel *Tender Is the Night* (1934) uses his experiences with his wife's mental illness. The characters are tragic because, like Gatsby, they fail the "test of reality".

ERNEST HEMINGWAY (1898–1961) also spoke for the Lost Generation. He drove an ambulance in World War I and then decided to stay in Paris and become a writer. His first novel, *The Sun Also Rises* (1926) is a portrait of young adults in the post-war era. The characters are young Americans living in Paris. Some had fought bravely for their country. But now they are completely useless in peacetime. Others in the novel are simply "expatriates", people without a homeland:

> You're an expatriate. You've lost touch with the soil. Fake[A]
> European standards have ruined you. You drink yourself to
> death. You become obsessed[B] by sex. You spend all your time
> talking, not working. You are an expatriate, see? You hang
> around cafés.
>
> [A] falsely copied [B] with the mind filled

Without hope or ambition, they try to enjoy each day as it comes. Their despair is similar to the despair of T. S. Eliot's *Waste Land*. Jake Barnes (the narrator of the novel) was wounded in the war. Now he is sexually impotent. But this word has a wider meaning in the novel. It symbolizes how all of the characters have been damaged by the war. Spiritually, they are all "impotent". Describing his own real impotence, Jake reports, "I did not care what it was all about. All I wanted to know was how to live with it." The other characters deal with their symbolic impotence in the same way. All they want to know is how to live in the emptiness of the world. In later writings, Hemingway develops this emptiness into the important concept of *"Nada"* ("nothingness" in Spanish). Sometimes we see this *Nada* as the loss of hope or the inability to become active in the real world. At other times, it is the desire for sleep, or even an easy death. The typical Hemingway hero must always fight against the *Nada* of the world. He must never give up trying to live life as fully as possible.

The simple style and careful structuring of Hemingway's fiction is famous. In his early Paris days, Gertrude Stein often advised him to "Begin over again – concentrate (*condense*)." The aim of his style was to "get the most out of the least". As we can see in the passage quoted above, Hemingway's sentences are usually short and simple. Only rarely does he use adjectives. He will sometimes repeat a key phrase (e.g. "You're an expatriate") to emphasize his theme. The language is rarely emotional. Rather, it controls emotions: it holds them in. The aim of this language is to suggest a kind of *stoicism*[8]. This same stoicism is often the main theme in Hemingway's stories.

Hemingway perfected his writing method by experimenting with the short story. His early short story collections, *in our time* (1924) and *Men Without Women* (1927), carefully mix psychological realism with symbolism. Like most of his novels, they are very easy to read. Therefore, the careless reader often misses the deeper meanings. "Many of his stories deserve to be read with as much awareness[9], and as closely, as one would read a good modern poem," (Carlos Baker). On the surface, *Big Two-Hearted River* (1925) is just a simple description of a fishing trip. When it was first published, some critics complained that it was boring, because nothing happens. Nick Adams – the hero–narrator of many other stories – is back home from the terrible war. He needs to find the "balance" of his life again, and fight off the feeling of *Nada*. As in all of Hemingway's works, the outer world (nature) is a metaphor for the spiritual world of the character. Nick travels through a countryside destroyed by a fire. This is a metaphor for his life after the war. Notice how the following description has both a "real life" level and a symbolic level. The "fire-scarred" land, which

[8] *stoicism*, patience and courage when suffering.
[9] *aware*, ready and watching; n. *awareness*.

the hero walks away from, probably symbolizes the war and his terrible memories of it:

> He walked along the road that paralleled the railway track, leaving the burned town behind in the heat, and then turned off around a hill with a high, fire-scarred hill on either side onto a road that went back into the country . . . His muscles ached and the day was hot, but Nick felt happy. He felt he had left everything behind, the need for thinking, the need to write, other needs. It was all back of him.

The story carefully describes each of the hero's actions as he fishes. Clearly, each action has a special, symbolic meaning. The hero makes fishing into a kind of ceremony. This ceremony slowly brings him back to spiritual health.

In *A Farewell to Arms* (1929), his famous anti-war love story, Hemingway again uses nature symbolically. The mountain symbolizes life and hope; the plain is the image of war and death. We soon learn to see rain as another symbol of death. Frederic and Catherine are lovers during the war. Their love is a special world in the middle of war: "We could feel alone when we were together, alone against the others." Finally they make their own separate peace by escaping to Switzerland. In Switzerland, there is no war. But their happiness is destroyed when Catherine dies in childbirth. Bitterly, Frederic compares human beings to ants caught in a fire. They are completely ignored by God.

By the thirties, Hemingway's special concentrated style began to lose its freshness. Part of the problem was that many other writers were copying this style in their own stories. Hemingway's heroes also began to lose their freshness. Like many other characters in the literature of the thirties, they were "tough-guy" heroes. In *To Have and Have Not* (1937), Harry Morgan is this kind of hero. He shows courage and stoicism in a collapsing world. At the same time, however, there is a change in Hemingway's moral themes. He stops writing about the individual alone. He is now interested in the relationship between people. "No matter how, a man alone ain't got no bloody chance," Harry Morgan says. *For Whom the Bell Tolls* (1940) deepens this idea into a moral system. The hero, Robert Jordan, is fighting against fascism in the Spanish Civil War. His experiences teach him to believe

A scene from Hemingway's novel For Whom the Bell Tolls, set during the Spanish Civil War; the movie starred Ingrid Bergman and Gary Cooper

in the value of sacrifice. Each individual is a part of a whole: mankind. Love becomes a wonderful, mysterious union: "One and one is one." At first, he learns this through love for a woman. But at the end, as he lies dying, he discovers a similar "union" with nature and the earth. Jordan has learned about the power of love – a new theme for Hemingway.

In *Across the River and into the Trees* (1950), we see a later development of the Hemingway hero. Like the author himself, he is ageing and has been deeply wounded by life. Like the hero of *Big Two-Hearted River*, he is a man of many personal ceremonies. Everything he does – loading his hunting rifle or even pouring a glass of champagne – is done in a special way. It is a way of protecting his self-respect. Some critics felt that his great themes were not as well developed in this story. *The Old Man and the Sea* (1952), however, is a strong work. Again the themes are heroism, stoicism and ceremony. This short, simple novel is a beautiful allegory of human life. An old Cuban fisherman catches a huge fish after a long, patient fight. But sharks[10] come and eat it down to the bones. The old man then returns with just a skeleton.

[10] *shark*, large, and often very dangerous, fish.

John Dos Passos

When tourists laugh at him, he does not complain. The reader sees this as a sign of true heroism. The old man showed courage in the fight and stoicism in defeat. This was the last great message from Ernest Hemingway. *The Old Man and the Sea* received the Pulitzer Prize in 1952. In 1954, Hemingway was awarded the Nobel Prize for Literature. As he entered his own old age, he felt his powers as an artist failing. In 1961, he shot himself with his favorite hunting gun.

Like Hemingway, JOHN DOS PASSOS (1896–1970) drove an ambulance during World War I. His *One Man's Initiation – 1917* (1920) was the first American novel about that war. Because it was written immediately after the war it is rather emotional, and is filled with hatred for all war. His *Three Soldiers* (1921) is less personal and has a broader, more historical view. It tells several different stories at the same time. It shows war as a huge machine which destroys individuals. Like other members of the Lost Generation, Dos Passos saw the modern, post-war world as ugly and dirty. To Dos Passos, only art, and the invention of new artistic styles ("modernism"), could save the world.

Dos Passos's first successful "modernist" novel was *Manhattan Transfer* (1925). Covering the period from 1900 to World War I, it describes the daily lives of a large number of New Yorkers. Pieces of popular songs are mixed with newspaper headlines and phrases from advertisements. The people often talk in a special poetic style, as in the writings of James Joyce. Although the book has many characters, the real character is New York City itself. It is a city filled with energy, excitement and the modern "strangeness" of the twenties. Clearly, in this and later novels, Dos Passos has been influenced by the techniques of the movies. For example, he uses the "montage techniques" of film directors like Griffith and Eisenstein. These directors increased the power of their movies by breaking up the usual flow of action into little pieces. They arranged these pieces into new patterns in order to show the meaning behind the action. They combined shots of a whole scene with "close-ups" which showed the feelings of individual people in the scenes. Dos Passos shows the relationship between individuals and large historical events in exactly the same way.

When the twenties ended, Dos Passos's literature changed its direction. *Manhattan Transfer* tried to show the purposelessness of history. In 1930, Dos Passos published the first volume of his great "U.S.A." trilogy, *The 42nd Parallel*[11]. The trilogy tries to show how individuals are part of the history of the age in which they live. All three books in the trilogy use movie techniques to tell the history of the entire nation in the early twentieth century.

When *The 42nd Parallel* first came out, there was great excitement in Europe as well as in America. The great French philosopher Jean Paul Sartre said, "I regard Dos Passos as the greatest writer of our time." Alfred Kazin (b. 1915), a brilliant young critic, called the book "Dos Passos's invention". The author tells his story in an entirely new way. Although it is an interesting story, the techniques (such as montage) are even more interesting. The book, opening in 1900, follows the movements of "Mac", a professional labor organizer. In many ways he is more symbolic than real. He appears wherever the "action" (strikes, revolutions) is. More than anything else, Dos Passos wanted to "catch the echo of what people were actually saying, in the style anyone might have said it".

The next novel in the trilogy, *1919* (1932), is more angry. It describes World War I as "the plot of the big interests". It shows the rise of the revolutionary spirit at the time of the Russian Revolution. Dos Passos's style is fast-moving and unemotional. It is filled with the

---

[11] *Parallel*, one of the lines of latitude parallel to the equator (the imaginary line round the middle of the world).

sounds, smells and colors of reality. In *1919*, he describes the horrors of war:

> The German offensive[A] was on, the lines were so near Paris the ambulances were evacuating[B] wounded directly on the base hospitals. All night, the stretcher cases[C] would spread along the broad pavements under the trees in fresh leaf in front of the hospital. Dick would help carry them up the marble stairs into the reception room . . . He had the job of carrying out buckets of blood and gauze[D] from which protruded occasionally a shattered bone or a piece of an arm or a leg. When he went off duty, he'd walk home achingly tired through the strawberry-scented early Paris dawn.
>
> [A] attack   [B] carrying . . . straight to   [C] wounded men lying on low frames
> [D] material for cleaning or covering wounds

The Big Money (1936), the third of the trilogy, describes post-war America, when "society has gone mad with greed". In all three books, his descriptions are extremely sharp and clear. This makes his books quite easy to read. But there are so many characters that the reader begins to forget them before the book is finished. This appears to be Dos Passos's plan. He is not telling the story of individuals, but of a whole era. Everyone is "damaged by the modern experience". When we add together all of the parts (the individual characters) of the trilogy, they do not create a single meaning. Rather, they show the *loss* of meaning which is the "modern condition".

The quality of Dos Passos's literature began to decline after this trilogy. At the same time, he slowly moved from the far left of American politics to the far right. Although he did write a fine biography of Thomas Jefferson in 1954, his last works seem rather unpleasantly patriotic and anti-Communist.

Dos Passos used large numbers of characters to represent an entire nation. WILLIAM FAULKNER (1897–1962), on the other hand, used a rather small number of characters. These represent the various levels of a single region: the South. They often reappear in later novels. Faulkner shared two things with the Lost Generation: its strong dislike for the post-war world and its belief in the value of art. His first novel, *Soldiers' Pay* (1926), is about a wounded soldier who returns home to the "wasteland" of post-war society. His second novel, *Mosquitoes*

*William
Faulkner*

(1927), is a rather dull tale about artists and art lovers in New Orleans in the twenties.

Faulkner's third novel, *Sartoris* (1929), shows a big change in his thinking. He decided that his own "little postage stamp of soil" in Mississippi "was worth writing about". His mythical Yokna-patawpha County became one of the most famous "mini-worlds" in twentieth-century literature. *Sartoris* is set in the South, after World War I. Bayard Sartoris, the ex-flyer, returns home. His dissatisfaction with life makes him want to destroy himself. He is unsure about his manhood. He looks for death in airplanes and automobiles. His careless courage reminds us of the Southern aristocrats who were his ancestors. The story contrasts modern people with characters from the past. It also contrasts the Sartoris family with the Snopes family. The Snopes family are "rat-like". They are disgusting, "low" people; they represent the new spirit of the South. This is the spirit of commerce and self-interest. The Snopes family becomes central characters in later Faulkner novels (*The Hamlet*, 1940; *The Town*, 1957 and *The Mansion*, 1959).

The Sound and the Fury (1929) is one of Faulkner's "modernist" masterpieces. It tells the tragic story of the Compson family from four different points of view: Benjy, the idiot; Quentin, his brother, who kills himself at Harvard; Jason, the evil, money-hungry brother; and Dilsey, the black servant who keeps the family together with her love. The novel contains many of the experimental features which appear in later Faulkner novels. One feature is the use of *limited point of view*. Each of the four characters sees reality only in his or her own way. Each lives in his or her own reality, completely separated from the others. The reality of Benjy (the idiot) is the most completely separate. Objects, places and people have a strange dreamlike quality when he talks. Faulkner's special technique of narration is another feature. The reader is put into the center of the story without any preparation. We must put together the facts of the story by ourselves, since the author does not help us. A good example of this occurs at the beginning of the novel. Faulkner does not tell us that this is a scene of people playing golf. Benjy, the idiot, is watching:

> Through the fence, between the curling flower spaces, I could see them hitting. They were coming toward where the flag was and I went along the fence. Luster (*the nurse boy*) was hunting in the grass by the flower tree. They took the flag out and were hitting. Then they put the flag back and they went to the table, and he hit and the other hit. Then they went on and I went along the fence.

In almost all of Faulkner's stories, time is treated in a special way. He uses the "continuous present" style of writing, which was invented by Gertrude Stein (perhaps Faulkner learned this from Sherwood Anderson, who was greatly influenced by Stein). Past, present and future events are mixed: "Yesterday and tomorrow are *Is*: Indivisible: One." Everything – including events from a century before – seems to happen at the same time. Everything is part of the "now" of the novel. Because of these techniques it is usually hard work to read a Faulkner novel. But the rewards are worth the effort. As Ratcliff, a character in *The Hamlet*, says:". . . if it ain't complicated up enough, it ain't right".

In the 1930s, Faulkner was becoming increasingly concerned with the evils of modern society. *Light in August* (1932) is considered by many to be another masterpiece. It shows how racism[12] has made the white community of the South crazy. The central character is Joe Christmas, a man who is half black and half white: he belongs to neither race. Unhappy and confused he murders the woman who had protected him. This gives the white community an excuse for killing him. *Absalom, Absalom!* (1936) is Faulkner's last truly "modernist" novel. Like all the other novels, this one is set in Yoknapatawpha County. It is a huge, historical story. Thomas Sutpen plans to establish a great family. But racism, psychological illness and a family tragedy destroy his plans.

Faulkner's descriptions of human goodness are as powerful as his descriptions of human evil. Often (but not always) his "good" people are black. Black or white, these people show their goodness in their relationship with nature and their ability to love. When he was given the Nobel Prize for Literature in 1950, Faulkner gave a short speech in which he described man as a spiritual being. The world of this spiritual being is based upon moral truths which never change. Ike McCaslin – the hero of the famous short story *The Bear* (1942) – speaks for the author:

> Truth is one. It doesn't change. It covers all things which touch the heart – honor and pride and pity and justice and courage and love. Do you see it now?

Courage and love are central themes in the poetry of E. E. CUMMINGS (1894–1962; he always wrote his name as "e. e. cummings"). He was the most joyful poet of the Lost Generation. Like the others, his first work was a novel about the war, *The Enormous Room* (1922). The book attacks both war and government. The French army had made a big mistake: they had put Cummings in prison as a spy. After the war, he joined the Lost Generation in Paris. There, he studied both writing and painting. In his poetry we can see the clear influence of both Gertrude Stein and the Cubist painters. The Cubists broke their paintings up into many different angles or "facets". Similarly, Cummings loved to break the traditional poem into unusual bits and pieces. "So far as i am concerned," he says in his *six nonlectures* (1952),

[12] *racism*, practices etc. that come from the belief that one's own race or color is better than others.

"poetry and every other art was and is and forever will be strictly and distinctly a question of individuality."

Cummings made every part of a poem express his own individuality. Some of his book titles are not even real words, such as the title of his book of poetry, & (1925). He rarely capitalized the words we usually capitalize (like his name). He sometimes uses capital letters in the middle ("SlOwLy") or at the end of words ("stopS"). He wanted us to look carefully at the individual word (and even the letters in the word). Therefore, his poems look very strange on the printed page:

why
don't
be
sil
ly
, o no in-
deed;
money
can't do (never
did &

never will) any
damn
thing
: far
from it; you

're wrong, my friend.

(1962)

Underneath this experimental surface, however, the themes of Cummings's poetry are surprisingly traditional. Emerson and Whitman have clearly influenced his message in this beautiful hymn to God and nature:

i thank You God for most this amazing
day: for the leaping greenly spirits of trees
and a blue true dream of sky; and for everything
which is natural which is infinite which is yes.

(1950)

e. e. cummings: a self-portrait

Cummings hated the large, powerful forces in modern life: politics, the Church, Big Business. He also disliked the coldness of science. Here, he uses warm, human images to attack science:

(while you and i have lips and voices which
are for kissing and to sing with
who cares if some oneeyed son of a bitch[A]
invents an instrument to measure Spring with?
[A] nasty fellow

Occasionally, his love poetry becomes rather obscene[13]. But to him, real love can only happen in complete freedom: "I value freedom; and have never expected freedom to be anything less than indecent." Just as Whitman liberated American poetry in the nineteenth century, Cummings liberated the poetry of the twentieth century.

"By the very act of becoming its improbably gigantic self," Cummings once wrote, "New York has reduced mankind to a tribe of pygmies[14]." The city had quite a different meaning to HART CRANE (1899–1932), the other important Lost Generation poet. Like many other twentieth-century poets, Crane rarely gives us a direct message through his poems. He is talking about feelings which cannot be understood intellectually. His poetry uses words for their musical qualities more than for their meaning. This makes his work rather difficult to understand. His real subject is modern city life, and the feelings which that life creates in all of us.

Hart Crane uses New York as a "symbolic landscape" in his long, famous poem *The Bridge* (1930). The poem is an epic[15] of American life. The glories of the past are contrasted with the "wasteland" of the post-World War I era. Crane got the idea for the poem when he was very poor and living in a cheap little apartment in New York. From his window, he could look out on the Brooklyn Bridge: "Through the bound cablestrands[16], the arching path upward, veering[17] with light". The bridge becomes a symbol of the relationship between man and God. At the same time, it is the bridge which unites the American nation: "Vaulting[18] the sea, the prairies' dreaming sod . . ." Clearly, Crane wanted his long poem to "sing of America", like Whitman's *Leaves of Grass*. He openly calls to the spirit of Whitman:

> Not soon, nor suddenly, – No, never to let go
>   My hand
>   in yours,
>   Walt Whitman –
>
>   so –

[13] *obscene*, going into usually unacceptable details about sex etc.

[14] *pygmy*, member of a race of very small people.

[15] *epic*, long poem telling a story of great deeds or history.

[16] *cablestrand*, strong thick wire rope.

[17] *veer*, change direction.

[18] *vault*, jump over.

Although he tries to share Whitman's joyous spirit, Crane's view of life is far darker and more tragic. He is much closer to Poe. In a later part of *The Bridge*, Crane meets Poe in a crowded subway[19]:

> And why do I often meet your visage here,
> Your eyes like agate[A] lanterns – on and on
> Below the toothpaste and the dandruff ads[B]?
>
> . . .
>
> And Death, aloft[C], – gigantically down
> Probing[D] through you – toward me, O evermore!

[A] hard precious stone   [B] advertisements for hair treatments   [C] above   [D] feeling the way

Death quickly found the tragic Hart Crane. At the age of thirty-two, he killed himself.

[19] *subway*, underground railroad train.

The Depression years: unemployed men eating free bread and soup

Chapter Twelve

The Thirties

The economic collapse of 1929 destroyed the happy, confident mood of America in the "Jazz Age" twenties. "It was borrowed time anyway," F. Scott Fitzgerald wrote. Millions of Americans lost their jobs as the nation entered the Depression era. America was entering a new period of social anger and self-criticism. The writings of Dreiser, Dos Passos, Upton Sinclair and Sherwood Anderson now had a strong "Leftist" flavor. Instead of experimenting with "modernist" literature, most writers turned to a new kind of social realism and naturalism. It showed the struggles and tragedies of ordinary people. But it also showed their strength, their energy and their hopefulness. The writing itself is strong, energetic and quite easy to read. It usually gives us a clear picture of the times.

In the early thirties, the first reaction to the Depression was a literature of social protest. There was a powerful Marxist "Proletarian Literature" movement. The main intellectual magazine of the era was the pro-Marxist *Partisan Review*, edited by Jewish intellectuals in New York. MICHAEL GOLD (1896–1967), editor of the Communist paper *The New Masses*, was a leading force in the movement. He wrote *Jews without Money* (1930) as a model for other "Proletarian" writers. It describes the terrible reality of his boyhood world: the dirty streets and poor houses, the gangsters, prostitutes and factories with awful working conditions. EDWARD DAHLBERG's *Bottom Dogs* (1930) and JACK CONROY's *Disinherited* (1933) are similar autobiographical novels of social realism.

Gold's novel was also the start of the "Jewish–American" novel, which became an important type of literature in the fifties and sixties. Gold describes the failure of the "American Dream" for those who had left Europe looking for a new and better life. This soon became a main

theme in Jewish–American literature. *Call It Sleep* (1935), by HENRY
ROTH, mixes Marxist and Freudian theory, Jewish mythology and a
stream-of-consciousness writing style. He describes a young boy
growing up in a poor area of New York. It is "a world that had been
created without thought of him".

In his *Note on Literary Criticism* (1936), JAMES T. FARRELL (1904–
1979) says that his own views are Marxist, "but not of the usual over-
simplified sort". His famous "Studs Lonigan" trilogy actually belongs
to the naturalist tradition of Norris and Dreiser. *Young Lonigan* (1932)
is about middle-class Irish–Catholic families in Chicago. Farrell
writes more about "spiritual poverty" than about economic poverty.
Using stream-of-consciousness techniques, he shows how the "black
dullness" of such a life can hurt the spirit of a teenager. Studs slowly
changes from an ordinary but intelligent youth into a brutal "tough
guy" of the streets. *The Young Manhood of Studs Lonigan* (1934) and
Judgment Day (1935) continue the story up to Studs's death at twenty-
nine. *A World I Never Made* (1936) starts a new trilogy, with a new
hero, Danny O'Neill. It continues to develop the theme of the spiritual
poverty of Irish–Catholic families: the emotional religion, the new
child every year, the money worries and the heavy drinking. Farrell's
fast-moving "documentary[1]" style almost always holds our interest.
We feel as if we are reading the "true story" behind the newspaper
articles of the era.

The novels of JOHN O'HARA (1905–1970) show a similar interest in
"documentary[1]" realism. They are tough, realistic descriptions of the
upper middle-class world. *Appointment in Samarra* (1934) is considered
his best novel. Its fast-moving story holds the reader until the main
character kills himself at the end: did society cause his death, or did he
die for more private reasons? In this novel and in his next, *Butterfield 8*
(1935), O'Hara creates an honest picture of twentieth-century
Americans. They are driven by money, sex and the struggle for a
higher position in society. In 18 novels and 374 short stories, O'Hara
recorded the changing American scene from World War I to the
Vietnam War. His *Sermons and Soda Water* (1960) is social history in the
form of three short novels, centered on a murder trial. In the
introduction O'Hara writes:

[1] *documentary*, (like) a presentation of facts in a movie or TV program.

I want to get it all down on paper while I can . . . I want to record the way people talked and thought and felt. I cannot be content to leave their story in the hands of historians and the editors of picture books.

The work of JOHN STEINBECK (1902–1968) represents a similar attempt to "get it all down on paper". In the thirties, his characters were "naturalistic" in the classic meaning of the word. We see them driven by forces in themselves and in society: fear, hunger, sex, the disasters of nature and the evils of Capitalism. Crime is often the result of these forces. Steinbeck even describes "innocent murders" – by Lennie the idiot in *Of Mice and Men* (1937), and by a betrayed husband in *The Long Valley* (1938). In all of his novels, Steinbeck combines a naturalistic way of looking at things with a deep sympathy for people and the human condition. We feel that he really does love humanity. Steinbeck's books search for the elements in human nature which are common to all people. He usually finds them in the family, the group and the nation, rather than in the individual. In a letter of 1933, he wrote:

The fascinating thing for me is the way the group has a soul, a drive, an intent . . . which in no way resembles the same things possessed by the men who make up that group.

Like some other writers in the thirties (Dos Passos and Thomas Wolfe, for example) Steinbeck often tried to paint large portraits of the "national spirit". To do this, he combined myth with his naturalism. To him, "westering" (the movement to the American West) had great significance as an American myth. The old pioneer grandfather in *The Long Valley* says:

When we saw the mountains at last, we all cried – all of us. But it wasn't getting here that mattered, it was the movement and the westering. We carried life out here and set it down the way those ants carry eggs . . . The westering was as big as God and the slow steps that made the movement piled[A] up and piled up until the continent was crossed.

[A] added

RESETTLEMENT ADMINISTRATION
Rescues Victims
Restores Land to Proper Use

John Steinbeck in 1937

A poster offering help to the victims of the "dust bowl" disaster which Steinbeck describes in his novel The Grapes of Wrath

In *The Grapes of Wrath* (1939), Steinbeck's finest novel, the characters are "larger than life". He is not simply describing the experiences of a single family of individuals. He is really telling the story of a great national tragedy through the experiences of that one family. The Joads, a family of farmers, must leave Oklahoma because of the great "dust bowl" disaster. Terrible winds have destroyed their land. They go west into California and work as fruit pickers. There, they experience the hatred and violence of the large California landowners. Steinbeck's description of this social injustice shocked the nation. In time, laws were passed to help people like the Joads. But the literary interest of the book is in its descriptions of the daily heroism of ordinary people. Slowly, they learn to work together as a group, and help each other. In her thick Oklahoma accent, Ma Joad explains: "Use'ta be the fambly was fust. It ain't so now. It's anybody." This "anybody" comes to include all of humanity. This is the meaning of daughter Rosasharn's act at the end of the book. When her own baby dies, she feeds her breast milk to a dying old man. To some critics, this last scene is too sentimental. Sentimentalism in various forms is seen as a weakness of many of Steinbeck's novels.

The use of mythical elements is less successful in *East of Eden* (1952). It tells the story of a family from the Civil War to World War I. Here, Steinbeck uses his naturalistic style to create a modern story based on the Bible story about the brothers Cain and Abel. The book became famous as a movie, starring James Dean. In 1960, Steinbeck traveled through small-town America with his dog, Charley. The book he wrote about this, *Travels with Charley* (1962), is filled with his own personal Transcendentalism. It is a quiet book which expresses the unity of all living creatures. In the same year, 1962, Steinbeck received the Nobel Prize for Literature.

A scene from the movie of Steinbeck's novel East of Eden, *starring James Dean*

THOMAS WOLFE (1900–1938) was another writer who tried to speak for all of America. He brought a voice of hope to the despair of the thirties. "I believe that we are lost here in America, but I believe that we shall be found." As optimistic as Walt Whitman, he thought "that the true discovery of America is before us ... the true fulfillment of our spirit, of our people, of our mighty[2] and immortal[3] land, is yet to

---

[2] *mighty*, very great.
[3] *immortal*, never dying.

come". He does not "celebrate" America in the same way that Whitman does. His work is almost completely autobiographical. He almost always describes America by recording his own personal experiences and feelings as an American. "I must mix it all with myself and America," he wrote.

In the introduction to his first (and most famous) novel, *Look Homeward, Angel* (1929), he states that the novel "represents my vision of my life to my twentieth year". The young hero, Eugene Gant, grows up in the cultureless world of a Southern town. He is a romantic artist, filled with a hunger to know all and feel all, whether pleasure or pain. He sets out on a trip for "the deeper waters of experience". From his train window Gant sees people passing in another train:

> They looked at one another for a moment, they passed and vanished[A] and were gone forever, yet it seemed to him that he had known these people, that he knew them far better than the people in his own train, and that, having met them for an instant under immense and timeless skies, as they were hurled[B] across the continent to a thousand destinations, they had met, passed, vanished, yet would remember forever.
>
> [A] disappeared   [B] thrown

Similar moments of sudden, deep understanding fill all of Wolfe's work. The style – long sentences with poetic repetitions – was his personal invention. His next novel, *Of Time and the River* (1935), is subtitled *A Legend of A Man's Hunger In His Youth*. It continues the story of Eugene Gant. These two novels (along with *The Web and the Rock*, 1939, and *You Can't Go Home Again*, 1940), are the story of a great journey of exploration. The aim is to reach "the city of myself, the continent[4] of my soul".

In his long essay, *The Story of a Novel* (1936), Wolfe describes writing *Of Time and the River*. He was filled with "a great black cloud". The cloud poured out on the page "in a torrential[5] and ungovernable flood". In fact, this was Wolfe's problem. He never knew when his story was finished. Since he could not organize his own writing, editor Maxwell Perkins of Scribner's publishing company had to help him.

[4] *continent*, one of the 7 great land masses of the world.
[5] *torrential*, like a fast-flowing river.

By cutting and shaping Wolfe's "formless manuscripts[6]", Perkins (who was also editor for Hemingway and Fitzgerald) turned them into novels. E. C. Aswell, of Harper's Inc. publishing company, did the same for *The Web and the Rock* and *You Can't Go Home Again* after Wolfe's tragic early death. Wolfe simply could not stay within the traditional shape of the novel. His fiction is "one great autobiographical mass". The feelings he wanted to express were too big. His details were so rich that it is often difficult to see the ideas and structure of his novels. But this may not have been Wolfe's personal failure. The American novel – like the European novel – was about to enter a period of crisis[7]. In the 1960s, with its "anti-novels", the traditional shape of the novel broke down completely. In this way, Wolfe may have been ahead of his time.

HENRY MILLER (1891–1980) was also unhappy with the traditional novel. He was much more of a rebel than Wolfe. In the thirties, when the other expatriate writers had gone home, Miller stayed on in Paris. Because his novels were considered obscene, he could not publish them in America until the 1960s. In fact, they were the "anti-novels" of the thirties. The opening chapter of his *Tropic of Cancer* (1934, Paris; 1961, New York) shows us the spirit of the man and his work, both comic and serious at the same time:

> This is not a book. This is a libel, slander, defamation[A] of character. This is not a book, in the ordinary sense of the word. No, this is a prolonged insult, a gob of spit in the face of Art, a kick in the pants to God, Man, Destiny, Time, Love, Beauty . . . I am going to sing for you, a little off key[B] perhaps, but I will sing . . . I will dance over your dirty corpse.
>
> [A] untrue attack   [B] out of tune

Like Wolfe's, all of Miller's work is basically autobiographical. But unlike Wolfe, he hated America: he called it an "air-conditioned nightmare[8]". In fact, as he wrote in *The Time of the Assassins* (1956), he was an anarchist[9]: "I had no principles, no loyalty, no code

[6] *manuscript*, the author's original piece of writing (formerly hand-written).

[7] *crisis*, dangerous time of change.

[8] *nightmare*, bad dream.

[9] *anarchist*, one who believes in no form of rule or control.

*Henry Miller
in later years*

whatever." In *The Cosmological Eye* (1939), he states that all his life he has "felt a great kinship with the madman and the criminal".

Beginning with extreme anger at "the way things are", Miller developed his own vision of how man should live. Laughter, freedom and joy should be the goals of life. His "Rosy Crucifixion" trilogy (*Sexus*, 1949; *Plexus*, 1953, and *Nexus*, 1960), written after his return to America, mixes serious statements about life with many extremely funny scenes. The trilogy celebrates freedom for both the mind and the body: "Joy is like a river. It flows ceaselessly ... we (*too*) should flow on and through, endlessly like music." His view of art and literature is the same: "You think a poem should have covers around it. The moment you write a thing the poem ceases. The poem is the present which you can't define[10]. You live it."(*The Cosmological Eye*) Elsewhere, he expresses this more simply: "Writing is life. What is written is death."

Miller settled in California's Big Sur region in the fifties. He became an important spiritual advisor to a new generation of rebels, the "Beats". Like many others, Karl Shapiro, the poet (see p. 189) considered himself a "Millerite": "I regard Miller as a holy man." But not all "Millerites" fully understood Miller's message. "People of all

[10] *define*, explain the exact meaning of.

sexes frequently turn up at Big Sur," Shapiro wrote in 1959. "They announce that they want to join the Miller Sex Cult. Henry gives them bus fare and a good dinner and sends them on their way." In the sixties, there were even more "Millerites" among the Hippie generation. To them, he was a "guru" of literature and of life.

ERSKINE CALDWELL (b. 1903) is not anybody's "guru", but he does share Miller's joyous and funny view of human nature. Like Miller, he wrote about sex and his sex scenes are often wildly funny. Almost always, somebody else is watching: visitors, old country blacks looking over fences, etc. Caldwell's free use of sex in the thirties shows a major change in popular fiction. After the success of *Tobacco Road* (1932), open descriptions of sex moved into the mainstream of American literature. Caldwell's low-class characters live on the poor land of the American South. They have foolish hopes for their useless land. Jeeter in *Tobacco Road* dreams of growing a lot of cotton on it. And Ty Ty, in *God's Little Acre* (1933), dreams of finding gold under his land. Realism is mixed with thick Southern humor. Often strange diseases make the characters look rather funny. One man cannot stop laughing; another man is terribly fat. As one critic has remarked, "Caldwell puts people into complex social situations while making them act like insects." These "insect" people have great energy and are full of hope. We laugh at them but we admire them. It is difficult to feel sorry for them.

The characters of NATHANAEL WEST (1902–1940) are also quite funny. West was one of the most unusual writers of the thirties. Other writers described people struggling against the social and economic problems of their times. West's people are too blind to struggle. They are trapped, but they don't know it. When we look at their silly, wasted lives, we want to cry and laugh at the same time. In his first novel, *Miss Lonelyhearts* (1933), a young newspaperman has an unusual job. He writes special advice for readers who send in letters about their personal problems. Throughout the book, he is called "Miss Lonelyhearts". This is part of the strange humor. The people who write letters to him at the newspaper have problems which are often horrible and grotesque. "I sit and look at myself all day and cry," a sixteen-year-old writes. "I have a big hole in the middle of my face that frightens people, even myself." No one can justify or even explain suffering. But the "Miss Lonelyhearts" of this world are "the priests of twentieth-century America". Therefore he tries – and finally fails–

to bring comfort to some of the sufferers.

West describes this world with the language of "black humor[11]". The sky looks "as if it had been rubbed with a soiled eraser". One character's tongue is "a fat thumb", his heart "a lump of icy fat", his feelings only "icy fatness". West's *Day of the Locust* (1939) describes the crowds of people who come to Hollywood, "the city of fantasies, myths, religions". The characters live half in their own impossible dreams and half in a nightmare reality. The book has many strange, frightening images (dead horses in swimming pools, etc.). West's real theme is the crowd itself, not the individual. The main character (Hackett), an artist, is planning a painting called "The Burning of Los Angeles". He wants to represent the end of the world. But he cannot find the right image. Then, at the opening of a new movie, the crowd riots[12]. Although he is injured, Hackett at last finds the violent details he needs:

> Despite[A] the agony[B] in his leg, he was able to think clearly about his picture. . . . Across the top, . . . a great bonfire of architectural styles . . . Through the center, winding from left to right, was a long hill street and down it, spilling into the middle foreground, came the mob[C] carrying baseball bats and torches. For the faces, . . . he was using the innumerable sketches he had made of people who came to California to die . . . the airplane, funeral and preview watchers – all those poor devils who can only be stirred by the promise of miracles and then only to violence.
>
> [A] in spite of   [B] great pain   [C] dangerous crowd

America of the thirties had another group of writers who hated the culture of the modern cities. They were a group of Southern poets, novelists and critics who called themselves "The Fugitives[13]". In 1930, they published a famous book of essays: *I'll Take My Stand: The South and the Agrarian Tradition*. It strongly criticized the business and commercial base of American society, and praised the farming

---

[11] *black humor*, being funny about cruelty, unpleasant or dangerous people or situations.
[12] *riot*, go out of control.
[13] *fugitive*, one who has run away.

WEST · RANSOM · TATE

(agrarian) traditions of the Old South. There, life had been peaceful, religious and "close to nature".

JOHN CROWE RANSOM (1888–1974), one of the three most important Fugitives, felt that modern industrial society divides human experience into too many separate little boxes. This "de-humanizes" us. The head (mind, intellect) is separated from the body (emotions, physical feelings). In the poem *Painted Head* (1927) he says that beauty is not only something in the mind:

> . . . Beauty is of body.
> The flesh contouring[A] shallowly on a head
> Is a rock-garden needing body's love . . .
> [A] thinly giving shape to

Ransom's poems are usually written according to the literary rules of the "New Critics". They are carefully written and need careful reading. His themes, however, are as old as man: love, death, the passing of beauty. He emphasizes the value of tradition, ceremony and manners. The language is modern, creating brilliantly clear pictures:

> The lazy geese, like a snow cloud
> Dripping their snow on the green grass,
> Tricking and stopping, sleepy and proud . . .
>
> (*Bells for John Whiteside's Daughter*, 1924)

Ode to the Confederate Dead (1926), by ALLEN TATE (1899–1979), another of the Fugitives, is about the Southern soldiers who fought in the Civil War. It tries to imagine their heroism and the "certainty" of their belief in their cause. But in the poem, he admits that such certainty, such belief, is difficult for modern man. The South of the Civil War period is now history. It is now too far away. Even the names of the dead are forgotten:

> Row after row with strict impunity[A]
> The headstones yield their names to the element,
> The wind whirrs without recollection[B];
> In the riven troughs[C] the splayed leaves
> Pile up . . .
> [A] no danger of punishment [B] remembering [C] hollows (where the earth over the graves has sunk)

Like Ransom, Tate feels that the ideal life is filled with faith and tradition. His carefully written poetry often uses old-fashioned language. He says that his technique "gradually circles around the subject, threatening it and filling it with suspense[14]".

Ransom, Tate and Robert Penn Warren created a new form of literary criticism, called "New Criticism". They stressed that each work of literature is a "world in itself". It is separate from the author's life and opinions. Meaning and form are closely related. Through "close reading", the New Critic finds the meaning. Then he studies the form to see the particular way in which the poet expresses that meaning.

ROBERT PENN WARREN (b. 1905), the third important Fugitive, wrote both poetry and novels. His lyric poetry, like Tate's, shows modern man suffering from loss of religious faith. A more important theme is the relationship between man and nature. Modern man has lost the harmony of this relationship. Nature is wiser and could teach us if we listened. That is the theme of the poem *Pondy Woods*. Buzzards look down on a man as he runs to escape death:

> We swing against the sky and wait;
> You seize the hour, more passionate
> Than strong, and strive with time to die –
> With Time, the beaked tribe's astute ally[A].

[A] clever friend

In his fiction, Warren turns to the politics and morality of the purely human world. *All the King's Men* (1946), his best novel, is about the misuse of great political power in a democratic society. It tells the story of a Southern politician who wants to do good but becomes power-mad. This is what finally destroys him.

With William Faulkner, Thomas Wolfe and the Fugitive writers, the American South became an important center of literature. The fame of the literary South grew even further when younger writers appeared in the forties and fifties. KATHERINE ANNE PORTER (1894–1980) first came to national attention with her "perfect" short stories in the 1930s. Like Hemingway, Faulkner and Fitzgerald, her best

[14] *suspense*, anxious waiting.

work is of the "symbolic realism" type. The reader first sees the surface story, with its "local color" and particular details. After this the reader becomes aware of a deeper meaning.

Porter's story *Flowering Judas* (1930) has the theme of the "unlived life". Laura, the heroine, is unable to give herself completely to anything – to her lover, her religion, or the revolution which is happening around her. Her dream, at the end of the story, pulls together all of the story's symbols. *The Jilting of Granny Weatherall* (1935) is a powerful description of the dying moments of an old woman who has "weathered it all" (come through all the difficulties of life). Strangely, in these last few minutes, her thoughts are not about her family. She is thinking about a man whom she was going to marry, but who had left her – "jilted" her – half a century before:

> The blue light from Cornelia's lampshade drew into a tiny point in the center of her brain, it flickered and winked like an eye . . . her body was now only a deep mass of shadow in an endless darkness . . . God, give a sign! For the second time there was no sign. Again no bridegroom[A] . . . She could not remember any other sorrow because this grief wiped them all away . . . Oh, no, there's nothing more cruel than this – I'll never forgive it. She stretched out herself with a deep breath and blew out the light.
>
> [A] man to be married (at a wedding)

Porter spent thirty years trying to write a "perfect" novel. *Ship of Fools* (1962) was the result of this effort. The novel is set in the years just before World War II. A large group of characters, including Germans with Nazi opinions and Jews, are traveling by ship to Europe. The story is really an allegory about the "voyage of life". Through the complicated relationships between the characters, Porter develops her theme: that "evil is always done with the co-operation of good". Critics still disagree about whether or not the novel is successful. To some, her view of human nature is too dark and unpleasant. But Porter is not the only American writer with such a dark view. The horrors of World War II destroyed the faith of many people in the basic goodness of human nature. For these people, *Ship of Fools* is a fine artistic statement of a terrible truth.

Norman Mailer, whose writing expressed the concerns of the 1940s and 1950s

Chapter Thirteen

The Forties and Fifties

When World War II started in Europe in 1939, most Americans wanted to stay out of it. "America first!" was a popular phrase at the time. People felt that America should worry about its own problems and forget the rest of the world. The Japanese attack on Pearl Harbor (on December 7, 1941) changed all that. By 1945, America was a world power with huge international responsibilities. This made Americans both proud and extremely uncomfortable.

World War II produced a large number of war novels, many of them quite good. The best novels of World War I had been the "experimental" works of Faulkner, Dos Passos and e. e. cummings. Those of World War II, however, belong to the naturalistic tradition. Usually they show the ugliness and horror of war in a realistic manner. They are naturalistic because they study the effect of war on soldiers and on ordinary people. Although the novelists hate war, they rarely show any particular kind of "political consciousness". Like most writers in the forties and fifties, they were no longer interested in the Leftist ideologies of the thirties. *Hiroshima* (1946), by JOHN HERSEY (b. 1914), tells the true stories of six Japanese people who experienced the destruction of their city by the atomic bomb. Hersey writes in a newspaper-like style, without opinion or emotion. The terrible facts themselves create powerful emotions in the reader. *Guard of Honor* (1948) by JAMES GOULD COZZENS (1903–1978) and *From Here to Eternity* (1951) by JAMES JONES (1921–1977) both look at the bad effects of army life on the minds of soldiers. Other important war novels include *Williwaw* (1946) by GORE VIDAL, *The Gallery* (1947) by JOHN HORNE BURNS, *The Young Lions* (1948) by IRWIN SHAW, *The Naked and The Dead* (1948) by NORMAN MAILER and *The Caine Mutiny* (1951) by HERMAN WOUK.

Senator Joseph McCarthy, who led the anti-Communist "witch-hunts", looking at a pamphlet which attacks him

After the war, America entered an "Age of Anxiety". The politics of America were influenced by two great fears. First, there was the fear of the Bomb; many Americans were sure there would be a war with the Soviet Union using atomic bombs. Also, in the late forties and early fifties, fear of Communism became a national sickness. Senator Joseph McCarthy often appeared on television, telling Americans that American Communists were destroying the nation. He led the country on a "witch hunt" against "Communist" intellectuals, writers and Hollywood figures. McCarthy seriously hurt the lives and careers of many Americans who were not really Communists.

American authors in the fifties show that they are very uncomfortable in the post-war world. The new political fears (of Communism and the Bomb) are less important to them than their own psychological problems in the new American society. It is not a period of important experiments in style. Rather, the most interesting authors are developing new and important themes. Many writers in this period try to find new answers to the old question, "Who am I?" Many black American and Jewish–American writers find the answer by looking at their own cultural and racial backgrounds. Others explore the ideas of modern philosophy and psychology. The young "Beat" writers use Oriental[1] religion for the same purpose. The new writers of the South, however, seem a little less "modern". In their work, we still feel the sad, heavy weight of the past. The central theme of their work, however, is often loneliness and "the search for the self". This makes their work deeply interesting to modern readers everywhere.

In the forties and fifties the South continued to produce some of the

[1] *Oriental*, of the East, especially India.

finest American writers. A new generation joined Faulkner and the Fugitive writers in a "Southern Renaissance". Like Faulkner, EUDORA WELTY (b. 1909) wrote about Mississippi. Her description of the Mississippi countryside in the novel *Delta Wedding* (1946) gives the feeling of a rich and sunny land. Sometimes it is like a mythical or fantasy world:

> The land was perfectly flat and level but it shimmered[A] like the wing of a lighted dragonfly. It seemed strummed, as though it were an instrument and something had touched it.
>
> [A] seemed to tremble in the sunlight

Welty's interest in myth is famous. On the surface, her writing is realistic. But she often gives us the feeling that there is another world behind the one she is describing. Her collection of connected short stories, *The Golden Apples* (1949), uses many elements from Greek mythology (e.g. Hercules' search for the "golden apples of the Sun").

The surface story in her much-admired short story *Death of a Travelling Salesman* (1936) is about a salesman who loses his way "on a road without sign posts" in backwoods Mississippi. He spends the night with some simple country people. The description of one of these people suggests that they belong to another world:

> He looked at least thirty. He had a hot, red face that was yet full of silence. He wore muddy blue pants and an old military coat stained[A] and patched[B]. World War ? Bowman wondered. Great God, it was a Confederate coat!
>
> [A] discolored   [B] mended

The next morning, Bowman leaves them. Standing all alone on the road, he dies of a heart attack:

> He sank in fright onto the road. . . . He felt as if all this had happened before. He covered his heart with both hands to keep anyone from hearing the noise it made.
>
> But nobody heard it.

Many of Welty's characters live and die alone. They don't understand either life or themselves. Occasionally, as in *Delta Wedding*, individuals do learn an important lesson about life: live it day by day.

FLANNERY O'CONNOR (1925–1964) was another Southern writer whose fiction suggests the reality of "another world". In O'Connor's case, this other world appears to be connected to her Roman Catholicism. For her, "the centre of existence is the Holy Ghost". But she rarely discusses religion directly. This is because "my audience are the people who think God is dead. At least these are the people I am conscious of writing for." On the surface, her stories and novels are filled with horrible events and grotesque characters. This makes her typical of the "Southern Gothic" school of writing. There are murderers, haters and madmen. The events and people are almost always part of a religious allegory.

Hazel, the hero of O'Connor's first novel, *Wise Blood* (1952), has crazy religious ideas. He wants to establish "the Church Without Jesus". Yet clearly, "the wild ragged figure who moves from tree to tree in the back of Hazel's mind" is Jesus. In *A Good Man Is Hard to Find* (1955), her most famous short story, a Southern family – parents, children and grandmother – are murdered by criminals. Before she is killed, the grandmother talks to one of the murderers about God. She sees that he, too, is one of the children of God. *The Violent Bear It Away* (1960) also has many terrible events. But it also ends with the main character moving "toward the dark city where the children of God lay sleeping".

The stories and novels of CARSON MCCULLERS (1917–1967) also clearly belong to the Southern Gothic tradition. There is an unnaturalness to most of her characters. Their pain is locked up inside of them, like a secret. We are rarely asked to share their pain. We only need to see that it is there. The horrors of life are a major theme in McCullers's work. They are described with careful coolness, and without any emotion. One critic describes her style this way: "it suggests fright striving for perfect control" (Alfred Kazin). Yet strangely, this "coolness" emphasizes the tragedy of lives lived in loneliness. This is the effect of the first line of her novel *The Heart Is a Lonely Hunter* (1940): "In the town there were two mutes[2], and they

---

[2] *mute*, person who cannot speak.

A scene from the movie of Carson McCullers's novel The Heart is a
Lonely Hunter

were always together." The two mutes quickly lose each other. One of
them moves on to another town, where he tries to make friends with
other lonely, separated people: a sad, music-loving girl and a black
doctor who is slowly dying of cancer. But the loneliness remains. In the
end, he kills himself.

The Southern towns of McCullers's stories are filled with race
hatred and other kinds of "lovelessness". Her physical descriptions
help us see this lovelessness. This is the opening description of her most
famous short story, *The Ballad of the Sad Café* (1951):

> The town itself is dreary[A] . . . If you walk along the main street
> on an August afternoon there is nothing whatsoever to do. The
> largest building, in the very center of town, is boarded up
> completely and leans so far to the right that it seems bound to
> collapse[B] at any minute.

[A] tired and uninteresting [B] certain to fall down

The characters in the story are unreal, like the characters of a myth:
Miss Amelia, a strong but lonely woman, falls in love with her cousin,
a hateful dwarf[3]. Again we have the theme of human separateness.

[3] *dwarf*, unnaturally small person.

Mary McCarthy

One person bravely tries to love. But the other person cannot, or will not, return this love.

MARY MCCARTHY (b. 1912), a Northerner, was another woman writer active in this period. Like F. Scott Fitzgerald, she used her novels to describe the life of her own generation. Her first novel, *The Company She Keeps* (1942), is a humorous tale of a young woman living in New York's Greenwich Village, a community of artists and intellectuals. It is an experimental novel, similar to some of the fiction of the twenties. *The Groves of Academe* (1952), about American college life, is actually an allegory about the evil political power of Senator Joseph McCarthy (not a relative). *The Group* (1963), her most famous work, tells the story of eight young women during the thirty years after their graduation, in 1933, from Vassar (the author's own college). The novel tells American social history through fiction. Her essays on literature and politics (*On the Contrary*, 1961; *Vietnam*, 1967; *Hanoi*, 1968; etc.) are also widely read and praised.

In the 1940s and 1950s, the Jewish–American novel grew in importance. These novels looked at the spiritual and psychological problems of mid twentieth-century life in a new way. They brought to American literature a new interest in the old problems of morality: "How should a good man live?" "What are our responsibilities towards others?" They also created a new kind of humor: the humor of self-criticism.

Saul Bellow

SAUL BELLOW (b. 1915) is the most important of the Jewish–American novelists. His first novel, *Dangling Man* (1944), is about a man waiting to be called into the army during World War II. Before the war, he had been a Communist. But now he is deeply confused. He sits in his room and thinks. He wants "to know what we are and what we are for, to know our purpose". He fails to find any answers. In fact, he decides that the world is meaningless and that his life has no purpose. He is joyful when he is called into the army. The army will give him his purpose. He will have orders to obey. The problem this character faces (and fails to answer) is an "existential" problem. According to the philosophy of Existentialism, man is completely alone in a meaningless world without God or absolute moral laws. We are completely free. But this is not always a happy freedom. Since we have no "God-given" nature, "free" choices and actions in life become extremely important. They determine our nature as human beings. Existentialist writers such as Sartre and Camus were becoming popular in America at this time.

The Victim (1947), Bellow's next novel, also has an Existentialist theme. The hero is unhappy with his life in New York City. The tall, faceless buildings and crowded streets seem inhuman. He feels "alienated", unconnected to the world around him. In *The Adventures of Augie March* (1953), Bellow moves from heavy seriousness to joyful humor. Unlike Bellow's Existentialist sufferers, this hero is not alienated from the world around him. As a young man, Augie leaves his poor Jewish family to explore the world. In the end, he learns that everyone has bitterness in their life. To him, the best thing to do is "to refuse to lead a disappointed life". The comic hero of *Henderson the Rain King* (1959) has an inner voice that shouts "I want, I want!" He moves to Africa to find "something more" in life. His search succeeds when he discovers the value of loyalty and love. *Herzog* (1964) has a far more serious and intellectual hero. He spends his time writing letters to friends, dead philosophers and to God. He too is searching for the meaning of life. Although he never finds its meaning, he does find contentment. He finds that he is "pretty well satisfied to *be*, to *be* just as it is willed (*by God*)".

Bellow's novels became a model for many new writers in the fifties. He had created for them a new kind of hero and a new kind of descriptive style. The Bellow hero lives actively inside his own mind. He has the whole world – including heaven and hell – inside his own head. He searches for answers in his mind, rather than for things in the outside world. However, Bellow's descriptive style makes this outside world very real. He makes us feel as if we are walking the streets and riding the subways along with the character.

Bellow often reminds us that he is writing about Jewish minds and Jewish experiences. *Mr. Sammler's Planet* (1970) is his saddest and most completely Jewish novel. Sammler's experiences in a Nazi concentration camp and in modern America make him lose his belief in God. He is a tragic old man who dislikes everything he sees. Bellow's recent work (e.g. *The Dean's December*, 1982) has been mostly autobiographical. In 1976 he received the Nobel Prize for Literature.

The fictional world of ISAAC BASHEVIS SINGER (b. 1904) is very different from Bellow's world. Singer came to America from Poland in 1933. Until fairly recently, he continued to write his sad but humorous tales about East European Jews in their traditional language, Yiddish. When his work was translated into English in 1950, he became popular with both Jews and non-Jews. For most American Jews, the old culture of Jewish superstitions and folk tales had died with their grandparents. Singer's stories – like *Gimpel the Fool* (translated into English by Saul Bellow in 1957) – brought this lost world back to them. It was the world which the Nazis destroyed in the thirties and forties. *The Family Moskat* (in English, 1950), *Satan in Goray*

(1955), and *The Magician of Lublin* (1960) are really portraits of a way of life, rather than stories about individuals. Unlike the "Jewish–Existentialist" writers of modern America, Singer introduces the humorous wisdom of the pre-war Polish–Jewish village to the non-Jewish world. For this achievement, he was awarded the Nobel Prize for Literature in 1978.

The Natural (1952), the first novel of BERNARD MALAMUD (b. 1914), is about an American baseball hero. Actually the story is based on an old Christian legend. Roy Hobbs is a wonderful athlete, but he is a moral failure. He could have been a real leader for his baseball team, but he helps the team cheat in a game instead. With *The Assistant* (1957), Malamud begins to use his own, Jewish–American, background as the basis of his novels. One of the main characters, Bober, is a Jewish grocery store owner. The other character, Frankie, is a young Italian gangster. After Frankie robs Bober's store, he feels terrible guilt. He returns and becomes Bober's assistant. In the end, Frankie becomes more Jewish than the real Jews. Malamud creates a language and style which make his story sound very Jewish. We can almost hear Bober's Yiddish accent when he speaks. His grammar is a mixture of English and Yiddish: "Why do I cry? I cry for the world. I cry for my life that it went away wasted. I cry for you." Frankie, himself, gives a very funny definition of Jewishness:

> The one that has got the biggest pain in his gut and can hold it the longest without running to the toilet is the best Jew.

Humor and tragedy contrast in Malamud's stories. *The Fixer* (1966) is a dark tragedy about Jews in pre-World War I Russia. An innocent Jew is put in prison for a crime he didn't commit. Even here, there are moments of humor. *The Tenants* (1971) is a comic novel about two writers. One writer is a Jew who wants to write a "great" novel. The other writer is a black revolutionary whose life is filled with sex and violence. In the end, the black revolutionary becomes a serious artist. The Jewish writer, on the other hand, becomes deeply involved with the politics and "free love" philosophy of the 1960s. Malamud's stories usually treat the Jewish tradition with gentle humor. The characters, including talking birds (*The Jewbird*, 1961) and talking horses (*The Talking Horse*, 1961) are all Jewish. We can hear the Jewish past both in the way they speak and in the way they think.

PHILIP ROTH (b. 1933) is another novelist of typical Jewish humor. But his themes are extremely different from those of Bellow, Singer or Malamud. He is much younger. He writes about Jewish–Americans who have become successful members of American society. In *Goodbye Columbus* (1959) and *Letting Go* (1962), he describes rich Jews who have fallen into the "swamp[4] of prosperity[5]". The Jewish families he describes are not attractive – with weak fathers, bitterly complaining mothers and stupid children. Some critics say that Roth seems to dislike Jews as a group. *Portnoy's Complaint* (1969) continues his attack on the Jewish family. A bright son is made psychologically ill by his typically Jewish mother, Sophie. Her only interests in life are money, playing mah-jongg and worrying about fatty foods. The story is filled with the unhealthy sexual fantasies of the hero, Portnoy. The humor is cruel and extremely funny. Portnoy is thinking about the suicide of a young pianist he knew:

> My favorite detail from the Nimkin suicide: even as he is swinging from the shower head, there is a note pinned to the dead young pianist's sleeve – "Mrs. Blumenthal called. Please bring your mah-jongg rules to the game tonight. Ronald."

Roth's fiction became even more fantastic with *The Breast* (1972). A Jewish professor, who is deeply confused about sex, turns into a huge female breast. Roth creates more unrealistic fantasies with *The Professor's Desire* (1977) and *The Ghost Writer* (1980).

J. D. SALINGER (b. 1919) is a Jewish–American writer with almost no strong ties to the Jewish tradition. His only novel, *The Catcher in the Rye* (1951), made him the most popular American writer among serious young people in the fifties and early sixties. An unhappy teenager, Holden Caulfield, runs away from the private school where he is living. To him, the school and his teachers are part of the "phony[6]" world of adults. Holden dreams of moving out West. He wants to "build a little cabin somewhere and live there the rest of my life . . . near the woods, but not right in them". But he soon realizes that "You

---

[4] *swamp*, dangerously wet land.
[5] *prosperity*, being rich.
[6] *phony*, false; unreal.

J. D. Salinger, author of
The Catcher in the Rye

can't find a place that is nice and peaceful, because there isn't any."
Holden's story ends with him under medical treatment. But even after
he gets well, he still refuses to believe in the phony adult world:

> A lot of people . . . keep asking me if I'm going to apply myself[A]
> when I go back to school next September. It's such a stupid
> question, in my opinion. I mean how do you know what you're
> going to do until you *do* it? The answer is, you don't. I *think* I
> am, but how do I know? I swear it's a stupid question.
>
> [A] work hard

The rest of Salinger's work is a series of short stories about the warm-
hearted, Jewish–Irish Glass family (*Franny and Zooey*, 1961; *Raise High
the Roofbeam, Carpenters*, 1963; and *Seymour*, 1963). In *A Perfect Day for
Banana Fish* (1948), he had already introduced Seymour Glass.
Seymour, an intelligent, artistic person, becomes mentally ill and kills
himself. The later Glass family stories tell us more about Seymour. It
becomes clear that he had been a person with a deep and wise view of
life. Buddy, his brother, explains that Seymour's death was caused by
"the blinding shapes and colors of his own sacred human conscience".
Buddy is using religious language here. Other stories also have a
religious message (usually Zen Buddhist). In the mid-sixties, J. D.
Salinger stopped publishing his work. In a recent interview, he said
that he was still writing but that he hated publishing his work. Perhaps
we will have to wait until after his death to see what he has been
writing.

NORMAN MAILER (b. 1923) does more than try to describe the existential pain of the modern world. He wants to be a leader. In *Advertisements For Myself* (1959), he says, "I will settle for nothing less than making a revolution in the consciousness of our times." A few years after he wrote this, a kind of revolution did happen (see Chapter 14), and Mailer has been closely connected with it. His books try to report on the psychological history of America while that history is still happening. Each book is closely connected to a particular moment in time. Mailer is not interested in creating "pure art", like Hawthorne or Henry James. Most critics agree that none of his novels, so far, can be called "great". However, many critics see him as an extremely influential personality in post-World War II American literature.

Mailer's first novel, *The Naked and The Dead* (1948), is a realistic, violent novel about World War II. An American general, filled with hate, sends thirteen soldiers on a hopeless attack. Because this attack could not achieve anything, their individual heroism and deaths have no meaning. Through this story, Mailer is expressing pessimism about post-war American society. The American general says, "You can consider the army as a preview[7] of the future." *Barbary Shore* (1951) and *The Deer Park* (1955) each describe this post-war world. Both America's fear of Communism and the movie dreams of Hollywood make it very difficult for people to see the reality of their lives. But there are characters who do see. They are a new kind of American hero. They express their anger and refuse to conform. In a famous essay, *The White Negro* (1957), Mailer describes this new American hero:

> A stench[A] of fear has come out of every pore of American life, and we suffer from a collective failure of nerve[B]. The only courage that we have (*seen*) has been the isolated courage of isolated people . . . One is a rebel or one conforms[C], one is a frontiersman of the Wild West of American night life, or else a square cell, trapped in the totalitarian tissues of American society.
>
> [A] bad smell   [B] loss of courage   [C] does the expected thing

[7] *preview*, private showing of a film etc. before the public showing.

Truman Capote pictured after the publication of his first novel,
Other Voices, Other Rooms

Mailer was strongly against the Vietnam War. *Why Are We in Vietnam?* (1967) mentions Vietnam only in the last sentence. But it is an allegory about the war – a boy and his father go on a cruel hunting trip (using helicopters) in Alaska. With *The Armies of the Night* (1968), Mailer began an interesting experiment: the "non-fiction novel". It is about an anti-war protest demonstration[8] in Washington D.C. (this protest actually happened). Mailer, as "the reporter", describes his thoughts and feelings during the demonstration. The subtitle of this book is *History as a Novel, The Novel as History*. More non-fiction novels followed. *A Fire on the Moon* (1970), about the American space program, asks whether real heroes can exist in the era of space technology. *The Executioner's Song* (1978) is about a man put to death in 1977 for murder. It is the true story of his life, from his childhood until his death. *Ancient Evenings* (1983) is a return to real fiction. In this long story about ancient Egypt, Mailer uses a rich poetic language. He re-creates a world far away from the "now" of the present day.

In Cold Blood (1966), by TRUMAN CAPOTE (1924–1984), is perhaps the most famous of the non-fiction novels. It is the terrifying story of

---

[8] *demonstration*, a crowd gathered to protest or demand something.

how a whole family was murdered. Capote's earlier work belongs to the "Southern Gothic" tradition. His *Other Voices, Other Rooms* (1948) and *The Grass Harp* (1951) are beautiful, painful stories about young boys growing up in the South. Many of the scenes take place at night, in a dreamlike reality. This is when the characters discover their real identity: an important theme in Capote's work. During the last ten years of his life, Capote wrote very little. He became a popular but sad figure on American television and in movies.

There were several important traditional poets writing in the forties and fifties. They began their careers with a great common experience: the war. Afterwards, however, they went on to develop their own highly personal kinds of poetic expression. In his *Fury of Aerial Bombardment* (1944), RICHARD EBERHART (b. 1904) looks at the horror of World War II and states that "History, even, does not know what is meant." But in most of his poetry, he expresses a romantic delight in life and nature:

> Then go to the earth and touch it keen[A],
> Be tree and bird, be wide aware
> Be wild aware of light unseen,
> And unheard song along the air.
>
> [A] eagerly   (*Go to the Shine That's On a Tree*, 1953)

THEODORE ROETHKE (1908–1963) was influenced by the psychological theories of Jung and Freud. He believed that when he opened up his private life, he was describing basic human nature. In *Open House* (1941), he says:

> My secrets cry aloud.
> I have no need for tongue.
> My heart keeps open house[A],
> My doors are widely swung.
> . . .
> I'm naked to the bone,
> With nakedness my shield,
> Myself is what I wear . . .
>
> [A] allows anyone to come in

RANDALL JARRELL (1914–1965) wrote some of the best poems about World War II. In *Losses* (1945), about bomber pilots, he describes the cruel meaninglessness of the war:

> In bombers named for girls, we burned
> The cities we had learned about in school –
> Till our lives wore out; our bodies lay among
> The people we had killed and never seen.
> When we lasted long enough they gave us medals;
> When we died they said, "Our casualties[A] were low."
> They said, "Here are the maps"; we burned the cities.
>
> [A] number of men lost

But Jarrell was much more than a fine war poet. His poetry often has deep psychological themes. He is surprisingly good at describing the thoughts and emotions of women. In *The Woman at the Washington Zoo* (1960), a woman looks at the animal cages and thinks of her own empty life. She imagines herself as one of the animals in the zoo: "Oh, bars of my own body, open; open!" But, "the world goes by my cage and never sees me." Then she cries, "You know what I was / You see what I am; change me, change me!"

During the war KARL SHAPIRO (b. 1913) also wrote fine war poetry. But after the war he turned to more joyful themes, like love. He does not stay with any one type of poetry. The content of the poem decides what form it will take. He is an admirer of Walt Whitman and Henry Miller. For him, poetry and life are almost the same: "Where are the poems that are already obsolete[9], leaves of last month ...? / Maybe I'll write them, maybe I won't, no matter."

ROBERT LOWELL (1917–1977) was a poet whose style and beliefs changed several times in his career. In his early books of poetry – in *Lord Weary's Castle* (1946) and *The Mills of the Kavanaughs* (1951) – he is deeply Roman Catholic. Often he writes directly to St. Mary the Virgin:

> O Mother, I implore[A] . . .
> Buckets of blessings on my burning head
>
> [A] beg for

[9] *obsolete*, out of date.

Lowell has been called a "poet of restlessness". He quickly lost his religious beliefs. His collection of poems *For the Union Dead* is a painful look at the culture of the late fifties:

> ... Everywhere,
> giant finned[A] cars nose forward like fish;
> a savage servility[B]
> slides by on grease.
>
> [A] with high wings (like fish's fins) at the back   [B] willingness to serve

In the poem *Skunk Hour* from the collection *Life Studies* (1959), he hears the word "love" used in a cheap, teenager's song:

> A car radio bleats,
> 'Love, O careless Love . . .' I hear
> my ill-spirit sob[A] in each blood cell,
> as if my hand were at its throat . . .
> I myself am hell,
>   nobody's here –
>
> [A] make the sound of caught breath when weeping

When Lowell mentions his "ill-spirit", he is talking about his own mental problems. In the fifties, he spent some time in a mental hospital. But he is also talking about the "ill-spirit" of the entire modern world. Because he can relate his private troubles to the troubles of his era, Lowell speaks for all of us.

The ill-spirit of the fifties was an important theme for the "Beat" movement. The Beats were the new rebel–heroes that Mailer described in *The White Negro*. They called themselves "Beats" because they felt beaten (defeated) by society, and because they loved the strong, free beat of jazz rhythms. Some were "hot" Beats. For them, fear of the future was part of the illness of modern society. They lived for the joy of the "enormous present" (Mailer's phrase). They enjoyed drugs, sex and wild trips around the country. Others were "cool" Beats. These, like the poet GARY SNYDER (b. 1930), looked for a deeper spiritual life through Zen Buddhism and other Oriental philosophies.

For all of the Beats, creating literature was a kind of performance. It

Allen Ginsberg in 1956

showed other people how deeply they *felt*. They often shouted out
their poetry in coffee houses, with jazz in the background. Clearly
Howl (1956), by ALLEN GINSBERG (b. 1926), was written to be shouted
out in a coffee house:

> I saw the best minds of my generation destroyed by madness,
>   starving[A] hysterical[B] naked,
> Dragging themselves through the negro streets at dawn
>   looking for an angry fix[C] . . .
>   . . .
> Moloch[D]! Solitude! Filth! Ugliness! Ashcans and unob-
>   tainable dollars! Children screaming under the stair-
>   ways! Boys sobbing in armies! Old men weeping in
>   the parks!

[A] needing food   [B] crying/laughing without control   [C] drug intake   [D] ancient
god demanding the gift of one's most precious possessions

Ginsberg is often called a modern Walt Whitman, because he uses
free-form poetry to praise the free life-style. His poetry almost always
has a message: defending drug-taking and homosexuality or attacking
American society and politics. He is still personally popular among

American young people today, but not as popular as he was in the fifties and sixties. He has always been interested in Zen Buddhism. He uses the Zen idea of "spontaneity" (unplanned action) in his poetry. Sometimes the results are quite good. This spontaneity can give emotional power to his poems. But it often causes carelessly written poetry.

LAWRENCE FERLINGHETTI (b. 1919) is another Beat movement poet. In *A Coney Island of the Mind* (1958), he describes the poet as a public performer:

> Constantly risking absurdity[A]
> > > and death
> > whenever he performs
> > > above the heads
> > > > of his audience
> The poet like an acrobat
> > > climbs on rime
> > > > to a high wire of his own making
> And balances on eyebeams
> > > above a sea of faces.

[A] seeming foolish

Like Ginsberg, the writing style of JACK KEROUAC (1922–1969) is influenced by the Zen idea of spontaneity. He wrote his novel *On The Road* (1957) "at a white heat" in a few weeks. But most critics complain that he should have planned it more carefully. It is the story of a group of Beats who travel westward across America. Symbolically, it is a trip from the "unfree" city to the emotional, spiritual and physical freedom of the West. The style of the book gives us the feeling that the journey is being made in a great hurry:

> It's time for us to move on. We took a bus to Detroit. Our money was running quite low. We lugged our wretched baggage through the station . . . Exhausted, Dean fell asleep in the bus that roared across the state of Michigan.

In later novels, *The Dharma Bums* (1958) and *Desolation Angels* (1965), he also describes people "on the road" to freedom. But their trips have a deeper, religious meaning. They are "inner journeys" to the meaning of life.

The experiments of WILLIAM BURROUGHS (b. 1914), another writer, had a strong influence on American writers in the sixties and seventies. From 1944 to 1957, Burroughs was a heroin addict. This experience creates the basic structure for his fiction. His novels are a complete dream world, filled with terrible nightmares. In *Junkie* (1953), his first novel, he says that "Junk[10] is not, like alcohol, a means to increased enjoyment of life. Junk is a way of life." In *The Naked Lunch* (Paris 1959; New York, 1963) and *The Soft Machine* (1961), Burroughs creates a confusing and extremely funny world. He breaks up images, sentences and words and recombines them in new ways. Like other Beats, he is a "spontaneous" writer. But when he describes his method, he sounds rather like Gertrude Stein:

> There is only one thing a writer can write about – what is in front of his senses at the moment of writing ... I am a recording instrument. I do not impose[A] "story", "plot" or "continuity".
>
> [A] force anyone to accept

Burroughs is announcing here the new direction for American literature in the sixties and seventies. He is saying that writers must now write about writing. In the fifties, writers had explored the theme of man's place in society. In the sixties, however, writers became more interested in a new question: "What is writing?" They began to experiment with completely new forms of literature: post-realism and the "anti-novel". Their new kind of writing made readers read in a completely new way.

---

[10] *junk*, street slang for heroin; *junkie* = heroin addict.

A student taking part in a demonstration against the Vietnam War at the University of California's Berkeley campus in 1970

Chapter Fourteen

The Sixties and Seventies

The 1960s were years of great cultural excitement and social pain. In the fifties, the Beats had called for a "revolution in consciousness". It began among college students in the sixties. They were the "Hippies". They looked for new experiences through love, drugs and Oriental religions. Many people called it a joyful "second American Revolution". But this was also the decade when John F. Kennedy, the young American President, was murdered and the country began a long, hopeless war in Vietnam. By the middle of the sixties, the streets were filled with angry young people demanding equal rights for blacks and an end to the Vietnam War. By 1970, the national mood was very unhappy. The war was going badly and Americans were losing their confidence.

Some writers of the sixties and seventies look deep into the nature of American values in order to understand what is happening in their souls. In many ways, they continue the psychological studies of the fifties. JOHN UPDIKE (b. 1932), for example, is concerned with how individuals live and view their own lives. In *Bech: A Book* (1970), the main character is a Jewish–American writer who worries about "people skimming[1] the surface of things with their lives". This describes the unhappy situation of the main characters in most of Updike's own novels. They are not satisfied with their everyday lives in modern society. They look for something below "the surface of things": myth, religion or just the happiness of their childhood. Harry Angstrom, the hero of *Rabbit, Run* (1960), cannot forget his successes as a high school basketball star. Now, as a married man, he feels dissatisfied and wants to escape. *Rabbit Redux* (1971) and *Rabbit Is Rich*

---

[1] *skim*, move quickly near or just touching (a surface).

(1981) show Harry as an older man. But he is still unhappy and confused. *The Centaur* (1963) combines realism with mythology. The hero, George Caldwell, is a high school teacher, but his students do not respect him. Only his son, Peter, understands and loves him. George's friend, Doctor Appleton, gives him some "modern" advice: "You believe in the soul. You believe your body is like a horse you get up on and ride for a while and then get off. You ride your body too hard. You show it no love. This is not natural."

The characters in Updike's later novels seem to have only their bodies. Their bodies have become more important than their souls. In *Couples* (1968), one character states: "People are the only thing people have left since God packed up[2]. By people, I mean sex." In his next books, Updike becomes the novelist of "the modern religion, sex". In *Couples* and *Marry Me* (1976), we see middle-aged couples trying to discover the "old mystery of Life" through sex. But these attempts always fail. In the era of anxiety, man seems to have lost the ability to achieve peace and happiness.

The sixties and seventies were also decades of important experiments in new forms for American fiction. These experiments developed in two different directions. One direction was the "factualized novel". Here, the author used the "facts" of history to create new and unusual forms of fiction. In *The Confessions of Nat Turner* (1967), WILLIAM STYRON (b. 1925) describes a young black slave who led a rebellion in 1831. Mostly using his own imagination, Styron takes us deep into the thoughts of the man. In *Ragtime* (1975), E. L. DOCTOROW (b. 1931) describes early twentieth-century America. He "re-tells" history by combining many real people, like Henry Ford, with invented characters. In *The Public Burning* (1977), ROBERT COOVER (b. 1932) goes even further. He uses real people – President Eisenhower and Richard Nixon – in a strange fantasy story about a real historical event. In these works, the dividing line between fact and fiction almost disappears.

In his book of short stories *The Death of the Novel* (1969), RONALD SUKENICK (b. 1932) describes another direction for American fiction: "post-realism". We can no longer be sure that there is a "real world" outside our own heads. "Reality doesn't exist," he says. Reality is

[2] *pack up*, stop working.

simply our experience, and fiction is only a way of looking at the world. Realist and naturalist writers used to depend upon psychology, sociology and the natural sciences[3] to describe reality. But these also are only "ways of looking at the world". Writers can still use these techniques, but only as part of the "game" of literature. "There is only reading and writing," Sukenick says, "which are things we do, like eating and making love, to pass the time." The most important writers of the sixties and seventies, including Nabokov (see p. 203), use this idea in various ways. They make it difficult for us to read their novels in the usual way. Often the style and the structure is far more important than the story itself. These writers use "distancing" techniques to create a space (or "distance") between the reader and the plot or characters. This distance helps us remember that we are reading a book, a thing created by the author, and not reality itself.

In certain important ways, *Catch-22* (1961) by JOSEPH HELLER (b. 1923) established the mood for American fiction in the sixties. The hero is a pilot in World War II, called Yossarian. He tries to prove that he is crazy so that he doesn't have to fight. But an Air Force rule (called "Catch-22") says that "anyone who wants to get out of combat[4] missions isn't really crazy". Therefore Yossarian fails. The same "Catch-22" works in ordinary life. It stops Yossarian from marrying the girl he loves: "You won't marry me because I am crazy, and you say I am crazy because I want to marry you." This kind of humor is "black humor" because it makes us laugh at the darkness in human life. It is the darkness of cruelty and of other things we cannot understand. We cannot understand life's "Catch-22" situations because they are absurd. They seem completely foolish and against reason. We may think we are free, but we are all controlled by the absurd language of society. The only characters who escape destruction in *Catch-22* are the ones who have mastered the language of absurdity. They succeed by being more absurd than the world around them. In a later Heller novel, *Good as Gold* (1979), the "Catch-22" is still at work. The main character is hired by the U.S. government and told, "Do anything you want, as long as it's everything we tell you to do. You'll have complete freedom."

[3] *the natural sciences*, biology (the study of living things), chemistry and physics (matter, natural forces).

[4] *combat*, fighting; a *combat mission* is an air attack.

Kurt Vonnegut

KURT VONNEGUT (b. 1922) is another master of black humor. During World War II, he was made a prisoner in Dresden, Germany. One night the city was fire-bombed by the British. He came out of the prison and found "135,000 Hansels and Gretels baked like gingerbread". (Hansel and Gretel are child-heroes of a German-based fairy tale; a wicked witch tries to bake them in her oven like gingerbread cakes.) The terrible experience of Dresden influenced Vonnegut as a writer. His first novel, *Player Piano* (1952) describes a future world of computers and other scientific machines. Humans have become completely useless. They live bored and unhappy lives. Then they rebel and begin destroying the machines. Soon, however, they find that they cannot live without the machines and they start them up again. His next novel, *The Sirens of Titan* (1959), is pure science fiction. Clearly, he enjoyed playing with this form of popular fiction. It is filled with ray guns, "space dogs", and armies of evil robots[5].

Mother Night (1961) is an experimental spy novel. Like *The Sirens of Titan* it is an escape from "serious fiction". For the first time, we see Vonnegut's typical style of short sentences (sometimes only one word) and short paragraphs. *Cat's Cradle* (1963) invents a false religion, based on "foma" (lies that make people happy). In one of its myths, man asks God about the world:

> "What is the *purpose* of all this?" he asked politely.
> "Everything must have a purpose?" asked God.
> "Certainly." said man.
> "Then I leave it to you to think of one for all this." said God.
> And He went away.

With this novel, Vonnegut's humor becomes very black. In this, and in his next few novels, life seems to be a terrifying joke.

Slaughterhouse-Five (1969) – Vonnegut's most important novel – had a strong influence on American fiction in the seventies (similar to *Catch-22*'s influence in the sixties). Here, for the first time, Vonnegut is able to use his experience of the Dresden fire-bombing in his literature:

> I thought it would be easy for me to write about (*the fire-bombing*) . . . but there is nothing to say about a massacre. Everybody is supposed to be dead . . . Everything is supposed to be very quiet after a massacre, and it always is, except for the birds.
>
> And what do the birds say? All there is to say about a massacre, things like "Poo-tee-weet"?

Billy Pilgrim, the childlike hero of *Slaughterhouse-Five*, is an American prisoner of war in Dresden. After the bombing, he becomes "unstuck in time" and bounces[6] around between different moments in his life. He is taken to the planet of Tralfamadore. This world uses a

---

[5] *robot*, a machine that can move like and do some of the work of a human being.
[6] *bounce*, move like a ball from surface to surface.

very different kind of knowledge. On Tralfamadore, even novels are written in a different way. Their novels are made up of:

> ... brief, urgent messages – describing a situation, a scene. We Tralfamadorians read them all at once, not one after the other ... the author has chosen them carefully, so that, when seen at once, they produce an image of life that is beautiful and surprising and deep. There is no beginning, no middle, no end, no suspense, no moral, no causes, no effects.

In fact, this is a description of *Slaughterhouse-Five* itself, and of Vonnegut's own experiment with post-realism. Real time is broken up into little bits and mixed together. This distances us from the story and makes us think about the book *as something written*. But in *Slapstick* (1976), *Jailbird* (1979) and *Deadeye Dick* (1982), Vonnegut turns away from experimentalism. Also, while the humor is still black, it is softer and less painful.

The Cannibal (1949), by JOHN HAWKES (b. 1925), combines two stories set in Germany. One is about the rise of the Nazis and the other is about a group of crazy people who walk through destroyed, post-war Germany. Again, events are "unstuck in time". The author keeps moving back and forth between the two stories and the two times in history. It is a horror story with murders and the eating of human meat. The style is extremely clear, like that of Flannery O'Connor and other American Gothic writers. *The Lime Twig* (1961) is another Hawkes horror story, this time about post-war England. The destroyed city becomes a symbol for the destroyed minds of the characters. Hawkes is more an "anti-realist" than a "post-realist". He makes no difference between fantasy and reality. We look at the outside world from inside the strange minds of his characters. In *Second Skin* (1964), we soon find that we cannot trust the narrator. For him, and therefore for us, fantasy becomes as real as reality. The complexity of Hawkes's fiction increases in *The Blood Oranges* (1971) and *The Passion Artist* (1979). The last novel is about an East European city of prisons and iron. It is a nightmare place. We feel we *should* understand the meaning of things there, but the meaning always changes. This method also distances the reader.

In *JR* (1975), WILLIAM GADDIS (b. 1922) finds other ways to distance his reader. The surface story is about a schoolboy criminal who makes money on the stock market[7]. But the boy and his story often disappear for more than a hundred pages (it is a very long novel). There are many long conversations, on the telephone and face-to-face. Often we don't know who is speaking to whom. But this, like the story about the boy, is not really important. The world he is describing is a nightmare place. Everything is deeply confused.

The Floating Opera (1956) and *The End of the Road* (1958), by JOHN BARTH (b. 1930), are typical "Existentialist" comedies (see p. 181). Barth's confusions are funny rather than nightmarish. The first novel is about a man who decides to kill himself because the world is meaningless: " 'Nothing has any value in itself,' I remarked, as coolly as though I had known it for years." He then decides to stay alive – because "there is no 'reason' for living (or for suicide)".

In the sixties, Barth became an important leader in the post-realist movement. "What the hell, reality is a nice place to visit but you wouldn't want to live there, and literature never did, very long," Barth once told a group of students. He began his attack on the traditions of realist literature with *The Sot-Weed Factor* (1960), set in Colonial times in Maryland. It is written like an eighteenth-century novel. Actually, it is a big joke. Barth is showing us how foolish such a novel becomes when written by a twentieth-century author. This is part of his theory that the literature of the present era is a "Literature of Exhaustion[8]" (this is the title of a famous essay by the author). Modern writers are experiencing the "used-upness of certain forms (*of literature*) or the exhaustion of older possibilities". In *Giles Goat-Boy* (1966), he tries to create new forms and possibilities. Like Vonnegut, Barth uses here the methods of science fiction to create a new myth (or allegory) for the world. The whole world is divided into two competing university campuses. Each campus is controlled by a computer. The computers are at the same time "perfectly logical" and completely crazy.

Lost in the Funhouse (1968) is about a family on a trip to the beach. Actually Barth is writing about the terrible problems of trying to write a story. He fills the story with worried comments about his own writing. Clearly, he is not satisfied with his own work: "What is the

[7] *stock market*, place (or system) for buying and selling shares in companies.
[8] *exhaustion*, being used up (*exhausted*) and finished.

story's theme?" "A long time has gone by without anything happening . . .." "To say that Ambrose's mother was *pretty* is to accomplish[9] nothing; the reader's imagination is not engaged." In the end the story breaks down completely. In *Chimera* (1972), Barth enters the story as a character and says, "I've lost track of who I am; my name's just a bundle of letters; so's the whole body of literature; strings of letters and empty spaces." Like Ronald Sukenick, he has decided that literature "does not exist". However, in later novels – *Letters* (1979) and *Sabbatical* (1982) – he becomes less experimental and more traditional.

In the fiction of DONALD BARTHELME (b. 1931), the "meaning" and the "story" often disappear. He loves to "embarrass" readers who look for these things. In the short story *View of My Father Weeping* (1970), for example, he introduces a character to the reader and begins to describe him. Then he makes the reader doubt the truth of what he is saying: "Yet it is possible that it is not my father who sits there in the center of the bed weeping. It may be someone else, the mailman, the man who delivers the groceries . . .." Often his stories have no real ending. He may just stop with "etc." In *Sentences* (1970), Barthelme sympathizes with the reader's problems in understanding this kind of writing. It is:

> . . . all a disappointment, to be sure, but it reminds us that the sentence itself is a man-made object, not the one we wanted of course, but still a construction of man, a structure to be treasured for its weakness, as opposed to the strength of stones.

Barthelme's descriptions rarely describe a reality beyond his own words. This is because to him, a writer's only reality is language. He believes that in the modern world, words have a life of their own. "There are worms in words!" he says. A typical Barthelme description is filled with the language of advertisements, popular magazines, book titles and worthless "party-talk". It shows us how meaningless our everyday conversations really are. "Oh, I wish there were some words in the world that were not the words I always hear!" cries Snow White in *Snow White* (1967), one of Barthelme's two novels (sometimes called

---

[9] *accomplish*, finish successfully.

"anti-novels"). Clearly, this is Barthelme's wish too. Instead, however, he has to use the old language to create new *non*-meanings:

> Went to the grocery store and xeroxed[A] a box of English muffins[B], two pounds of ground veal and an apple. In flagrant violation[C] of the Copyright Act[D].
>
> [A] photocopied   [B] bread-like cakes   [C] openly breaking   [D] law against copying other people's work

Each reader of this will get from it (or give to it) a different meaning. This is what Barthelme wants: he wants "creative readers".

WILLIAM H. GASS (b. 1924), like Barthelme, shares the post-realists' way of thinking. "Reality is not a matter of fact, it is an achievement," he says in his collection of essays, *Fiction and the Figures of Life* (1970). Writers do not record reality, they create it. "A good novelist", he says, "must keep us kindly imprisoned in his language." This is because "there is absolutely nothing beyond (*language*)". His *Omensetter's Luck* (1966) and *In the Heart of the Heart of the Country* (1968) explore the possibility of combining the essay form with fiction. Critic Alfred Kazin complains that there is "too much of the classroom" in Gass's work. But others enjoy the way he uses ideas, rather than plot, to organize his stories.

VLADIMIR NABOKOV (1899–1977) also experimented with the language and form of fiction. Like other writers in the fifties, sixties and seventies, he does not try to copy reality in his fiction. He believes that fiction *is* a kind of reality: "the invention of art contains far more truth than life's reality". His novels are often quite complicated because they have many levels of meaning. Some, however, like *Pnin* (1957), are easy to read and are quite funny. The story of *Lolita* (1958) is told by a middle-aged man, Humbert Humbert, while he waits for his murder trial. He describes his passion for a twelve-year-old girl and his murder of a man named Quilty. But there is much more to this novel than its plot. Since he only has words to play with, Humbert Humbert uses the names of places, people and things to create a large, complicated game. "Fiction is the most urgent game," Nabokov writes, "a contest[10] of minds with the reader."

---

[10] *contest*, struggle for victory.

A scene from Nabokov's novel Lolita, showing Lolita and Humbert Humbert

Pale Fire (1962), Nabokov's most experimental novel, has an unusual structure. It claims to be an explanation (with footnotes) of a 999-line poem by one of the characters. It has several different levels of reality. One level is the poem itself. Another level is the discussion of the poem. A further level is the world of politics and murder in which the poet and the other characters live and die. *Ada* (1969), another complicated "game", is about a man's lifelong love for his sister. It is set in a strange world where Russia and America are the same country and where there is no difference between the past and the present. In all of his work, Nabokov is an artist who tries to "defeat time and destroy reality".

Like Vonnegut, RICHARD BRAUTIGAN (1935–1984) was a popular writer among the Hippies of the sixties. Like John Barth, he loved to play with older forms of literature. His first novel, *A Confederate General from Big Sur* (1964), begins like a typical realist story about the Civil War. He describes a battle the way Stephen Crane (see p. 88) does in *The Red Badge of Courage*. Suddenly, the description becomes post-realist. Northern soldiers are attacking the Southerners:

At the instant of contact, history transformed their bodies into statues. They didn't like it and the attack began to back up along the Orange Plank Road. What a nice name for a road.

A new and different kind of battle develops: the battle is between the story and the book (as a thing) itself. In the middle of a description, the author tells us to "turn to page 19 for Robert E. Lee. Turn to page 103 for an interesting story about alligators." The book wins the battle and becomes "free" of its two stories (one is about the Civil War; the other is about a modern Hippie). At the end of the book, there is no clear ending. Instead, there are many, many possible endings: "endings going faster and faster, more and more endings, faster and faster until the book is having 186,000 endings per second".

Brautigan's *Trout Fishing In America* (1967) is not really about trout fishing, of course. He is only using the *form* of a book about fishing to create new forms of fantasy. There is a character called "Trout Fishing In America Shorty". And later, the author buys a "used trout stream" from a place that sells parts from broken automobiles. *In Watermelon Sugar* (1968) is about a peaceful, Hippie-like society called iDEATH. Objects there often do not even have names. They are just "things": "I sat down on something that looked like a wheel and watched Margaret take a forgotten sticklike thing and poke around in a pile of things." A character asks the narrator: "What's your book about?" He answers, "Just what I am writing down, one word after another." Brautigan's later books play "games" with other forms of literature: the horror story, the Western and the mystery story.

The novels of THOMAS PYNCHON (b. 1937) are not post-realist. His stories have plots and the things he writes about are mostly real. He is unusual because he seems to know everything. His descriptions of historical events, philosophy, medicine, strange religions, unusual literature and modern science are based upon a deep knowledge of these things. When *Gravity's Rainbow* (1973) was published, one group of critics compared it to Melville's *Moby-Dick*. At the same time, *Scientific American* (one of the world's best magazines about science) seriously studied the interesting scientific ideas in the novel.

Pynchon's novels try to create the "emotion of mystery". His main characters become "detectives", spending their lives trying to understand strange mysteries. But their search is hopeless because the mysteries are far too big. In *V* (1963), the mystery is a woman called V. Who is she? What is she? Her life is closely connected to many of the important events in European history, from 1898 to 1956. The book suggests that all of these events are part of one great mystery. V's son, Herbert Stencil, is sure that she is a part of this mystery. But as he searches, her meaning and physical shape keep changing. She has a glass eye with a clock in it, and feet that can be taken off. While Stencil searches through the past, we also watch the life of Benny Profane. He is a funny, low-class person, "a tourist through the streets and sewers of the present". One theme of the novel seems to be the question, "What is 'now'?" Can we understand it by understanding the secrets of the past? Perhaps Benny has the answer: just live it moment-by-moment. In *The Crying of Lot 49* (1966), Oedipa Maas explores the mystery of an ancient European secret society. Is it still alive in today's California? Again the mystery seems to include all of human history. Its bigness defeats Oedipa, and she breaks down completely:

> She hoped she was mentally ill; that that's all it was. That night she sat for hours, too numb[A] even to drink, teaching herself to breathe in a vacuum. For this, oh God, *was* the void[B].
>
> [A] unable to feel   [B] empty space

The plot of *Gravity's Rainbow* is too difficult for most readers. The real hero is not a person, but a scientific *thing*: the German V2 rocket of World War II. Wherever the main character (Slothrop) makes love to a woman in 1944 London, a V2 rocket explodes soon afterward. Slothrop searches for the answer to this mystery. He soon discovers a basic Pynchon truth: everything is related to everything else. Slothrop gets one "answer" from an African tribesman who worked for the Germans: "War was never political at all, the politics was all theatre ... secretly it was being dictated by the needs of technology." But the V2 rocket means much, much more. It is like the great white whale in *Moby-Dick*: "It is impossible to think of the rocket without thinking of human fate," a German scientist says. Like Melville's whale, the rocket "answers to a number of different shapes in the dreams of those who touch it".

The novels of JERZY KOSINSKI (b. 1933) are about the "self" all alone in the world. His first and most famous novel, *The Painted Bird* (1965), is about a young child walking through Poland in World War II. He is a kind of "painted bird" because he looks different from everyone else. He is dark (perhaps Jewish) and the people he meets are blond, white and stupid. The boy saves his own life by lying about who he is. The main hero of the stories in *Steps* (1968) also uses lies to escape the stupid cruelty of people around him. The hero of *Being There* (1971) is a simple gardener who doesn't know how to read. He only knows about gardening. But when other people hear him talk about gardening, they believe he is really talking about life, using complicated metaphors. They mistake him for a great man of deep wisdom.

The works of JOHN GARDNER (1933–1982) often deal with philosophical questions: *The Sunlight Dialogues* (1972) and *Nickel Mountain* (1973), for example. In *Grendel* (1971), he retells the old Anglo–Saxon legend of *Beowulf* (about a long battle between the hero Beowulf and the monster Grendel). The story is sympathetic to the monster. Like Vonnegut and Brautigan, KEN KESEY (b. 1935) was popular among the Hippies. His *One Flew Over the Cuckoo's Nest* (1962) is a black-humor novel about a hospital for the mentally ill. By the end of the book, the doctors and nurses seem more crazy than their patients.

After the mid-seventies, American fiction began to move away from the post-realist and post-modernist experiments of the sixties and early seventies. *them* (1969), *The Childwold* (1976) and *A Bloodsmoor Romance* (1982), by JOYCE CAROL OATES (b. 1938), are a return to Gothic literature. She realistically describes the people who must live in the dark and destructive society of America. Unlike the post-realist experimenters, Oates thinks that "art, especially prose fiction, is directly connected with culture, with society". In her carefully written short stories, she often describes the difficulty of finding (and keeping) love in the modern world. The strange, funny characters of JOHN IRVING (b. 1942) are also concerned about love. In his novel *The World According to Garp* (1978), he describes the deep relationship between a young, talented novelist (Garp) and his very strange mother. Garp's kind and loving nature seems too good for the real world. In the end, he is murdered by a crazy, hate-filled girl.

America lost one of its most important young poets with the suicide of SYLVIA PLATH (1932–1963) at the age of thirty-one. Because she often writes about aloneness, pain and death, many critics like to

Sylvia Plath

compare her to Emily Dickinson. But Plath's pain seems to be stronger
and more terrible:

> I am inhabited by a cry
> Nightly it flaps out
> Looking, with its hooks, for something to love.
>
> I am terrified by this dark thing
> That sleeps in me;
> All day I feel its soft, feathery turnings, its malignity[A].

[A] hatred   (*Elm, 1962*)

In her only novel, *The Bell Jar* (1963), she describes a young woman's
fight with mental illness and suicide. The heroine chooses to live in the
end. But one month after the book was published, Sylvia Plath herself
chose to die.

The poet JAMES DICKEY (b. 1923) is "much more interested in man's relation to the God-made world, the universe-made, than to the man-made". Much of his poetry is about nature. He says that "the growing up of seasons out of dead leaves, the generations of animals and man (*are*) very beautiful to me". In the poetry of JOHN ASHBERY (b. 1927), there is often a feeling of sadness. Like many other artists in the modern age, he seems to believe that we can never understand ourselves or the world around us:

> One must bear in mind[A] one thing
> It isn't necessary to know what that thing is.
> All things are palpable[B], none are known.
> [A] remember [B] easily felt

> (1967)

A. R. AMMONS (b. 1926) is another poet who talks about the problems of "knowing". In this poem, from his collection *Tape for the Turn of the Year* (1965), he shows the influence of Walt Whitman:

> if we looked only by
> what we know,
>   we couldn't turn our
>   heads:
>   if we were at the
>   mercy of what
> we understand,
> our eyes couldn't see:
>   discovery is
>   praise
>   understanding is
>   celebration

It is often said that the two main themes of modern American literature are money and sex. They seem to have replaced, in many cases, the great old themes of fate and evil. But in general, American literature still expresses optimism about man's possibilities in the future. The basic American "flavor" still combines humor and celebration.

James Baldwin

Chapter Fifteen

The Twentieth-Century Black Writer

One of the most important themes in twentieth-century American history is the struggle of black Americans for their human and social rights. In 1863, during the Civil War, President Abraham Lincoln had ended the slavery of blacks. But their position in American society remained very bad. In the South especially, government laws were used to keep black Americans in a low social position. There was also a powerful organization called the Ku Klux Klan which often used violence against blacks. Around the Turn of the Century, large numbers of blacks began moving from the South to the cities of the North. In such cities as New York, their situation was somewhat better. In the North, young black artists and writers began their long struggle for social justice for their people.

In literature, this struggle began with *The Souls of Black Folk* (1903) by w. e. b. du bois (1868–1963). This book is a work of sociology, rather than of fiction. It describes the effects of white American racial prejudice on the minds of blacks. Also, for the first time in American literature, it describes the special culture of American blacks. This culture unites them into a single "nation". Du Bois also uses this theme of "black cultural nationalism" in his novels, *The Quest of the Silver Fleece* (1911) and *Dark Princess* (1928). In the thirties, Du Bois became interested in Africa. For him, it is the spiritual and cultural home of all blacks:

> This (*Africa*) is not a country, it is a world, a universe of itself and for itself, a thing Different, Immense . . . It is a great black bosom where the spirit longs to die. It is life, so burning so fire encircled that one bursts with terrible soul inflaming[A] life.
>
> [A] setting fire to one's soul

Near the end of his life, Du Bois wrote his most complete study of America. He did this in the three novels of his "Black Flame" trilogy (1957–1961). Through his main character, Manuel Mansart, he carefully describes the history of American blacks through the first sixty years of the twentieth century.

The era of the 1920s is often called the Jazz Age. Jazz, a musical form created by Southern blacks, became an important part of white culture at this time. For the first time, the names of black musicians and black writers became famous among all Americans. In Harlem, a northern part of New York City, black writers began the "Harlem Renaissance". The writers in this movement were influenced by the experimental styles of European and American literature. They tried using these forms to talk about the experience of black people in American society. The best writers in the Harlem Renaissance were able to create works of high artistic quality. *Cane* (1923), by JEAN TOOMER (1894–1967), is the most famous work of the movement. *Cane* combines poetry with short stories. The first part is about black women in the South. Toomer sees a natural beauty in them. He describes girls doing their hair in the morning:

> As they kneel there, heavy-eyed and dusky . . . they are two princesses in Africa going through the early morning ablutions[A] of their pagan prayers.
>
> [A] ceremonial washing

The next section of *Cane* moves to Washington D.C. It uses the experimental language of the literature of the twenties. In the city, blacks cannot feel comfortable and free. His descriptions, therefore, are full of locks and prisons:

> There is a sharp click as she fits into her chair. The click is metallic like the sound of a bolt being shot . . . The house contracts about him. It is a sharp-edged metallic house. Bolted to the endless rows of metallic houses.

LANGSTON HUGHES (1902–1967) was another leader of the Harlem Renaissance. Not only was he an important poet, he also helped many other black writers to get their works published. In his own poetry, he sometimes experiments with the jazz and blues rhythms of black music. Elsewhere, as in *Dream Variations* (1922), he is more interested in producing the images of fast-moving jazz music, than in reproducing its rhythms. He celebrates the joy of motion:

> Dance! Whirl! Whirl!
> Till the quickday is done
> . . .
> Night coming tenderly
>   Black like me . . .

Hughes's early work does not directly attack white society for its racial hatred. His protests are made softly, like sad wishes. In *I, Too* (1925), he adds to Walt Whitman's songs of America:

> I, too, sing America.
>
> I am the darker brother.
> They send me to eat in the kitchen
> When company comes . . .

Black workers at a country store in North Carolina in the 1930s

In the fifties, his poetry begins to express more anger. In *Harlem* (1951), he seems to be warning whites that there might be an explosion of black violence, if blacks cannot get social justice for themselves. He asks:

> What happens to a dream deferred^A?
>
> Does it dry up
> like a raisin in the sun?
> Or fester^B like a sore
> And then run?
>
> . . .
>
> *Or does it explode?*
> ^A delayed   ^B go bad

COUNTEE CULLEN (1903–1946), the third important Harlem Renaissance poet, did not want to be just a "black" poet. He wanted to be a poet for all mankind. But will the world really listen to a black poet? This is the meaning of the sadness in the famous last lines of his poem *Yet Do I Marvel* (1925):

> Yet do I marvel at this curious thing:
> To make a poet black and bid him sing!

Cullen's themes are love (both its joys and sorrows), beauty, and the shortness of life. Still, behind these themes, he clearly feels the pain of being black in America:

> So in the dark we hide the heart that bleeds,
> And wait, and tend^A our agonizing^B seeds.
> ^A look after; cultivate   ^B bringing (a harvest of) great pain

The next step in black literature was to bring "the heart that bleeds" out of hiding. This is what RICHARD WRIGHT (1908–1960) does in a number of works using powerful realist techniques. The five short stories in his *Uncle Tom's Children* (1938) give a detailed description of the violence which Southern white society uses against blacks. In his autobiography, *Black Boy* (1945), Wright explains that "All my life had shaped me for the realism, the naturalism of the modern novel."

In his novel *Native Son* (1940), Wright uses naturalist techniques to describe the social and psychological pressures on his black hero. For the first time, we see a black writer describe the violence in a black man. The novel's hero, Bigger Thomas, murders a white woman and then murders his own lover. The novel surprised and frightened many white readers when it was published. Until *Native Son*, black writers had always described blacks as victims of white violence. But Wright knows that the social situation of blacks causes them to become violent, too. Bigger feels he lives "on the outside of the world peeping in through the fence". The novel often uses language similar to the language of Frank Norris, the naturalist novelist. To Bigger, the world of white people is:

> . . . a sort of great natural force, like a stormy sky overhead, or like a deep swirling river stretching suddenly at one's feet in the dark.

Bigger's fear of the white world causes confusion. And this confusion leads to his crimes. At the end of the novel, Bigger realizes he is part of "suffering humanity". Many critics compare Wright's naturalism in this novel with that of Dreiser's *American Tragedy*. Both works see human nature as basically good. It is society, rather than the individual, which is really bad.

In his short story *The Man Who Lived Underground* (1945), Wright created an interesting new metaphor for the way blacks are "invisible" in American society. RALPH ELLISON (b. 1914) uses this same metaphor in his *Invisible Man* (1952), perhaps the most famous novel in black American literature. The hero is a nameless black individual who also lives "underground", in a hole in New York City. He is "invisible" because the people around him "see only my surroundings, themselves, or figments[1] of their imagination". According to Ellison, the problem is that whites cannot see blacks as individual people. Whites only see their own stupid (and wrong) idea of what a black is. The hero of the story had been a "good boy" in the South. He "spoke well" and could say "just the right things" to black college presidents and white businessmen. But by being so good, he is really a

---

[1] *figment*, something we believe although it is not real.

Civil Rights leader Dr. Martin Luther King addressing a crowd of 70,000 people in Chicago in 1964

"Black anger": a protest in New York

"nothing man". He is still the black victim of white society. The world is full of lies. And the hero seems to believe each lie before he discovers it is really a lie. Both whites and blacks use lies for their own benefit. *Invisible Man* does more than describe American social injustice. Looking at the reality of America through the eyes of the hero, we see its absurdity. This is what makes him hide in his hole. The humor of the novel is quite similar to the absurd "black humor" we find in the works of Vonnegut and Barthelme.

In the 1960s, many blacks and young whites joined together in the huge Civil Rights movement. Its purpose was to change the laws which hurt blacks. Its call was for "freedom now!" Although it succeeded in changing the laws, many other problems remained. For many blacks, real freedom was coming too slowly. They called for "Black Power" to fight for their own economic and social rights. In the writings of JAMES BALDWIN (b. 1924), we see the rising anger of blacks in the sixties. Baldwin's first novel, *Go Tell It on the Mountain* (1953), is a story about religion in Harlem. The central character is a boy deeply troubled by religious thoughts. We see how race, sex and religion influence the lives of people in a small Harlem church. Religion creates deep, strong emotions in these people. But these religious emotions also destroy their ability to see the real world. *Giovanni's Room* (1956) is about a young American black in Paris. He must choose between love for a man (his "true love") and love for a woman. Both of these novels deal more with psychological problems than with the race problem. In *Another Country* (1962), however, Baldwin begins to describe the moral confusion and race hatred of American cities. The long first chapter is about Rufus, an unhappy black jazz musician. Rufus realizes that he "had not thought at all about this world and its power to hate and destroy". Soon, however, he finds himself filled with anger:

> Sometimes I lie here and I listen, listen for a bomb, man, to fall on this city and make all that noise stop. I listen to hear them moan[A]. I want them to bleed and choke, I want to hear them crying.
>
> [A] make the low sounds of one in pain

At the end of the first chapter, Rufus kills himself.

In Baldwin's collection of essays *The Fire Next Time* (1963) and his play *Blues for Mister Charlie* (1964), this anger explodes as the main theme. Up to this time, Baldwin had believed that non-violent methods could solve America's race problems. But here, he seems to support violence. He is giving a warning to white society. His novel *Tell Me How Long the Train's Been Gone* (1968) is the story of Christopher, a young black nationalist. He is forced to use violence to defend himself. In each of these works Baldwin uses his anger to make excellent literature. *If Beale Street Could Talk* (1974), however, is a story of young love. It shows Baldwin moving away from the strong emotions of the sixties. Since then he has written another novel (*Just Above My Head*, 1979), film scripts, film criticism and a children's book. Sadly, none of these have the high literary quality of his best work in the sixties.

The anger of LEROI JONES (b. 1934) sometimes seems like hate. For a while, around 1965, he wrote plays and poetry which openly stated that blacks are better than whites and that whites are evil. He changed his name to an African name: Amiri (*prince*) Baraka (*blessedness*). His essays at this time became very violent. In *Home: Social Essays* (1966), he says that "The Black Artist's role[2] in America is to aid in the destruction of America as he knows it." Elsewhere, he demands "poems that kill". His poetry uses the dialect of poor blacks. Many of his plays were presented in black-only theatres. Still, Jones is an extremely important voice in modern American literature. He is a master of the short, free-verse lyric. His poems of love (*for a lady i know*) and of pain (*Preface to a Twenty Volume Suicide Note*) have a quiet beauty that is widely admired. In *An Agony, As Now* (1964), he even seems to suggest that the part of him that hates whites is different from the part of him that experiences the pain of life:

> I am inside someone
> who hates me. I look
> out from his eyes. Smell
> what fouled tunes come in
> to his breath.

[2] *role*, part to play (as on the stage or in a movie).

Amiri Baraka (LeRoi Jones)

In the late fifties, Jones had been close to the Beat writers Allen Ginsberg and Jack Kerouac. We see the Beat influence in his experimental novel *The System of Dante's Hell* (1965). Most of Jones's plays, however, attack white society. *Dutchman* (1964) is a symbolic play about a black man and a white woman. But the symbols are not very clear. Perhaps the man is Christ and the woman the Devil. Perhaps he is Adam and she is Eve. *Slave Ship* (1967), which Jones wrote for black-only theatres, is a powerful drama of human suffering. The slaves speak Swahili (an African language) in the play much more than they speak English. They often moan and groan, filling the stage with the sounds of terrible pain. In 1973, Jones became a Communist leader. His more recent plays show blacks and whites joining in a revolution to destroy their evil society. He has completely turned away from his old anger. *The Motion of History* (1978) even has a humorous black nationalist. He is like a machine which sings again and again, "The white man is the devil." Clearly, Jones no longer completely believes this.

Gwendolyn Brooks

The poetry of GWENDOLYN BROOKS (b. 1917) also tells of the tragedy of black life in America. But, as she says in the introduction to her poetry collection *Annie Allen* (1949), she tries to "present Negroes (*blacks*) not as curios[3] but as people". Later, even when "black anger" began to enter her work, Brooks continued to express herself with great beauty. *Malcolm X* (1968), one of her most famous poems, uses sexual images to describe this black revolutionary leader. He is "the father of a new, frightening strength".

In his *Autobiography of Malcolm X* (1965), ALEX HALEY (b. 1921) describes the spiritual growth of this man: his painful childhood, his prison years, his years of anti-white hatred and his religious "awakening" (through Islam) to a love for all people. Haley, a newspaperman,

---

[3] *curio*, something unusual to add to a collection.

went on to write *Roots* (1976). It is the author's own search for his family beginnings (his "roots"). The novel (and the television movie) had a deep influence on both blacks and whites. For the first time, huge numbers of ordinary whites started thinking about the tragic past of the blacks in America. Some black writers, however, state that they do not want whites to pity them. In her *Black Judgement* (1968), NIKKI GIOVANNI (b. 1943) writes:

> I really hope no white person ever has cause to write about me because they never understand . . . and they'll probably talk about my hard childhood and never understand that all the while I was quite happy.

We cannot really say that the years of "black anger" are over. There will probably be new explosions in the coming years. As long as the black experience in America remains different from that of other Americans, there will continue to be a "black literature". This literature now has a long and rich tradition.

Tennessee Williams, Southern playwright

Chapter Sixteen

Drama

In the nineteenth century, the American theatre had many fine actors, but no great playwrights. The American public demanded entertainment rather than art. Most plays were pure melodramas[1], filled with tears and moral lessons. The good were always rewarded and the wicked were punished. In the bigger theatres, a lot of money was spent to make the productions as big and exciting as possible. They often showed fights and sometimes even a huge earthquake or a fire. As the technology of theatre productions advanced, they became more and more realistic.

The movement toward realism in the story of the play was far slower. BRONSON HOWARD (1842–1908) was the first important realist in American drama. In such plays as *The Banker's Daughter* (1878), *Young Mrs. Winthrop* (1882) and *The Henrietta* (1887), he carefully studied two areas of American society: business and marriage. He made audiences at the time "think uncomfortable thoughts" about both of these. But Howard's dramatic techniques were still the old-fashioned techniques of melodrama.

WILLIAM DEAN HOWELLS, the realist novelist, was also active in the attempt to modernize the American theatre. He wrote at least thirty-six plays. But only one was really successful, *A Counterfeit Presentment* (1887). Howells was more successful as a critic and an organizer. In 1892, together with Hamlin Garland (another important realist novelist), he established the First Independent Theatre in Boston. Its purpose was "to encourage truth and progress in American Dramatic Art". It was also a model for the "Little Theatre" movement.

The Little Theatre movement began around 1912. It was a revolt

---

[1] *melodrama*, play which is very exciting but unlike real life.

Eugene O'Neill at Provincetown, where his plays were performed by the Provincetown Players

against the big theatres, such as those on Broadway in New York City, whose main interest was making money. The "Little Theatres" were to be art theatres. Between 1912 and 1929, there were over a thousand Little Theatres across the country. The most famous of these were the Washington Square Players in New York City's Greenwich Village, and the Provincetown Players in Massachusetts. These two theatres are important in literary history because they introduced the world to EUGENE O'NEILL (1888–1953).

With O'Neill, American drama developed into a form of literature. He freed it from the character types of melodrama (the "pure" heroine, the kindly old father, etc.). Through his many plays he brought a wide range of new themes and styles to the stage. Each play is an exploration of the human condition. His deep seriousness is shown by the fact that he wrote only one comedy (a very good one), *Ah, Wilderness!* (1933). In 1936, O'Neill won the Nobel Prize for Literature.

O'Neill's father was a famous actor. This man had spent his entire career playing one role, the lead role in *The Count of Monte Cristo*. Remembering his childhood, O'Neill writes, "my early experience with the theatre through my father made me revolt against it. I saw so much of the old, artificial romantic stuff that I always had a sort of contempt for the theatre." As a result, O'Neill turned away from his family. He became a heavy-drinking sailor for a number of years. This taught him much about the ugly underside of society; the world of cheap hotels and sailors' bars. When he began to write plays these experiences were his first material. They helped him to change the old characters of melodrama into realistic characters.

O'Neill's work was excellent from the beginning. His *Bound East for Cardiff* (1916) described a sailor dying on board the ship *S. S. Glencairn*. This and three other plays of the "*S. S. Glencairn*" series were produced by the Provincetown Players in the fall of 1917. The mood of the plays is dark and heavy. The theme of each play goes beyond the surfaces of life to study the "forces behind life".

In all of O'Neill's work, fate is one of these forces. In *Anna Christie* (1920) and in many other plays, fate is symbolized by "that ole devil, sea". Psychology is another of these "forces behind life". In fact, O'Neill often uses the new psychology of Freud to deepen his dramas. He was one of the first playwrights to study the struggle inside a character's mind between conscious motives and unconscious needs. While most of his plays are realistic in form, he experimented with anti-realistic techniques. He sometimes "distorted[2]" reality in order to "express" the inner meaning (or problem) in a play. *The Emperor Jones* (1920) and *The Hairy Ape* (1922) are important examples of this "expressionism". In order to show the sailors in *The Hairy Ape* as caged animals, prisoners and robots, O'Neill calls for an "expressionistic" setting:

> The treatment of this scene, or any other scene in the play, should by no means be naturalistic . . . The ceiling crushes down upon the men's heads. They cannot stand upright. This accentuates[A] the natural stooping posture[B] which shovelling coal . . . (*has*) given them. The men themselves should resemble those pictures in which the appearance of Neanderthal Man is guessed at.
>
> [A] makes more noticeable   [B] way of standing   [C] early (Stone Age) men

[2] *distort*, put out of shape.

The form of each of O'Neill's plays is based upon the special dramatic needs of that play. As one critic notes, "he never echoes[3] himself" from play to play. In *Strange Interlude* (1928), the play's most important "action" happens inside the minds of the main characters. We listen to them thinking. O'Neill takes the stream-of-consciousness technique from the novel and "dramatizes" it. The characters allow the audience to hear their inner thoughts. Although the experiment is successful, we find no "echo" of it in the author's later work.

Desire Under the Elms (1924) is a completely realistic drama set in nineteenth-century New England. Its theme is sexual desire and the desire for land. The structure of this tragedy is like a Bible story. But O'Neill gives the story Freudian meaning. O'Neill also used themes and techniques from Greek tragedy in such plays as *The Great God Brown* (1926) and *Mourning Becomes Electra* (1931). In his last years, the plays become increasingly autobiographical. *A Moon for the Misbegotten* (1952) explores the spiritual problems of the American family (probably O'Neill's own). *Long Day's Journey into Night* (1956) is considered by many critics to be a triumph of realistic drama and O'Neill's finest play. It is about human responsibility and love-hate within a family. The action takes place in a single day. The father and his sons bitterly discuss the past, while waiting for their drug-addict mother to come downstairs. When night comes, we recognize it as a kind of tragic "night of the soul".

The twenties and thirties were a high point in American drama. O'Neill was followed by such talented authors as SUSAN GLASPELL (1882–1948), MAXWELL ANDERSON (1888–1959), PAUL GREEN (1894–1981), ROBERT SHERWOOD (1896–1955) and THORNTON WILDER (1897–1975).

The best plays of ELMER RICE (1892–1967) are works of social criticism. His *Adding Machine* (1923), a completely expressionistic drama, shows its hero as a victim of the machine age. His *Street Scene* (1929), a realistic play, shows the failure of social idealism. CLIFFORD ODETS (1906–1963) also wrote plays reflecting the social concerns of the American Left in the 1930s. His optimistic *Awake and Sing!* (1935) has been called "*the* play about the Depression era". Today, however, his work is viewed as "too ideological". It expresses the political

---

[3] *echo*, (make) a sound that comes back.

opinions which were popular in the thirties. These opinions seem less important to us today.

After World War II, TENNESSEE WILLIAMS (1911–1983) and ARTHUR MILLER (b. 1915) brought new life into American drama. It was an especially difficult time for artists and intellectuals. During the thirties, American plays often showed individuals as "types" (the immigrant, the "average citizen", the rich man, etc.). Starting in the late forties, however, the individual began to be shown in a different manner. He was an "alienated" person: he had the feeling of *not belonging* to any group. He was a lonely person, separated from society and other people. The most famous plays of both Williams and Miller take the alienation of modern man as their basic theme. One of Williams's characters complains that, "We're all of us sentenced to solitary confinement[4] inside our own skins – for life."

In 1945, Tennessee Williams began his career as a Broadway playwright with *The Glass Menagerie*. It is a "memory play": scenes from the past and the present are mixed. A small family lives in the closed world of a small apartment: a struggling mother, her shy, crippled daughter and her dissatisfied son. The son, who is the narrator, has left the family and is now remembering the scene. Laura, the daughter, has escaped from life into the timeless world of her imagination. She is one of the many "gentle creatures" destroyed by life in Williams's plays. Blanche Dubois, in *A Streetcar Named Desire* (1947), also lives in a world of unreality. She tries to hide her age with powders and soft lighting: "I don't want realism . . . I want Magic! . . . Yes, yes, magic! I try to give that to people. I misrepresent things to them. I don't tell the truth, I tell what ought to be the truth." Williams's characters often express a fear of reality, and of the destructive power of time.

Tennessee Williams was brought up in the South. We can clearly see elements of the Southern literary tradition in his work. The first of these elements is his complicated feelings about time and the past. The past is usually looked upon with sadness, guilt or fear. Like many other Southern writers, he describes his society as a kind of "hell" of brutality[5] and race hatred. Its sick spirit is present in all his plays.

---

[4] *solitary confinement*, being shut alone in a prison.
[5] *brutality*, animal-like cruelty.

*The actress Vivien Leigh
in a 1949 production of
Tennessee Williams's play
A Streetcar Named Desire*

Often, the South's moral sickness is described in sexual terms. Such themes as brutality and immorality are strong in *Orpheus Descending* (1957); *Suddenly Last Summer* (1958); *Sweet Bird of Youth* (1959), and in *A Streetcar Named Desire*.

At first, Williams appears to be a realist playwright. In fact, however, the language of his plays is sometimes close to poetry. Situations and characters are distorted; they are made "larger than life". Like Edgar Allan Poe (who was also a Southerner), Williams specializes in "Gothic" tragedy. His tragedies are not ordinary, everyday tragedies. They happen in a reality distorted by the imagination of the playwright. They are "Gothic" because they show the horrors of the soul. This element becomes even clearer in Williams's later plays. In *The Frosted Glass Coffin* (1970), characters are described in the language of horror and nightmare. One character "closes his cataract-bound[6] eyes and opens his jaws like a fish out of water. After a few moments, a sound comes from his mouth which takes the full measure of grief." A character in *I Can't Imagine Tomorrow*

---

[6] *cataract-bound*, blinded by a growth.

(1970) describes a nightmare world which is completely Poe-like:

> Dragon Country, the country of pain, is an uninhabitable
> country which is inhabited, though. Each one crossing
> through the huge, barren[A] country has his own separate track
> to follow across it alone . . . In this country of endured but
> unendurable pain each one is so absorbed, deafened, blinded
> by his own journey across it, he looks for no one else crawling
> across it with him.
>
> [A] where nothing grows

From his first plays through his last, Williams seems to see life as a
game which cannot be won. In one way or another, almost all of his
characters are defeated. But his message does not end there. As
Maggie, the heroine of *Cat on a Hot Tin Roof* (1955), says: ". . . life has
got to be allowed to continue even after the *dream* of life is over."

The world of Tennessee Williams is ruled by irrational[7] forces. The
world of Arthur Miller, however, is quite rational. He believes that
things happen for a reason. Unlike Williams, he believes that "life has
meaning". This makes his plays seem more intellectual than
Williams's. The past has a direct influence on the present in Miller's
plays. "We live in a world made by men and the past," he says. "Art
makes the interconnections palpable. People are connected to each
other through responsibility." Often in his plays, characters learn to
take responsibility for their past actions.

This is the theme of Miller's first Broadway play, *All My Sons* (1947).
Joe Keller, the main character, learns that "the consequences of
actions are as real as the actions themselves". During the war his
company made aircraft engines. Mistakes in some of the engines
caused the deaths of American pilots. At the trial, Joe successfully
escaped "responsibility". But the problem of his guilt will not go
away. He is shown a letter from his dead son. In the letter, the boy says
that he is killing himself because of his father's actions. This shock
causes Joe to admit his own guilt. He now realizes that the dead pilots
were "in a way, all my sons". He then shoots himself.

Miller's plays are rather similar to the plays of Henrik Ibsen (the

[7] *rational*, to be explained by reason; *irrational* = against reason.

A 1949 production of Arthur Miller's Death of a Salesman

great nineteenth-century naturalist playwright). They often set up a
dramatic situation in order to prove an intellectual point. Miller
himself says that he has been strongly influenced by Ibsen. Miller
learned from Ibsen the technique of giving the audience information
about past events little by little. The new information (like the dead
son's letter) changes the way we see the present situation. Little by
little, false ideas of reality are erased and the underlying truth comes
out.

All of these elements can be seen in Miller's best-known play *Death
of a Salesman* (1949). Willy Loman, an ageing salesman, cannot
understand his lifetime of failure. His business is failing and his favorite
son hates him. The play shows that all of these failures are caused by
false dreams. Clearly, one of these false dreams is the American Dream
of financial success. Willy judges his own value as a human being by
his own financial success. In order to succeed, he must "sell" himself:

> The man who makes an appearance in the business world, the
> man who creates personal interest is the man who gets ahead[A].
> Be liked and you will never want.
>
> [A] is successful

But Willy cannot succeed in "selling himself". This failure means to
him that he is a failure in life. And as the play progresses, we discover
why Willy's son, Biff, hates him. Ever since he was a little boy, Willy
has been filling Biff's head with false dreams of success. These dreams
have ruined Biff:

I never got anywhere because you blew me so full of hot air I could never stand[A] taking orders from anybody! . . . I'm not bringing home any more prizes any more, and you're going to stop waiting for me to bring them home!

[A] bear

In the end, Biff achieves "self-knowledge". He accepts responsibility for his own failure and can shout, "I know who I am!" But Willy never wakes from his dreams. In the end they even cause him to kill himself.

The Crucible (1953) is set in seventeenth-century New England, during the witch trials. During this time of public fear and panic, a single individual (John Proctor) decides to take responsibility for his own actions. The theme of this play (and of his *View from the Bridge*, 1955) is that social evil is caused by individuals who do not take responsibility for the world they live in. All Miller's plays show a deep faith. They show that moral truth can be found in the human world. In 1979, he wrote: "My effect, my energy, my aesthetic[8] lies in finding the chain of moral being in the world . . . somehow."

In 1958, the American theatre was in a period of crisis. O'Neill was already dead. And the most successful years of both Miller and Williams seemed to be over. Drama critics of the major newspapers, therefore, started to look beyond the huge theatres of Broadway for good drama. They found it in the much smaller "theatre-like spaces" of Off-Broadway. The big discovery of 1958 was *The Zoo Story* by

[8] *aesthetic*, sense of beauty.

Arthur Miller with his wife, the actress Marilyn Monroe

EDWARD ALBEE (b. 1928). By the early 1960s, Albee was widely considered to be the "successor" to Miller and Williams.

Many of Albee's plays seem to be influenced by the European "Theatre of the Absurd" movement of the fifties and sixties. The basic philosophy of this movement was that traditional realism only shows life as it "seems to be"; and that in fact, life is meaningless (absurd). Art should reflect the meaninglessness (absurdity) of life. In the Theatre of the Absurd, therefore, dramatic action shows this meaninglessness. The style of *The Zoo Story* is "absurdist". The conversation between the two characters, Peter and Jerry, shows the great difficulty which people have communicating. They simply don't understand each other. Jerry gives Peter a knife and makes Peter kill him. With this self-sacrifice, and his talk of love, Jerry becomes a Christ figure. Actually, the play's message is not "absurd" at all. Albee is really saying that people can and must break out of their aloneness. Peter cannot return to being a person all alone in the world after his experience with Jerry. He is now united with Jerry through guilt.

Although Albee often uses the methods of the Absurdists, he is really a social critic and satirist. This is clear in his next important play, *The American Dream* (1961). It is an attack on the false values which have destroyed the real values in American society. The American Dream (represented by the handsome but somehow inhuman Young Man) speaks of its emptiness: "I have no emotions. I have been drained, torn asunder[9] . . . I let people love me . . . while I know I cannot relate . . . I know I must be related *to*. I let people love me . . . touch me . . . draw pleasure from my presence . . . from the fact of me . . . but, that is all it comes to . . . And will always be thus." *Who's Afraid of Virginia Woolf?* (1962), Albee's most famous work, has a similar theme. George and Martha have a marriage based upon a fantasy, a false dream. Since they couldn't have children, they invented an imaginary son. When George "kills" the son, he destroys their fantasy world. Can their marriage now survive in a world of pure reality? Albee gives no clear answer, but he appears hopeful.

Albee's later work, however, is far less hopeful. About his play *Quotations from Chairman Mao Tse-Tung* (1968), he says:

[9] *asunder*, to pieces.

I am becoming less and less certain about the resiliency[A] of civilization. Maybe I am becoming more and more depressed[B] by the fact that people desire to live as dictatorships tell them to.

[A] ability to spring back   [B] saddened

In this extremely experimental play, one character is Mao. He does nothing but quote himself from his famous little red book. Another character does nothing but quote lines of sentimental poetry. Each character is caught in his own little world. Their words seem unconnected to any real meaning. In his *Counting the Ways* and *Listening* (both 1977), even the word "reality" has lost its meaning. The characters spend their time remembering a "past" which probably never happened. In all of his plays, Albee's language is wonderful. But in his recent plays, he seems to doubt the reliability of language itself: "We communicate and fail to communicate by language . . . My characters tend to be far more articulate[10] than a lot of other people's characters. That is one of the problems, I suppose." Like the novelist Thomas Pynchon, Albee seems to doubt that art can explain life.

JACK GELBER (b. 1932) is another important recent playwright. In *The Connection* (1959), his drama about the life of a drug addict, the audience takes an active part in the play itself. The rich language of *Texas Trilogy* (1973–1975) by PRESTON JONES (1936–1979) and the dramatic imagery of SAM SHEPARD (b. 1943; *Cowboys*, 1964; *Seduced*, 1979) have also been widely praised. Black writers (see Chapter 15) like JAMES BALDWIN (*Blues for Mister Charlie*, 1965), LEROI JONES (*The Slave* and *The Toilet*, 1964) and ED BULLINS (*Goin' a Buffalo*, 1968) have had a great influence on serious American drama. By the 1980s, other black writers were beginning to cross from "black theatre" to mainstream Broadway theatre.

In general, Americans have been more interested in their nation's film art (movies) than in its "serious" stage drama. Unfortunately, this has meant that new stage talents have not been supported as much as they should be.

[10] *articulate*, able to express thoughts clearly.

A poster for one of the very popular Tarzan movies, based on the novels by
Edgar Rice Burroughs

Chapter Seventeen

Popular Fiction

The writers covered in this chapter are all creators of light or popular literature. Their stories and characters are loved by millions and millions of American (and foreign) fans[1]. Few of them are "serious artists". But their books are a very important part of America's culture. You will find that you are familiar with at least some of them. Many of their works are now well-known Hollywood movies. American humor, mystery stories, Westerns and science fiction are now part of the culture of the whole world.

Since the time of Benjamin Franklin, Americans have loved to laugh at themselves. GEORGE ADE (1866–1944), like many writers before him, used many funny American characters in his stories and plays: the fast-talking salesman, the stupid farmer, the fat and slightly dishonest politician. DON MARQUIS (1878–1937) wrote humorous story-poems. These include the much-loved stories about Archy the cockroach[2] and Mehitabel the cat. Archy lives in a newspaper office and loves the cat. At night, he writes love poems to her by jumping down on the keys of a typewriter. OGDEN NASH (1902–1971) also wrote humorous poetry. He took his subjects from everyday life: "What is life? Life is stepping down a step or sitting on a chair, / And it isn't there." He writes about the "little disasters of life": boring parties, nasty children and friends who talk too much.

DOROTHY PARKER (1893–1967) wrote humorous short stories and poems. They are usually about silly and unpleasant upper-class ladies. Describing one of these ladies on her wedding day, Parker says, "she looked as new as a peeled egg". Behind Parker's humor there is usually

[1] *fan*, admirer.
[2] *cockroach*, large insect sometimes found in houses.

a message of social criticism. In the poem *Epitaph for a Darling Lady*, she describes the useless life of one upper-class lady:

> Shiny day on shiny day
> Tumbled in a rainbow clutter^A
> As she flipped them all away,
> Sent them spinning down the gutter^B.

^A many-colored confusion ^B roadside ditch to carry away rainwater

ROBERT BENCHLEY (1889–1945) became known to most Americans by appearing in movies in the thirties and forties. He always played a very well-dressed – but very confused – professor or businessman. In his humorous essays and stories – *Why Does Nobody Collect Me?* (1935), *One Minute Please!* (1945), etc. – his characters usually think of themselves as very important people. They are quite funny when they get angry. They always seem to have big problems with little things like fountain pens, folded road maps or wrapping up Christmas presents. As a writer, Benchley often finds the typewriter to be "an especially cruel enemy". He becomes crazy with anger when:

> . . . owing to some technical fault which I don't understand, the letters begin getting dimmer and dimmer . . . On such occasions I start very quietly hitting the keys harder and harder, muttering, "Oh, you won't, won't you?" until I am crashing down with both fists on the keyboard and screaming, "Take that – and *that*!"

The gentle humor of JAMES THURBER (1894–1961) is even better known to Americans. His most famous character is Walter Mitty, a "little man in an overcoat that fitted him badly". Walter loves books of great adventures. He uses them to hide from his strong, nasty wife. In his dreams he is always a cowboy or some famous hero. Even the names of Thurber's books are funny: *Is Sex Necessary?* (1929), *The Middle-Aged Man on the Flying Trapeze* (1935) and *Men, Women and Dogs* (1943). He was also a fine cartoonist.

E. B. WHITE (b. 1899) was close friends with Thurber. He and Thurber wrote *Is Sex Necessary?* together. White's own books of humor – *Another Ho Hum* (1932), *Alice Through the Cellophane* (1933), *Every Day*

Is Saturday (1934), etc. – are rarely as funny as Thurber's. But his *Charlotte's Web* (1952), a book for children, is very famous. Charlotte is a smart little spider. She saves her friend, the pig, from being killed by the farmer. She writes messages to the farmer in her web like: "This is a wonderful pig!"

DAMON RUNYON (1880–1946) was a newspaperman who wrote funny stories about gangsters, show-girls, gamblers and the world of bars and horse racing. His dialogue is always in the present tense. This way of speaking was quite common among lower-class Americans at this time. Some of his best stories – like *Guys and Dolls* (1931) – have been made into famous movies. RING LARDNER (1885–1933), another newspaperman, wrote humorous (but often sad) short stories. Like Runyon, he was a master of dialogue. But Lardner's message is often more serious than Runyon's. He often describes the "little cruelties" which ordinary people often commit against each other in everyday life.

In many ways, Edgar Allan Poe was the inventor of the modern mystery (or detective) story. From the 1920s through the early 1950s, there was a kind of "golden age" of the American detective novel. Thousands of such novels were published during this time. They were usually printed as cheap paperback books. People would buy them, read them in a few hours and then throw them away. So unfortunately, very few of the oldest ones exist today. MARY ROBERTS RINEHARD (1876–1958) was one of the first famous mystery writers. Her novels usually follow the same story pattern, from *The Circular Staircase* (1908) to *The Swimming Pool* (1952). The setting is usually an old house, shut off from the outside world. The detective is an intelligent lady who works all alone. She hears footsteps and secret conversations. These help her to solve the mystery.

"Ellery Queen", one of the best-known writers during this golden age, was really two writers: FREDERIC DANNAY (b. 1905) and MANFRED LEE (1905–1971). Both the plots and the titles of the novels have a certain pattern: *The Roman Hat Mystery* (1929), *The French Powder Mystery* (1930), *The Dutch Shoe Mystery* (1931), etc. Queen's best stories are enjoyable even for highly intelligent readers. It is fun, but hard work, to guess "who did it?" However, in the last Queen novels (like *A Fine Place To Live*, 1971), the old pattern becomes boring.

REX STOUT (1886–1975) created one of the best-known characters in

A scene from the movie of Raymond Chandler's detective novel The Big Sleep, starring Humphrey Bogart and Lauren Bacall

detective fiction – the fat, brilliant Nero Wolfe. Wolfe is a little like Sherlock Holmes. He usually solves his mysteries by sitting at his own desk and thinking carefully. DASHIELL HAMMETT (1894–1961) created a new and seemingly realistic kind of detective story. He destroyed the old pattern of the thoughtful, brilliant detective hero. Hammett's detectives become confused along with everybody else. Crime fills every part of society, from the top to the bottom. Even the detective is caught in this world of crime. Reason and clues[3] rarely help him solve the mystery. He must use violence, just like the gangsters. Sam Spade, Hammett's most famous detective character, is "hard-boiled[4]". He knows the whole world is "dirty". He rarely shows his emotions. *The Maltese Falcon* (1930) was made into a famous movie in the thirties, with Humphrey Bogart as Sam Spade.

RAYMOND CHANDLER (1888–1959) created the Philip Marlowe series of detective novels. Marlowe tries to be "hard-boiled", like Sam Spade. But he is more idealistic and romantic. Like Hammett's New York City, Chandler's Los Angeles is a world of lonely people,

[3] *clue*, something that helps (a detective) to find an answer to a problem.
[4] *hard-boiled*, hardened by experience, showing no feelings.

unhappy people, crazy people and criminals. Marlowe drives around the city looking for a "lead" to solve a murder. The author's style helps us feel that the bars, night clubs, apartment houses and rich homes of Marlowe's Los Angeles are very real places. In fact, the best parts of Chandler's novels – *The Big Sleep* (1939), *Farewell, My Lovely* (1940), *The Little Sister* (1949) – are often their realistic details. Many critics praise his *Long Goodbye* (1953) as one of the few detective novels which is also first-class literature.

ERLE STANLEY GARDNER (1889–1970) created the famous "Perry Mason" series of novels. Perry is really a lawyer, rather than a "private eye" (detective). There are eighty-two Perry Mason stories, from *The Case of the Velvet Claws* (1933) to *The Case of the Postponed Murder* (1973). They are all popular because the stories move quickly and are easy to read.

ZANE GREY (1872–1939) made the Western novel as popular as the detective story in America. His seventy-seven novels, about cowboys and "outlaws" in the Wild West, seem quite old-fashioned today. His heroes are always brave and morally good. Many of his stories – *Riders of the Purple Sage* (1912), *The Lone Star Ranger* (1915), *West of the Pecos* (1937) – were made into movies in the twenties and thirties.

EDGAR RICE BURROUGHS (1875–1950) was also a writer of adventure stories. His *Tarzan of the Apes* (1914) is about a young white boy who is brought up by monkeys in Africa. It was the first of twenty-five Tarzan novels. Burroughs was also a creator of space adventure stories: *A Princess of Mars* (1917), *The Master Mind of Mars* (1928) and *Pirates of Venus* (1934). In these, heroes fight strange monsters to save beautiful princesses on faraway planets. None of these tales show a deep interest in or knowledge of real science. Therefore, they cannot be considered real science fiction.

The horror stories of H. P. LOVECRAFT (1890–1937) often have themes which come closer to science fiction. Lovecraft invented a basic myth for all his tales: "The Cthulu Mythos". In the days before human beings, our planet Earth was ruled by fish-like people. Their God was Cthulu. Then their civilization was destroyed by man. The fish-like people are always trying to get back their power on our planet. They always fail but they keep trying. Lovecraft wrote more than sixty "Cthulu" stories. Myths and invented histories like this have now become an important part of modern science fiction.

Real science fiction uses the facts of science to create imaginary worlds. It started becoming popular in the thirties. The stories were published in cheap magazines with names like *Amazing* and *Wonder*. The best of these was *Astonishing Magazine*. The editor of this magazine chose writers who had a good knowledge of modern science. He had them write stories about the machines of the future. What would life be like when there were robots and space travel? Scientific knowledge was used to make "possible futures" seem probable.

Most of the famous, older American science fiction writers started by publishing in this magazine. One of them was ISAAC ASIMOV (b. 1920). His *I, Robot* (1950) is a fine example of early modern science fiction. He created a morality for robots: they must never harm a human being. The robots in his stories often seem to act strangely. But by the end of the story, we see that they have really been acting in a quite logical (and moral) way. Asimov strongly believes in the goodness of science and of man-made machines. His four *Foundation* novels (1951, 1952, 1953 and 1983) are even more famous. Human beings have an empire which includes tens of thousands of planets. But the empire is slowly dying. Asimov invents a new science, "psychohistory", for these stories. This new "science" helps a secret organization see the future.

PHILIP K. DICK (1928–1982) also has a favorable opinion of science. But his best work also shows a deep interest in psychology. His robots are highly intelligent thinking machines. Often they have mental problems. They ask, "Who am I?" Dick's novel *Do Androids Dream of Electric Sheep?* (1968; made into the movie *Blade Runner*) gives us a very sad picture of such robots.

ROBERT A. HEINLEIN (b. 1907) wrote *Stranger in a Strange Land* (1961), an extremely popular novel among college students in the sixties and seventies. Many of his books, like *Starship Troopers* (1959), describe a boy learning to become a man. Almost all of his work contains some political or social criticism about the modern world.

The Martian Chronicles (1950), by RAY BRADBURY (b. 1920), is a very poetic novel. It is really a series of stories about man's attempt to make Mars into a planet like our own Earth. Humans destroy the old culture of the Martians (just like the early Americans destroyed the old culture of the Indians). All of Bradbury's novels – including *Something Wicked This Way Comes* (1962) and *The Halloween Tree* (1972)

– study the relationship between man and nature.

FRANK HERBERT (b. 1920) is best known for his *Dune* (1965; now a movie). This novel creates a strange new world (the desert planet of Dune). Herbert's careful descriptions of the details of life on this planet make it seem very real. The hero, Paul Atreides, is one of the best-developed characters in science fiction. *The Dosadi Experiment* (1978) shows a future world in which technology is used for evil purposes.

URSULA LE GUIN (b. 1929) is the leading woman writer in science fiction. Her style is extremely clear and "pictorial". Her best work is *The Left Hand of Darkness* (1969). It describes a planet called Winter. The people there freely change from male to female or female to male whenever they want. Le Guin shows us how different our world would be if we did not have our differences between male and female. We see a strong interest in eastern religions in her work. Often her theme is "balance": good/evil, male/female, life/death, etc.

PHILIP JOSÉ FARMER (b. 1918) uses an interesting idea in his "Riverworld" series (*To Your Scattered Bodies Go*, 1971; *The Fabulous Riverboat*, 1971; *The Dark Design*, 1977). Everyone who ever lived is brought back to life again. Famous people from different eras of human history meet and have adventures together.

In addition to the writers mentioned above, we must remember that Kurt Vonnegut, Jerzy Kosinski and Richard Brautigan have written science fiction-type novels. Similarly, science fiction writers like Bradbury and Le Guin have written excellent works of "serious" fiction. Increasingly, science fiction has become an important "laboratory[5]" for experimenting with new forms of fiction. Soon, perhaps very soon, it will be recognized as an important form of literature. Our everyday world is becoming very much like the world described in science fiction. Many of the problems studied by science fiction writers – like intelligent robots and the possible destruction of our planet – have already become the issues of the real world of today.

[5] *laboratory*, scientist's workroom.

Glossary of literary terms

aesthetic	sense of beauty
allegory	a story (etc.) in which the characters and events represent good and bad qualities; adj. *allegorical*
associations	connections in the mind
ballad	short story told in the form of a poem
best-seller	book that very many people buy
black humor	being funny about cruelty, unpleasant or dangerous people or situations
blank verse	poetry (*verse*) without rhymes
canto	one of the main divisions of a long poem
coincidence	two events that happen, by chance, at the same time
comedy	a play, often amusing, always with a happy ending
contemporary	of (or at) the same time – today or when an author was writing
couplet	two lines (of poetry) together, ending in the same sound (*rhyme*)
criticism	judging the good and bad points of writing etc.; a critic does this; v. *criticize*
culture	the particular way of living and thinking of a society, including its art
depict	draw a picture of; describe; n. *depiction*
dialog	conversation written down
document	piece of writing that gives support
documentary	(like) a presentation of facts in a movie or TV program
drama	serious (writing of) plays for the theatre
edition	printing (of a book) with changes
epic	long poem telling a story of great deeds or history
episode	one event or happening in a book

era	period in history
essay	short piece of writing on a single subject
fiction	stories from a writer's imagination
folklore	stories (*folk tales*), customs and beliefs of a racial or national group
free verse	poetry in a form that does not follow any regular pattern
genre	particular kind of writing
Gothic novel	eighteenth-century story of mystery and horror set in lonely places
idealism	living life according to one's *ideals*: what one considers perfect; adj. *idealistic*
ideology	set of ideas that may point the way for society
image	a picture brought into the mind by words; *imagery* = the use of such words
impression	effect produced on the mind; *impressionistic* = trying to give an impression without describing in detail
inspire	cause a flow of fine feelings or great thoughts
irony	a use of words which are clearly opposite to one's meaning, often laughingly (as when one says "What beautiful weather!" on a day of very bad weather); adj. *ironic, ironical*
journalism	writing for newspapers
legend	old story passed down (possibly based on actual events)
light verse	poetry without a (very) serious purpose
lyrical	expressing strong feelings, usually in song-like form; also *lyric* as adjective
manuscript	the author's original piece of writing (formerly hand-written)
melodrama	play which is very exciting but unlike real life
metaphor	a way of expressing one idea by naming another thing to which it can be compared (not using "as" or "like") – example: "the *roses* in her cheeks"

meter	arrangement of words in regular groups of strong and weak beats in poetry
montage	a piece of writing made from separate parts combined together
mood	a state of the feelings
motive	cause (reason, desire etc.) of a person's actions
Muckraker	one who collects the shameful facts (*muck* = dirt) about people
myth	ancient story with magic elements; *mythical* = of or like myths; *mythology* = collection of myths
narrator	person who tells (*narrates*) the story (*narrative*)
naturalism	the idea that art and literature should present the world and people just as science shows they really are
neoclassical	new (*neo-*) or modern style based on ancient Greek or Roman writing
novel	book-length story; *novelist* = a writer of novels
obscene	going into usually unacceptable details about sex etc.
optimistic	believing that good will win in the end
pamphlet	short book of a few pages
personality	character
pessimism	the belief that in this world evil is more powerful than good
phase	stage of development
playwright	writer of plays for the theatre
plot	set of events that make up a story
preface	the writer's introduction to his or her book
prose	written language which is not poetry
publish	print and sell (books etc.); *publisher, publication*
quatrain	group of 4 lines of poetry in fixed form
realism	showing things as they really are
review	critical essay on new books etc.; *to review* = to consider or reconsider the value of
rhythm	expected beat or movement

romanticism	admiring wild (not man-made) beauty and feelings (emotions) – not thought
satire	making the reader laugh at the faults in people or ideas
sentimental	expressing (too much of) tender feelings; *sentimentalism* = too great an interest in such feelings
sermon	religious address
sonnet	14-line poem with definite rhyme patterns
stanza	one of the groups of lines that make up a poem
suspense	anxious waiting
symbol	something that represents an idea; adj. *symbolic*; *symbolism* = a use in literature of symbols to represent real things, feelings etc.
target	the thing one aims at (in satire etc.)
tension	anxiety in a situation or between people
theme	subject (of a piece of writing etc.)
tragedy	serious play for the theatre, with a sad ending; any very sad event; adj. *tragic*
Transcendentalist	one who believes that man can find truth through his own feelings – see Chapter 4
trend	direction of development
trilogy	a group of 3 books related in subject but each complete in itself
trochaic	using trochees, feet of two sounds, stressed followed by unstressed ($\acute{}\ \smile$)
utopia	a perfect country (as described in Sir Thomas More's *Utopia*, 1516); adj. *utopian*

Table of historical and literary events

The names of writers in this table are arranged in order of the dates (as given in brackets after the writer's name) of publication of the first work named in the text.

| YEARS | PROSE | | |
	NON-FICTION	FICTION	
1601–1650	Captain John Smith (1608) Roger Williams (1644) John Cotton (1645) Thomas Hooker (1648) Edward Johnson (1650)		
1651–1700	Increase Mather (1684)		
1701–1750	Cotton Mather (1702) Robert Beverley (1705) **Benjamin Franklin** (1722) William Byrd (1728) Jonathan Edwards (1733)		
1751–1800	**Thomas Paine** (1776) **Thomas Jefferson** (1776) Crèvecoeur (1782) Alexander Hamilton (1787)	William Hill Brown (1789) H.H. Brackenridge (1792) Gilbert Imlay (1793) Charles Brockden Brown (1798)	
1801–1850	**R.W. Emerson** (1836) W.H. Prescott (1837) M. Fuller (1845) G. Bancroft (1848) (Lowell) F. Parkman (1849) (Poe) **H.D. Thoreau** (1849)	**Washington Irving** (1809) **James Fenimore Cooper** (1821) J.K. Paulding (1831) J.P. Kennedy (1832) Edgar Allan Poe (1833)	W.G. Simms (1835) R.H. Dana (1840) **Nathaniel Hawthorne** (1843) **Herman Melville** (1846)
1851–1900	**Oliver Wendell Holmes** (1857) W.E. Channing (1873) Lafcadio Hearn (1890)	Harriet Beecher Stowe (1852) (Holmes) **Mark Twain** (1865) Louisa May Alcott (1868) **Henry James** (1876) J.C. Harris (1880) W.D. Howells (1882) Sarah Orne Jewett (1886)	E. Bellamy (1888) Ambrose Bierce (1891) H. Garland (1891) **Stephen Crane** (1893) H. Frederic (1896) Frank Norris (1899) Theodore Dreiser (1900)
1901–1910	**Henry Adams** (1904) Ida Tarbell (1904)	(Adams) W. Churchill (1901) Ellen Glasgow (1902) **Jack London** (1903) **O. Henry** (1904)	Edith Wharton (1905) **Upton Sinclair** (1906) James Branch Cabell (1907)
1911–1920	(Du Bois) (Pound) Van Wyck Brooks (1915) H.L. Mencken (1919)	W.E.B. Du Bois (1911) Zane Gray (1912) Willa Cather (1913) Edgar Rice Burroughs (1914) Booth Tarkington (1918) Sherwood Anderson (1919)	Floyd Dell (1920) **F. Scott Fitzgerald** (1920) Zona Gale (1920) **Sinclair Lewis** (1920) John Dos Passos (1920)

POETRY	DRAMA	HISTORICAL
Anne Bradstreet (1650)		1607 *Jamestown* founded 1619 *Slaves* from Africa to Southern colonies 1620 *Mayflower* Puritans 1624 *Virginia* an English royal colony
Michael Wigglesworth (1662)		1675–76 *Indian Wars* 1685 *New York* an English royal colony
		Accelerating immigration Expansion of *slave trade*
Philip Freneau (1771) John Trumbull (1773) Joel Barlow (1787) Timothy Dwight (1788)	Thomas Godfrey (1767) Royall Tyler (1787) William Dunlap (1789)	1754–63 *French and Indian War* 1765 British *Stamp Act* 1770 *Boston Massacre* 1773 *Boston Tea Party* 1776 DECLARATION OF INDEPENDENCE
W.C. Bryant (1817) (Emerson) **H.W. Longfellow** (1832) J.R. Lowell (1846) (Thoreau) (Poe)		1815–50 *Westward* expansion 1846–48 *Mexican War* 1849 California *gold rush*
Walt Whitman (1855) **Emily Dickinson** (1862) J.G. Whittier (1866)	B. Howard (1878) (Howells)	1860 *Abraham Lincoln* President 1861–65 CIVIL WAR 1870–90 *Railroad* expansion 1898 *Spanish–American War*
W.C. Williams (1909)		1901 *Theodore Roosevelt* elected President 1903 First powered *airplane flight*
Ezra Pound (1911) Vachel Lindsay (1914) Carl Sandburg (1914) Amy Lowell (1915) E. L. Masters (1915)	**Eugene O'Neill** (1916)	1914–18 WORLD WAR I 1917 *America* enters the War 1920 *Women* given the vote

YEARS	PROSE	
	NON-FICTION	**FICTION**
1921–1930	**Gertrude Stein** (1928) (Eliot)	e.e. cummings (1922) **William Faulkner** (1926) **Ernest Hemingway** (1926) James Thurber (1929) E. Dahlberg (1930) (Toomer) M. Gold (1930) K.A. Porter (1930) Thomas Wolfe (1930)
1931–1940		Damon Runyon (1931) John O'Hara (1934) Erskine Caldwell (1932) **Henry Miller** (1934) J.T. Farrell (1932) H. Roth (1935) E.B. White (1932) **John Steinbeck** (1937) Jack Conroy (1933) Richard Wright (1938) Erle Stanley Gardner (1933) Raymond Chandler (1939) N. West (1933)
1941–1950	John Hersey (1946)	Mary McCarthy (1942) **Norman Mailer** (1948) **Saul Bellow** (1944) Irwin Shaw (1948) Gore Vidal (1946) John Hawkes (1949) R.P. Warren (1946) Isaac Asimov (1950) Eudora Welty (1946) Ray Bradbury (1950) J.H. Burns (1947) J.G. Cozzens (1948)
1951–1960		James Jones (1951) **James Baldwin** (1953) J.D. Salinger (1951) W. Burroughs (1953) Herman Wouk (1951) **John Barth** (1956) R. Ellison (1952) Jack Kerouac (1957) B. Malamud (1952) Vladimir Nabokov (1957) Flannery O'Connor (1952) Philip Roth (1959) **Kurt Vonnegut** (1952)
1961–1970	Alex Haley (1965) LeRoi Jones (1965) W.H. Gass (1970)	R.A. Heinlein (1961) W. Styron (1967) J. Heller (1961) P.K. Dick (1968) R. Brautigan (1964) R. Sukenick (1969) (Gass) D. Barthelme (1970) F. Herbert (1965) **John Updike** (1970) J. Kosinski (1965) Truman Capote (1966)
1971–1985		John Gardner (1972) T. Pynchon (1972) E.L. Doctorow (1975) W. Gaddis (1975) R. Coover (1977)

POETRY	DRAMA	HISTORICAL
(Stein) Marianne Moore (1921) T.S. Eliot (1922) L. Hughes (1922) **Robert Frost** (1923) Wallace Stevens (1923) Jean Toomer (1923) R. Jeffers (1924) A. MacLeish (1925) Countee Cullen (1925) Allen Tate (1926) Hart Crane (1930) J.C. Ransom (1930)	Elmer Rice (1923)	1927 First nonstop solo flight across Atlantic 1929 The DEPRESSION begins
		The DEPRESSION continues 1933 *F.D. Roosevelt* elected President 1934 *"Dust bowl"* disaster 1939 WORLD WAR II begins in Europe
T. Roethke (1941) R. Eberhart (1944) Karl Shapiro (1944) R. Jarrell (1945) **Robert Lowell** (1946) Gwendolyn Brooks (1949)	**Tennessee Williams** (1945) **Arthur Miller** (1947)	1941 Japanese bomb *Pearl Harbor*. U.S. enters World War II 1945 *War ends* in Europe (May) and the Far East (August). U.S. a world power
Allen Ginsberg (1956) **Sylvia Plath** (1960)	Edward Albee (1958) Jack Gelber (1959) (Baldwin)	1950–53 *Korean War* 1950–54 *McCarthy* purges 1958 *First satellite* launched 1960 *Kennedy* elected President
A.R. Ammons (1965) (Jones)	Sam Shepard (1964) (Jones) Ed Bullins (1968)	1962 *Cuban missile crisis* 1963 *Kennedy assassinated* 1963–73 *Vietnam War* 1968 *Martin Luther King assassinated* 1969 U.S. lands *first man on moon*
	Preston Jones (1973)	1972–74 *Watergate scandal;* President Nixon resigns 1981 *Reagan* elected President

Index

Writers named in the book appear in the index with dates of birth and death. Where there is more than one reference, the number in **bold** type shows the page on which the main discussion of the writer's work begins.

Acknowledgements

Special thanks to: George Farina, who initiated the project; John Edlund, who collaborated in the original planning; and Prof. Takagi Taikan, for valuable advice and encouragement.

We should like to thank the following for permission to reproduce the photographs:

BBC Hulton Picture Library for pages 49, 79, 104, 116, 124, 142, 210, 222, 228, 230; The Bettmann Archive for pages 36, 43 (right), 53, 68, 74, 88, 93, 99, 101 (above), 113, 133, 135, 145, 150, 153, 157, 160, 164, 181, 187, 198, 224; Boston Museum of Fine Arts for page 62; The British Library for pages 23, 65, 66, 101 (below); Her Majesty the Queen for page 84; The Library of Congress for pages 71, 82, 96 (above and below), 213; Mansell Collection for pages 10, 11, 17, 18, 29, 31, 40, 43, (left), 55, 58; Mary Evans Picture Library for pages 32, 64; MGM/UA for pages 122, 204, 234, 238; Museum of Modern Art, New York for page 164; The New-York Historical Society for page 87; New York Public Library Astor, Lenox and Tilder Foundations for page 26; Paramount for page 149; Popperfoto for pages 108, 128, 180, 231; Topham Picture Library for pages 168, 176, 185, 191, 216 (below); UPI for page 194; UPI/Bettmann Newsphotos for pages 174, 208, 219, 220; U.S. Information Service for page 216 (above).

We are unable to trace the copyright holders of the pictures on pages 4, 7 and 14, and would appreciate any information which would enable us to do so.

We are grateful to the following for permission to reproduce copyright material:

the author's agents for the poem 'An Agony. As Now' by Amiri Baraka (Leroi Jones); Jonathan Cape Ltd on behalf of the Estate of Robert Frost and the editor, and Henry Holt & Co Inc for the poems 'Stopping by Woods on a Snowy Evening' and 'The Road Not Taken' from *The Poetry of Robert Frost* ed Edward Connery Lathem, US edition Copyright 1916, 1923, © 1969 by Holt, Rinehart and Winston. Copyright 1944, 1951 by Robert Frost; Carcanet Press Ltd and Viking Penguin Inc for an extract from the poem 'Poem in Three Parts' by John Ashbery from *Selected Poems* (UK title) and *Self-Portrait In A Convex Mirror* (US title) Copyright © 1974 by John Ashbery; Doubleday & Co Inc for extracts from the poem 'Open House' by Theodore Roethke from *The Collected Poems of Theodore Roethke*, Copyright 1941 by Theodore Roethke; Faber and Faber Ltd and Farrar, Straus & Giroux Inc for an extract from the poem 'For the Union Dead' from *For The Union Dead* by Robert Lowell, US edition Copyright © 1956, 1960, 1961, 1962, 1963, 1964 by Robert Lowell, and an extract from the poem 'Skunk Hour' from *Life Studies* by Robert Lowell, US edition Copyright © 1956, 1959 by Robert Lowell; Faber and Faber Ltd and Harcourt Brace Jovanovich Inc for an extract from the poem 'The Waste Land' from *Collected Poems 1909–1962* by T S Eliot; Faber and Faber Ltd and Alfred A Knopf Inc for the poem 'Anecdote Of The Jar' by Wallace Stevens from *The Collected Poems of Wallace Stevens*, US edition Copyright 1923 and renewed 1951 by Wallace Stevens; Faber and Faber Ltd and Macmillan Publishing Co for an extract from the poem 'Silence' by Marianne Moore from *The Complete Poems of Marianne Moore* (UK title) and *Collected Poems* (US title) Copyright 1935 by Marianne Moore, renewed 1963 by Marianne Moore and T S Eliot; Faber and Faber Ltd and New Directions Publishing Corporation for an extract from the poem 'In a Station Of The Metro' by Ezra Pound from *Collected Shorter Poems* (UK title) and *Personae* (US title) Copyright 1926 by Ezra Pound; the author's agents and New Directions Publishing Corporation for an extract from the poem 'Constantly Risking Absurdity' from *A Coney Island Of The Mind* by Lawrence Ferlinghetti, Copyright © 1958 by Lawrence Ferlinghetti; Grafton Books, A Division of the Collins Publishing Group, and Harcourt Brace Jovanovich Inc for the poem 'why don't be' from *Complete Poems 1913–1962* by E E Cummings, Copyright © 1963 by Marion Morehouse Cummings, and an extract from the poem 'i thank you God for most this amazing' from *Complete Poems 1913–1962* by E. E. Cummings, Copyright 1947 by E E Cummings, renewed 1975 by Nancy T Andrews; Harcourt Brace Jovanovich Inc for an extract from the poem 'Chicago' from *Chicago Poems*